RACING
WEIGHT

RACING
WEIGHT

*How to Get Lean for
Peak Performance*

Matt Fitzgerald

Boulder, Colorado

1830 55th Street
Boulder, Colorado 80301-2700 USA
303/440-0601 · Fax 303/444-6788 · E-mail velopress@competitorgroup.com

Distributed in the United States and Canada by Ingram Publisher Services

Library of Congress Cataloging-in-Publication Data
Fitzgerald, Matt.
Racing weight / Matt Fitzgerald.
   p. cm.
Includes bibliographical references and index.
ISBN 978-1-934030-51-6 (pbk.: alk. paper)
1. Endurance sports—Training. 2. Endurance sports—Physiological
aspects. 3. Athletes—Nutrition. 4. Body weight—Regulation. I. Title.
GV749.5.F58 2009
613.7'1—dc22

                                2009037500

For information on purchasing VeloPress books, please call 800/234-8356 or visit www.velopress.com.

This book is printed on 100 percent recycled paper (80 percent minimum recovered/recycled fiber, 30 percent post-consumer waste), elemental chlorine free, using soy-based inks.

Recipes (Chapter 13) by Pip Taylor
Cover and interior design by *the*BookDesigners
Cover photographs by John Segesta
Composition by Lisa Liddy, the Printed Page
Illustrations by Samuel A. Minick
Interior photographs by Jonathan Devich, p. 202; Getty Images, pp. 189, 191, 193,
   196, 197, and 198; Brad Kaminski, p. 188; MarathonFoto, p. 195; Robert Murphy,
   pp. 194, 200, and 201; Victah Sailer, p. 190; and Eric Wynn, p. 199

09   10   11 / 10   9   8   7   6   5   4   3   2   1

CONTENTS

Acknowledgments vii

Introduction 1

1   Body Weight, Body Fat, and Endurance Performance 9

2   How to Determine Your Optimal Performance Weight.................21

3   Tracking Your Progress..39

4   Seasonal Considerations 53

5   Sport-Specific Racing Weight Considerations 69

6   Guidelines for Beginners...83

7   Improving Your Diet Quality 93

8   Balancing Your Energy Sources.. 111

9   Nutrient Timing...131

10 Managing Your Appetite..147

11 Training for Racing Weight 165

12 What the Pros Eat... 185

13 Endurance Fuel 203

14 The Role of Supplements...235

Appendix: Recommended Strength Exercises for

    Endurance Athletes 249

References 271

Index...279

About the Author...288

ACKNOWLEDGMENTS

I wish to express my heartfelt gratitude to the following persons whose various contributions made this book possible, and better than it would have been otherwise: Hunter Allen, Lance Armstrong, Jason Ash, John Berardi, Jeremiah Bishop, Anna Cummins, Nataki Fitzgerald, Donovan Guyot, Ryan Hall, Wesley Howarth, Renee Jardine, Scott Jurek, Megan Kalmoe, Hunter Kemper, Linda Konner, Tera Moody, Connie Oehring, Chip Peterson, Andy Potts, Kikkan Randall, Shannon Rowbury, Kip Russo, Pip Taylor, Dave Trendler, Rafael de la Vega, Chrissie Wellington, Simon Whitfield, and Phil Zajicek.

INTRODUCTION

How would your performance change if you were at your optimal body weight? Imagine what it would feel like to set out on a run weighing 10 pounds less than you do right now. How much would it affect your efficiency, your endurance, or more simply, your self-image? When was the last time you saw a marked improvement in your fitness? Do a few extra pounds stand between you and a faster race? Chances are it was your quest for optimal body weight that led you to pick up *Racing Weight*.

When I was almost done writing this book I received an e-mail, in my capacity as content director of Competitor Running, from Darwin Fogt, a Los Angeles–based physical therapist, who invited me to stop by his facility at my convenience and try out his Alter-G antigravity treadmill. I had been dying to step onto one of these machines since I first heard about them a couple of years earlier, so I readily accepted his offer.

The Alter-G allows the user to walk or run at the equivalent of as little as 20 percent of his or her body weight by increasing the air pressure within an airtight tent that seals around the user's waist and thereby lifts the runner. Many elite runners, including two-time Olympian Dathan Ritzenhein, use it to train through injuries that prevent them from running on their full body weight. Others, such as NCAA champion Galen Rupp, use it to increase their running volume without increasing their risk of injury.

My epiphany came when Fogt zipped me into his Alter-G, increased the belt speed to my normal jogging pace, and then reduced my effective body weight to 90 percent. Instantly I felt as if I had become 10 percent fitter. Scooting along at a 7:00/mile pace was utterly effortless. It was not a feeling of gross artificial assistance, like running on the moon. Rather, it felt like normal running, only so much better.

While I was motivated to write this book by a belief that body-weight management is critical to performance in endurance sports, I don't think I fully appreciated it until I effectively lost 15.5 pounds instantaneously on the Alter-G. It was a stunning lesson. I left Fogt's facility feeling twice the sense of urgency about spreading the messages of this book as I had felt when I started writing it.

Another motivation for writing this book was my awareness that many endurance athletes struggle to manage their body weight effectively and frequently go about it all wrong. Some of the most extreme examples are to be found in the elite ranks, where money and glory are at stake. In the 2005 documentary film *What It Takes*, three-time Hawaii Ironman® world champion triathlete Peter Reid confessed to going to bed so hungry that he suffered from headaches during periods when he was trying to lose weight. In 2008, world champion cyclist Marta Bastianelli of Italy was banned from competition after one of her blood samples tested positive for an illegal diet drug. Bastianelli admitted that she took the drug after receiving pressure to lose weight from her coaches.

As these examples indicate, professional endurance athletes know that controlling their body weight and body fat is critical to achieving maximum performance, but reaching optimal race weight never requires an athlete to go to bed hungry or take illegal diet drugs.

It's not just the pros who worry about getting leaner and are confused about the best way to do so. Recently I assisted exercise scientists from Montana State University in conducting a survey of endurance athletes concerning their attitudes about their body weight and their weight-management practices. More than three thousand cyclists, runners, triathletes, and other endurance athletes responded. Most were serious competitive athletes who trained at least one hour a day, five days a week. The results of the survey, which were presented at a meeting of the Society for Behavioral Medicine in Montreal, Canada and published in the *Annals of Behavioral Medicine* (Ciccolo et al. 2009), were quite interesting.

Seventy-four percent of respondents labeled themselves as "concerned" or "very concerned" about their body weight. Fifty-four percent said that they were dissatisfied with their body weight. These figures are almost identical to those that come from surveys of the general population, despite the fact that the general population is quite a bit heavier than most of the people who took the Montana State survey, nearly all of whom fit the medical definition of healthy weight.

> A RUNNER WEIGHING 160 POUNDS HAS TO MUSTER ABOUT 6.5 PERCENT MORE ENERGY TO RUN THE SAME PACE AS A RUNNER WEIGHING 150 POUNDS.

While striking on one level, these findings did not surprise me. That's because, as a sports nutritionist and endurance sports expert, I am accustomed to communicating with and helping endurance athletes who are concerned about and dissatisfied with their body weight. As a runner and triathlete myself, I share their concern and, at times, their dissatisfaction.

The nature of the endurance athlete's concern and dissatisfaction is somewhat different from the nonathlete's, however. The nonathlete is typically motivated to shed excess body fat by the desire to look better, and perhaps also by the desire to improve his or her health. Endurance athletes care about looking good and being healthy too, but they are equally concerned about their sports performance, and they know that excess body fat is the enemy of performance in every endurance sport. For example, a runner weighing 160 pounds has to muster about 6.5 percent more energy to run the same pace as a runner weighing 150 pounds—a difference I felt powerfully on Darwin Fogt's antigravity treadmill while running at 90 percent of my actual 157-pound body weight.

Whereas two-thirds of American adults in the general population are overweight, most of the athletes who took the Montana State survey had body-mass indices that fell within the healthy range. Yet nearly three-quarters of these endurance athletes reported being heavier than the weight they consider optimal for peak performance in their sport—hence their dissatisfaction. Do these men and women suffer from a distorted body image? By and large, no. They simply have different standards for their bodies, and they struggle to attain them just as nonathletes struggle to meet their own, more relaxed standards. You probably know exactly what I'm talking about.

Why do so many endurance athletes struggle to reach and maintain their optimal performance weight? For largely the same reasons that nonathletes struggle to avoid becoming obese. Our modern lifestyle is different from that of our early ancestors in two important ways that promote excessive weight gain: We have easy access to cheap, high-calorie foods, and we are much less active than our forebears were.

Our early ancestors lived on wild plants, nuts, seeds, and the occasional piece of fish or meat—mostly low-calorie foods and usually just enough of them to supply the energy required to get more food. Today we still have the option to eat like hunter-gatherers, and many nutrition authorities urge people to do so, but it's not a realistic solution for most of us. We have come to prefer the taste of high-calorie foods such as cheeseburgers (which, of course, did not exist until less than a century ago) to low-calorie foods such as vegetables, and we feel compelled to eat what's put in front of us even though the portions have never been larger, nor has food or the promotion of food ever been so ubiquitous.

What's more, early humans had to work much harder and burn a lot of calories for every meal, foraging through woods and fields or stalking game for hours, whereas today we just sidle up to a fast-food drive-thru window or press "Start" on the microwave oven. Endurance athletes have one major advantage over couch potatoes—we are hardly sedentary. But even most endurance athletes spend more time sitting around than our hunter-gatherer ancestors did, and we are no less plagued by the overabundance of cheap, high-calorie processed foods than our sedentary counterparts.

So if the weight concerns of endurance athletes and nonathletes share a common cause, is their solution also the same? The answer to this question is "yes and no." Certainly, a balanced, natural diet is the most effective means to manage weight for endurance athletes and nonathletes alike. However, the weight management goals of endurance athletes are somewhat different from those of nonathletes, and some of the challenges that endurance athletes face on the path toward optimal performance weight (rather than toward the basic "healthy body weight" that most nonathletes pursue) are also different. Endurance athletes, then, generally require their own special approach to weight management. For example, low-carbohydrate diets are an effective weight-loss strategy for nonathletes, but for endurance athletes they are a recipe for disaster because they starve the muscles of the primary fuel they need for endurance performance.

There are hundreds of books that tell nonathletes how to lose weight to look better and be healthier. Yet although endurance athletes are just as concerned about their weight as nonathletes, there has not been a single book showing endurance athletes how to get leaner and lighter to improve their performance (*and* to look better and be healthier). *Racing Weight* addresses the unique body-weight and body-composition management needs of athletes like you who compete in endurance sports ranging from mountain biking to triathlon. In the following pages, you will find all of the information you need to set appropriate body-weight and body-composition goals and to achieve them safely and easily through scientifically grounded dietary and training practices.

The Racing Weight solution is based on the idea that the human body is highly adaptable and readily accommodates to the demands that are made on it, whether it is a demand to store excess body fat or a demand to shed it. Stimuli such as diet, workouts, watching TV, and other life-style habits are like messages to the body, telling it to "Fatten up in case food becomes scarce later" or "Get leaner so you can pedal up and over mountains more easily." Achieving your optimal performance weight is a matter of lining up your training, nutrition, and other lifestyle habits in a way that sends your body a consistent message: "Keep the muscle, lose the fat, and take your performance to the next level." This book shows you how to send this message to your body.

PART I ("Finding Your Racing Weight") covers the importance of being light and lean if you want to perform better and gives you some unique new tools to determine your own optimal performance weight and to track your progress toward it. In this section you will also find chapters that address seasonal considerations (which cover topics such as managing your weight during the off-season versus the competitive season) as well as sport-specific nutritional challenges and tips for beginning endurance athletes.

PART II ("Five Steps to Your Racing Weight") presents a five-step plan to get leaner and lighter in a way that maximizes performance and all-around health. Each step in the plan is based on the latest advances in the science of weight management, especially as they relate to endurance athletes, and on the practices that are proven to work best in the real world. Here's a quick synopsis of the Racing Weight plan for body weight optimization:

STEP 1: IMPROVE YOUR DIET QUALITY. Step 1 in my Racing Weight plan is to improve your diet quality, or the amount of nutrition you get from each calorie in your diet. Increasing the nutrition-per-calorie ratio of your diet will enable you to get all the nutrients you need for maximum performance from fewer total calories, thus enabling you to become leaner. An effective way to improve your diet quality is to grade or score the quality of your current diet and continue to score your diet quality as you make efforts to improve it. Nutrition scientists have come up with various ways of measuring diet quality. Most of these approaches are a bit too complex to be useful to the average endurance athlete, so I created a simplified diet-quality scoring system that you will find very easy to work with and that will help you nourish your body for health and endurance performance. In Chapter 7, I will give you all of the information you need to track and improve your Diet Quality Score.

STEP 2: BALANCE YOUR ENERGY SOURCES. There are three main sources of energy for the human body: carbohydrate, fat, and protein. The body uses each of these three "macronutrients" in different ways. There are also different types of these same macronutrients—carbohydrates, fats, and proteins—that affect the body in slightly different ways. Consuming the right balance of macronutrients and the right balance of carbohydrate, fat, and protein types will help you achieve your optimal performance weight. In Chapter 8, I will show you how to properly balance your energy sources to get leaner.

STEP 3: TIME YOUR NUTRITION. *When* you eat affects your body as much as *what* you eat. The timing of your food intake has a big impact on what's known as energy partitioning, or what becomes of the calories you consume. There are three main destinations of food calories in your body: muscle, fat cells, and energy. If you want to become leaner, you need to shift the balance of energy partitioning so that more calories are incorporated into your muscles, fewer calories are stored in your fat tissues, and more calories are used to supply your body's immediate and short-term energy needs. This shift will lead to more metabolism-boosting lean tissue and less health-jeopardizing fat tissue.

Interestingly, you can often achieve this objective with little or no reduction in the total number of calories that enter your body. We're really talking about redirecting calories once they've entered your body, not about decreasing the number of calories that enter your body in the first place. The practice of nutrient timing, or consuming the right nutrients at the right times throughout the day, will enable you to partition your energy more effectively and achieve your racing weight. In Chapter 9, I will show you how to practice nutrient timing the way many top endurance athletes do.

STEP 4: MANAGE YOUR APPETITE. Appetite is important. It is your body's built-in mechanism for food intake regulation, and its job is to drive you to eat enough to meet your body's energy and micronutrient needs, and no more. The appetite mechanism works very well under normal circumstances, having survived millions of years of evolutionary testing to the benefit of our health. But our modern lifestyle does not constitute "normal circumstances" in relation to the environment in which most of our evolution took place. Consequently, we can't rely entirely on our appetite to ensure that we don't overeat.

In recent years, scientists have learned a great deal about how the appetite mechanism works. Understanding how your appetite works will put you in a better position to manage it effectively so that you consume only the number of calories you need to maximize your performance—and no more. In Chapter 10, I will explain what science has taught us about how the human appetite works and give you some simple practices to manage your appetite in a way that helps you achieve your optimal performance weight.

STEP 5: TRAIN RIGHT. Training errors are common in every endurance sport, even at the highest levels of competition. Many of these training errors not only limit performance but also prevent athletes from becoming as lean as they could be. Training methods continue to evolve at the elite level of each endurance sport. In Chapter 11 I will identify the most rewarding changes you can make to your training to raise your level of performance and achieve or maintain your racing weight.

PART III of this book ("The Racing Weight Menu") provides resources that will help you put the Racing Weight plan into practice. Chapter 12 presents sample food journals from elite athletes in several different endurance sports. These examples are not to be copied exactly, as there are important differences between the caloric needs of world-class endurance athletes and those of most amateurs, but they do provide some practical ideas and inspiration.

In Chapter 13, you will find 21 delicious and easy-to-prepare breakfast, lunch, and dinner recipes that will fuel your body for endurance performance and help you achieve your racing weight, plus a few deliciously wholesome dessert recipes. These recipes were created by professional triathlete and dietitian Pip Taylor.

Finally, Chapter 14 discusses the limited role of supplements in achieving your racing weight. Most nutritional supplements are useless. This generalization includes the supplements that endurance athletes most commonly use to shed excess body fat, but a select few supplements can be helpful for some athletes when used appropriately. In the concluding chapter of this book, I will tell you about these supplements, all of which should be considered strictly optional.

All of the guidance presented in this book, in addition to being scientifically grounded and tested in real-world practice, reflects the practices that I rely on in my own training. I struggle as much as any endurance athlete to optimize my body weight for performance, and the Racing Weight plan works for me. So come on, let's do this together.

ONE

BODY WEIGHT, BODY FAT, AND ENDURANCE PERFORMANCE

I was a Lance Armstrong fan before most Americans had ever heard of him. It's not uncommon for runners to be casual fans of other endurance sports. I became a runner at age 12 and became a casual cycling fan three years later, when Greg LeMond won his first Tour de France. Lance burst into prominence in 1993, when he won the World Championship Road Race at age 21. I rooted for him thereafter and was saddened when he announced in 1996 that he had cancer. Because we are the same age, the revelation shook me, both as a fan and with the realization that a similar card could be dealt to me.

I met Lance for the first time on September 4, 1997, which happened to be the day he announced that the doctors who had helped him beat cancer had cleared him to return to professional bike racing. The announcement was made at the Interbike bicycle-industry trade show in Las Vegas, which Lance was attending on behalf of sponsors and I was attending on behalf of *Winning* magazine. Lance was far from being the household name he is today, but at age 26 he was already a legend to fans of American cycling—a two-time Tour de France stage winner, two-time Olympian, and world champion.

Nevertheless, he was a good deal more accessible back then. I got to him by walking up to his coach, Chris Carmichael, and telling him I wanted an interview. The next day I sat down with Armstrong alone— well, alone save for the presence of my friend and colleague Jimmy, who insisted on tagging along to stare—and peppered him with questions for a full hour.

Lance has become the world's most followed Pied Piper in the fight against cancer, but in 1997 his foundation was just getting off the ground, and all of his cycling fans, myself included, expected him to just walk away from cancer now that he had beaten it. The first question I asked him was whether he was sick of talking about cancer. He surprised me by replying that he intended to continue talking about cancer until he died or the disease was cured. When I asked Lance whether he felt he had the potential to energize cycling spectatorship in the United States, he told me he was a lot more interested in energizing the cancer community.

A reputation for arrogance preceded him, but I was surprised to find Lance to be humble, introspective, and grounded. I asked him whether there was a silver lining to the cloud of his experience with cancer, and he said, "Oh, yes, definitely. It's probably the best thing that ever happened to me, in terms of growing as a person, in terms of my family growing closer, even though we were very close before, and my friends, and a lot of other people around the world. I think it was a good lesson. It taught me a lot about the preciousness of life and a lot of the stuff around it that we always take for granted—our health, our family, our friends, our support, our jobs. They can all be taken away, and I never really realized that before."

Lance was also physically different from the young man I had heard and read about. To be specific, he seemed a lot skinnier. And in fact he was. In the first chapter of his career Lance had been among the biggest, most muscular riders in the peloton, but cancer had stripped some of that mass from his body. The transformation turned out to be a boon to his dream of winning the Tour de France. Lance had only been able to complete one of the four Tours he had ridden before cancer, and in that one he finished in 36th place. He just had too much bulk to carry across France and up and over the Alps and Pyrenees for three weeks. The new, leaner, lighter Lance was as potent a time trialist as ever but a much better climber. This new strength helped propel him to seven straight Tour de France victories after cancer.

Although cancer had changed Lance's body, it took a conscious effort to prevent his body from changing back in the years that followed his recovery. Cancer did not destroy his "linebacker genes." Aware that he performed better with his leaner physique, Lance carefully controlled his diet and training to ensure that he kept it. He organized his nutrition, exercise, and overall lifestyle to send a consistent message to his body: that it was to stay lean, light, and powerful as long as he still held the desire to win another Tour de France. When he retired from racing in 2005, Lance's linebacker genes took over again, and when he came out of retirement three and a half years later, he had to repeat the slimming process, and he did.

Do you need to get cancer and lose a lot of weight to become a better endurance athlete? Absolutely not! Lance's story is just a particularly salient example of the importance of leanness, and in many cases lightness, to endurance sports performance. Lance Armstrong was already one of the world's best one-day racers before his body changed, but only by taking advantage of that change did he become capable of winning a three-week tour.

There are countless other examples of champion athletes who elevated their performances by changing their bodies. Usually the change involves shedding excess body fat, and perhaps a bit of excess muscle. But sometimes endurance athletes need to gain muscle to improve their performance. In 2008, Dara Torres, at age 41, attempted to qualify for her fifth U.S. Olympic swim team. To counteract the physical effects of aging, Torres incorporated an intensive dryland training regimen into her program. In the run-up to the Olympic Trials, she performed four 60-to-90-minute functional strength sessions per week with Florida Panthers strength-and-conditioning coach Andy O'Brien. The result was a chiseled physique, complete with six-pack abs (a rarity among swimmers) that drew a lot of attention during the Beijing Games. More importantly, Torres swam better than she had in her 30s, 20s, or teens, qualifying for the U.S. team in the 50-meter and 100-meter freestyle and winning silver medals in the 50-meter freestyle and two relay events.

The message here is that form and function are closely related in endurance sports. Physiology is destiny. Your body weight, lean-muscle mass, body-fat percentage, body-mass distribution, and body-fat distribution affect your performance. They are not the only factors that affect your performance—there are plenty of invisible ones as well, such as the density of aerobic enzymes in your muscle cells—but these anthropometric variables are as important as any other factors. And they are also malleable. Your genes place limits on how much muscle and fat you can gain and lose, but within these limits there is a fair degree of adaptive potential. The right training and nutrition practices will optimize your physique for the type and level of performance you seek, much as they did for Lance Armstrong and Dara Torres.

THE RIGHT BODY FOR THE JOB

Thankfully, there is no single, ideal body type for any specific endurance sport. The variety you see in the physiques of world-class cyclists, runners, and other endurance athletes can be surprising. For example, the winner of the 1997 Tour de France, Jan Ullrich, stood 6 feet tall and raced at 162 pounds. The winner of the 1998 Tour, Marco Pantani, was 5 inches shorter and more than 30 pounds lighter. Nevertheless, there are certain parameters of body size, proportion, and composition that are characteristic of successful athletes in each endurance sport.

The Cross-Country Skier's Body

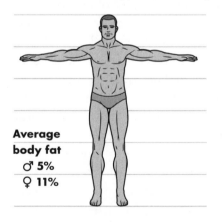

**Average
body fat**
♂ 5%
♀ 11%

Elite-level cross-country skiers are typically average to slightly above average in height. The average height of male Olympic cross-country skiers is 5 feet 10 inches and that of their female counterparts is 5 feet 7 inches. Height provides a mechanical advantage for poling, which is important to the generation of forward thrust in cross-country skiing. However, with height comes mass, and mass is the enemy of performance in cross-country skiing because it increases gravitational and frictional resistance. That's why you don't see as many 6-foot-5 athletes on the competitive ski trails as you do on, say, the volleyball court.

The typical elite-level cross-country skier is light, but not as light as elites in cycling and running. The average female Olympic cross-country skier weighs 141 pounds and the average male weighs 165 pounds. The relative heaviness of cross-country skiers compared to some other types of endurance athletes is due to their need for greater upper-body strength, and with strength comes muscle mass. Former U.S. champion Kris Freeman is typically proportioned for an elite male cross-country skier. He stands 5 feet 11 inches and weighs 170 pounds.

While they may be slightly bigger than other endurance athletes, cross-country skiers are among the leanest athletes in any sport. The average male Olympian has just 5 percent body fat and the average female only 11 percent.

The Cyclist's Body

There is more than one body type in cycling. The typical physique varies by specialty. Climbers tend to be short of stature and very light. At 5 feet 7 inches and 130 pounds, Marco Pantani was not unusually tiny for a climbing specialist. *Domestiques* and time-trial specialists are typically bigger than the climbers. Whereas power-to-weight ratio is the critical variable in climbing, in time

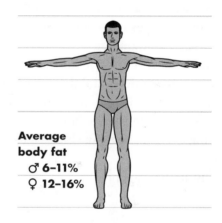

Average body fat
♂ **6–11%**
♀ **12–16%**

trialing, it is raw, sustainable power output that matters most. Virtually every road-cycling course has some elevation change, though, so it's best not to be too heavy. American David Zabriskie, a three-time U.S. time-trial champion, has a typical time-trialist build at 6 feet and 147 pounds. Sprinters need to have the ability to sustain high levels of power output over long distances so that they can arrive at the finishing stretch at the head of the peloton, but once there they need the capacity to churn out massive wattage numbers in a short, all-out effort. Sprinters therefore have the most massive legs in cycling and are bigger generally than other cyclists. Sweden's Magnus Backstedt, a Tour de France sprint-stage winner, raced at 210 pounds.

Overall, though, cyclists in all specializations have similar body types. They have twiggy upper bodies like those of runners but with far more muscular legs. Cyclists have greater leg muscularity because the legs do essentially all of the work in cycling, whereas running is a whole-body activity. In addition, the body gets a lot of "free energy" from ground impact in running, whereas in cycling the leg muscles must provide all of the energy for forward motion except when one is riding downhill.

A very low body-fat percentage is another hallmark of successful cyclists. The range of body-fat percentage among male riders in the European peloton is 6 to 11 percent, with an 8 percent average. The range among elite female cyclists is a very low 12 to 16 percent.

The physical demands of cross-country mountain biking (as distinct from downhill mountain bike racing, which is not an endurance sport) are very similar to those of hilly and mountainous courses in road cycling. Thus, the body type of the cross-country mountain biker is the same as that of the climbing specialist in road cycling: very light and lean. Indeed, the top cross-country mountain bikers and the top climbers in road cycling not only have the same bodies but are sometimes the very same athletes at different points in their careers. The classic case is that of Australian Cadel Evans, who went on to finish second two years in a row in the Tour de France, on the strength of his climbing, after winning a world championship as a mountain biker.

The Rower's Body

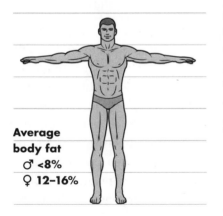

Average body fat
♂ <8%
♀ 12–16%

Rowing is the only endurance sport in which body mass is an actual advantage. Larger rowers have more muscle mass with which to apply force to the oars, which in turn apply force to the water, propelling the boat forward. Of course, more muscle means more power in every endurance sport, but unlike in other endurance sports, that mass comes at no cost in rowing, because there is no gravitational resistance to be overcome and the extra body weight has very little effect on frictional resistance between the boat and the water. Indeed, size is such an advantage in rowing that larger and smaller rowers compete in separate divisions.

Steve Redgrave had a typical, male world-class rower's build. At 6 feet 5 inches, and 225 pounds, Redgrave won five rowing gold medals in five Olympics for Great Britain. Anna Cummins is only slightly above average in size for a champion female rower. A member of the U.S. women's eight team that won gold in Beijing, Cummins stands 6 feet tall and weighs 170 pounds.

Yet you won't find any 300-pound elite rowers, and there are three reasons for this. First, rowing is as much a technique sport as it is a pure power sport. Beyond a certain point, muscle mass gets in the way of technique. You could say that you don't see any rowers with arms like bodybuilders for the same reason you don't see any Major League pitchers with such arms. Pitching a baseball is a power action, but it also requires a whip-like arm motion that is inhibited by excess mass. Second, rowing is also an aerobic sport, and many of the muscle characteristics that support aerobic metabolism cancel out those that support muscle growth. Top rowers are born with aerobically powerful muscles, and they further develop aerobic muscle characteristics in training, thus limiting their muscle-mass gains. Finally, rowing training consumes a lot of calories, keeping the athlete's body-fat percentage low, and a human being can become only so heavy with a body composition as lean as that of the typical elite rower.

How lean are top rowers? There is a difference between heavyweight and lightweight rowers in average body-fat percentage. Lightweight rowers tend to be leaner in part because of their special efforts to make weight. Studies have shown average body-fat percentages in the range of 12 to 16 percent for female lightweights and below 8 percent for male lightweights. The averages are slightly higher among heavyweights.

The Runner's Body

Top distance runners are notoriously light and skinny. Men's marathon world-record holder Haile Gebrselassie of Ethiopia weighs a scant 117 pounds. Women's 5,000 meters world-record holder Tirunesh Dibaba, also Ethiopian, weighs 97 pounds. And it's all muscle. Exercise physiologists William McArdle, of the City College of New York, and Frank Katch, of the University of Massachusetts (McArdle, Katch, and Katch 2005), among many others, have compiled body-composition

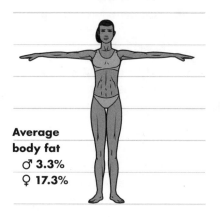

Average body fat
♂ **3.3%**
♀ **17.3%**

data on elite athletes in a wide variety of sports, across a number of studies, and found an average body-fat percentage among elite, male marathon runners of just 3.3 percent—lower than in any other sport—and an average body-fat percentage among female distance runners of 17.3 percent—lower than for every sport except bodybuilding and (of all things) the modern pentathlon.

Body weight is anathema to the distance runner because the runner must move his or her body against gravity—that is, upward—with every stride. A study by researchers at the University of Georgia (Cureton and Sparling 1980) found that a body-weight increase of 5 percent reduced performance by 5 percent in a 12-minute test run.

While you certainly already knew that distance runners are lean and light, you might not have known that elite female runners are average to above average in height (women's marathon world-record holder Paula Radcliffe is 5 feet 8 inches) whereas men are shorter than average. Furthermore, both male and female elites have narrow hips and smaller-than-average feet, and they carry a disproportionate amount of their lower body mass in the upper thighs and less in their lower thighs and shins. All of these features promote running economy.

The Swimmer's Body

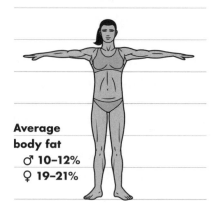

Average body fat
♂ **10–12%**
♀ **19–21%**

Swimming is not a natural human activity, so it is no surprise that the typical elite swimmer's body has some unusual characteristics. Successful swimmers are typically tall—often very tall—with unusually long torsos and arms that enable them to slip through the water efficiently and take long strokes. They also have large feet and loose ankles, which add power to the kick. Many elite swimmers are double-jointed in their elbows, knees, and ankles, an anomaly that helps them apply more body-surface area against the water over a greater joint range of motion and thereby produce greater forward impulse.

Swimmers carry more fat than other endurance athletes, although they are still significantly leaner than nonathletes. Fat is more buoyant than muscle, and buoyancy reduces water resistance, so a little extra "insulation" is beneficial to the swimmer as long as it is evenly distributed on the body. The typical male, elite swimmer has 10 to 12 percent body fat, and the typical female has approximately 19 to 21 percent.

An interesting question is whether body-fat percentages are somewhat higher in swimmers than in other endurance athletes because athletes with more body fat tend to excel in swimming, or because swim training does not reduce body-fat levels as much as other aerobic activities, or because swimmers eat more than other endurance athletes. The notion that athletes with more natural fat excel in swimming is contradicted by the many examples of top swimmers, such as Barb Lindquist, who have become triathletes and become leaner. (Lindquist qualified for the 1988 U.S. Olympic Trials in swimming and represented the United States in the 2004 Olympic Triathlon.) But a study by researchers at the University of Florida (White et al. 2005) found that volunteers ate 44 percent more after swimming in cool versus warm water. This finding suggests that the extra layer of insulation that swimmers carry is an adaptive response to frequent exposure to cold water, mediated through the appetite. If so, it's a beautiful example of the body's deep intelligence, and how the body naturally changes its form and composition to meet the specific demands placed upon it.

The Triathlete's Body

As you might expect, the triathlete's body is a hybrid of the swimmer's, cyclist's, and runner's bodies. Pro triathletes tend to be tall, but not as tall as pure swimmers, and there are plenty of shorter triathletes who do quite well. (At 5 feet 4 inches, Australian Greg Welch is one of only two athletes ever to win the ITU Triathlon World Championship, the Duathlon World Championship, and the Ironman World Championship.) Furthermore, the combination of run training and bike training results in legs that are more muscular than those of pure runners and less muscular than those of pure cyclists.

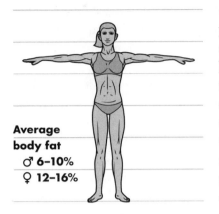

Average body fat
♂ 6–10%
♀ 12–16%

Interestingly, while most champion triathletes have national-class ability in each of the three triathlon disciplines, virtually none has truly world-class ability in one any of the three. A handful of Olympic-caliber swimmers have crossed over to become dominant triathletes, but nobody that I know of has ever transitioned between the highest level of running or cycling and triathlon, in either direction. Of course there's Lance Armstrong, who was already a competitive pro triathlete at age 16 (though one hampered by a relatively weak run) before he became one of the best cyclists of all time. It seems that past a certain point, the body becomes less suited to the other two disciplines as it becomes better suited to any single one of them. Triathlon demands its own special body type that is distinct from that of the swimmer, cyclist, and runner.

One thing that triathletes do have in common with all other endurance athletes is a lean body composition. Average body-fat levels in male and female pros are 6 to 10 percent and 12 to 16 percent, respectively.

THE IMPORTANCE OF BEING LEAN

This review of the body types of endurance athletes should have convinced you that a low body-fat percentage is the only anthropometric characteristic common to elite athletes in all endurance sports. Not only are top-level athletes quite lean, but body composition is an excellent predictor of performance at all levels of these sports. For example, in one study (Hecht et al. 2007), researchers found that the average body-fat percentage among age-group (i.e., non-elite) participants in an Ironman triathlon was 17 percent for males and 27 percent for females. These values are lower than average for the general population, but much higher than the values seen in the pros. And sure enough, when the researchers matched body-fat percentages against finishing times, they found that the men and women with the leanest bodies were also the fastest.

Why is a low body-fat percentage so closely associated with better performance in all endurance sports? It's simple. Body fat makes only a minimal positive contribution to endurance performance, by providing an energy source. But fat is not the limiting fuel source in any race; carbohydrates are. What's more, any excess body fat beyond the essential level required for basic health worsens endurance performance. Therefore one of the natural adaptations that the intelligent body makes in response to intensive endurance training is loss of body fat. Specifically, training increases fat metabolism more than it increases appetite. As a result, food intake is insufficient to replace all of the body fat lost during and between workouts, and the athlete becomes leaner. Performance increases as body fat is lost because of gains in efficiency. The runner has less gravitational resistance to overcome, the swimmer is more hydro-dynamic, and so forth. Also, as body-fat levels go down, aerobic capacity goes up, because muscle has less competition from fat tissue for oxygen and fuel. Endurance athletes who are genetically lean and who become leaner more readily in response to training tend to perform better than their competitors who are not so genetically blessed.

WHAT YOU CAN DO

You cannot change your height, the width of your hips, the length of your feet, or any of several other anthropometric variables affecting endurance performance that I have discussed in this chapter. You can't change your genetic potential for leanness, either. But you can reduce your body-fat percentage (and thereby adjust your weight) to the level that is optimal for performance in your chosen endurance sport given your unchangeable genetic constraints.

If endurance training automatically pushes body composition toward the optimal level of leanness, and if you are not just beginning as an endurance athlete, then why haven't you reached your optimal racing weight and body-fat percentage already? The answer, as I suggested in the introduction, is that the modern lifestyle, with its high-calorie processed foods and all-day sitting, tends to counteract the effects of training. In addition, certain common training errors keep many athletes above their optimal racing weight and limit their performance.

In effect, your training and the rest of your lifestyle are sending your body mixed messages. Errors aside, your training is telling your body, "Let's get leaner," while at the same time your diet (or certain features of your diet) and your inactivity outside of workouts are telling your body, "Let's fatten up!" Your body is very intelligent, and it is perfectly capable of "getting the message" and becoming a lean, mean, racing machine if you are willing to bring your overall lifestyle into line with that goal. In Part II we will begin to do just that. First, however, let's determine your optimal racing weight, set an initial racing-weight goal, and track your progress toward this target—measures that in themselves will help you get leaner by enhancing your focus, awareness, and motivation.

HOW TO DETERMINE YOUR OPTIMAL PERFORMANCE WEIGHT

I magine yourself devoting the next few months to getting in great shape. You train consistently and progressively, pushing hard enough to reach beyond previous limits, yet remaining cautious enough to avoid injuries and overtraining. Your diet is managed with equal care. You load up on wholesome foods and keep the indulgences to a minimum, providing your body with abundant fuel and raw materials for repair and maintenance but without excess. The whole process culminates in a big race in which you achieve a breakthrough performance.

If you weighed yourself on the day of this race, the scale would almost certainly display a different number than your current weight—probably a smaller number. This number represents your *optimal performance weight*—that is, the weight that is associated with your highest athletic performance level. (In reality, as we shall see, it may take you longer than one training cycle—a period of training typically lasting 12 to 24 weeks and culminating in a peak race—to reach your optimal performance weight. But for the purposes of this example let's assume that you are within one training cycle of your optimal performance weight.)

As we saw in the previous chapter, body weight affects performance in every endurance sport. Therefore, as you train and fuel your body toward peak performance, your body adjusts its mass (and composition) to accommodate the demands you're making on it. This change is as significant as any other of the many adaptations that your body makes to accommodate your demand for higher performance, including growth of the heart muscle, greater blood vessel elasticity, and increased muscle glycogen fuel storage.

The process is not as straightforward as simple weight loss, however. Suppose now that, after your big race, you allow yourself to get out of shape and gain some weight. A couple of months pass and—predictably enough—you begin to grow weary of feeling soft and slow and, remembering your optimal performance weight, you set a goal to reclaim it. Except this time, in your haste, you try to get there more quickly by dieting—that is, by sharply cutting your food intake. It seems to work—on one level, anyway. Before long, the scale displays the same reading it did on the day of your last big race. But there's a problem: You're not nearly as fit. That's because you've undernourished your body and consequently lost a lot of muscle along with some fat. So while your body weight is the same as it was when you were in peak shape, your body composition is different—you have a higher body-fat percentage.

You see, when you're in peak shape, you are not only at your optimal body *weight* but you're also at your optimal body *composition*. It's important to consider both of these factors, because it's possible to be at your optimal body weight without being at your optimal body composition and vice versa. From here on, then, I will use the single term "optimal performance weight" (and alternatively, and more casually, "racing weight") to refer to the combination of optimal body weight and optimal body composition.

There is no simple formula for determining your optimal performance weight. Most endurance athletes calculate it by working to achieve peak fitness and then measuring their weight and body composition at that time. But what is peak fitness? Even when you've just had the best race of your life, how do you know you couldn't perform even better in the next training cycle? Your highest performance level is fundamentally unknowable, except in retrospect, and so, therefore, is your optimal performance weight. Even so, most endurance athletes know when they are close to the highest performance level they are capable of achieving in their sport. And by definition, if you're close to your ultimate performance level, you're close to your optimal performance weight. So although optimal performance weight cannot be determined with perfect certainty, it can be quantified within a small margin of error.

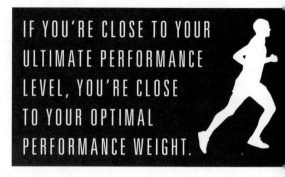

IF YOU'RE CLOSE TO YOUR ULTIMATE PERFORMANCE LEVEL, YOU'RE CLOSE TO YOUR OPTIMAL PERFORMANCE WEIGHT.

It is still useful to estimate your racing weight because it allows you to pursue your optimal performance weight as a semi-independent goal. Having such a target will encourage you to fine-tune your training and nutrition in ways that optimize your weight and body composition faster and enhance the performance benefits that you get from approaching your optimal performance weight.

Creating an advance estimate of your optimal performance weight is also helpful for those who feel that they are not as lean as they should be even when they are in peak shape. There are plenty of endurance athletes whose performance is held back by an apparent inability to reach their optimal performance weight. Obviously, these people cannot determine their optimal performance weight simply by stepping on a body-fat scale on the day of a big race. The problem is not that the definition of optimal performance weight as an athlete's body weight and composition at peak fitness fails to apply to everybody. The problem is that an apparent inability to reach optimal performance weight prevents some athletes from achieving peak fitness.

In this chapter I will show you a simple, step-by-step process that you can use to determine your optimal performance weight through the actual training process. I will also show you a unique method of estimating your optimal performance weight before you achieve it. Although this estimate is almost certain to be slightly too high or too low, it will increase the likelihood that you eventually do reach your optimal performance weight, whatever it turns out to be. But before we get into all of that, let me warn you against thinking of the number you identify by the end of this chapter as a *definitive* calculation of your optimal performance weight.

ESTIMATING YOUR RACING WEIGHT

Most adults have some sense of how much they should weigh. If you picked a man or woman on the street at random and you asked this person to name his or her ideal body weight (don't ever try this experiment!), this person would most likely be able to give you an exact number without hesitation.

Where do such numbers come from? I'll tell you where they *don't* come from: They don't come from the body-weight tables and formulas created by health experts. These tables and formulas, which include height-weight charts used by life insurance companies and body-mass index guidelines used widely by doctors, are far too general to help individual men and women determine an *ideal* body weight. Their main purpose is to quantify the relationships between body size and health throughout the population so that life insurance companies can better judge the risk of insuring their customers and so that doctors have a statistical basis for advising their overweight patients to slim down. Consider the specific example of body mass index (BMI), which is your weight in kilograms (1 kg = 2.2 lbs.) divided by the square of your height in meters (1 m = 3.28 ft.). All of the possible BMI values are lumped into just four classifications, which are based on health risks:

BMI	Classification
Below 18.5	Underweight
18.5–24.9	Normal
25–29.9	Overweight
Above 30	Obese

These broad classifications are not really helpful in determining ideal body weight for most individual men and women—where "ideal weight" could reflect optimal health or the weight at which you look your very best. For example, a person who stands 5 feet 5 inches tall is considered to be of "normal weight" whether he or she weighs 150 pounds (at 24.96 BMI) or 114 pounds (at 19.0 BMI). Presumably, at that height, your healthiest and sexiest body weight is somewhere in that 37-pound range—but where exactly?

Medical science can't say. First of all, there is no single body weight that is optimal for every person of any given height (I'll explain why momentarily). Nor does medicine have metrics that would enable doctors to pinpoint any single person's optimal body weight. The medical definition of optimal body weight, if it existed, would certainly be the weight at which a person's body functions best. But how do we define functioning best? Theoretically, tests of heart disease risk factors, insulin sensitivity, kidney function, aerobic capacity, sleep quality, and so forth could be used to triangulate this number with some degree of precision, but now we're in the realm of experimentation. In other words, this method could not work prescriptively. It could not identify your optimal body weight until you had already achieved it.

So, then, if we cannot determine ideal body weight using BMI charts and height-weight tables, how does the average person determine his or her ideal body weight? One factor is past experience. Many men and women who are not satisfied with their current weight can look back to a time when they were more satisfied, and they yearn to weigh what they weighed then. The mirror is another important factor. Most people have a sense of how they would like to look and, by looking in the mirror and mentally subtracting the excess body fat they see, can estimate how much weight they would have to lose to look that way. You are probably getting closer to identifying that number already.

Nobody knows our bodies better than we do ourselves, so there's no reason to doubt the general validity of such methods of determining an ideal body weight. However, they are not perfect. In our society, on the one hand, all too many people, women especially, develop an unhealthy you-can't-be-too-thin mentality that causes them to chase an unrealistically low body weight. On the other hand, there is also evidence that as people become heavier and heavier, our perceived ideal body weight is also inflating. In other words, while there are more people today who wish they were lighter than they are, as a population we no longer dream of being as light as we used to dream of being. If the average person 20 years ago weighed 160 pounds and wanted to weigh 150 pounds (this is a gross oversimplification for the sake of illustration), then the average person today weighs 175 pounds and wants to weigh 160 pounds. Whereas in the past people wanted to attain what was perhaps a closer-to-true ideal weight, today most people simply want to be not quite so fat while still believing they want to attain their ideal weight.

Athletes are in a similar predicament to that of the general population with respect to weight. There is no formula that can tell you, as an endurance athlete, what your optimal performance weight is. While we do have information about the weight and body composition of elite athletes in the various endurance sports, this information cannot serve as a tool to help other endurance athletes in the same sport determine their own optimal performance weight. After all, weight and body composition are determined largely by our genes. A Wake Forest University study (Hsu et al. 2005) found that body-fat percentage is 64 percent inherited. Lean parents tend to have lean children and fat parents tend to have fat children, regardless of differences in lifestyle. This means that if your parents carry a lot of excess body fat, it is unlikely that you can ever become as lean as the top athletes in your sport, most of whose parents are also naturally lean.

It is not necessarily impossible, though. Lifestyle still controls roughly 36 percent of your body-fat percentage, and it even affects the very genes that regulate your body composition. Finnish researchers (Mustelin et al. 2008) recently compared "discordant" identical twins (one obese, one not obese) and "concordant" identical twins (both non-obese) and found that while both twins in the pairs with one obese member were more likely to have certain genes that slowed metabolism, making them predisposed to obesity, these genes were significantly less active in the non-obese member of the discordant pairs, who tended to have a much higher fitness level. These results suggest that exercise switches off some of the genes that work to make you fat, making it almost as though you had not inherited these genes in the first place.

> LIFESTYLE CONTROLS ROUGHLY 36 PERCENT OF YOUR BODY-FAT PERCENTAGE.

Besides genetic influence, another factor that makes optimal performance weight nearly impossible to estimate is the long-term influence of your lifestyle, body weight, and body composition throughout your life. As most of us know from experience, body fat is easier to put on than to take off. This is because storing excess fat on your body is different from other forms of storage, such as dumping grain into a silo. After all, dumping grain into a silo does not change the silo. But the fat that you add to your body during periods of weight gain affects your whole body in lasting ways that make this fat resistant to subsequent breakdown. Your insulin sensitivity decreases, making it harder to build and fuel muscle tissue and easier to store even more body fat. Your appetite adjusts to support a higher body weight. And if you reduce your eating, despite your increased appetite, your resting metabolism slows down, at least temporarily, to conserve those fat stores, much as you might switch to driving a smaller car to conserve gas in response to rising fuel prices. In sum, gaining fat alters your body's "set point" for weight and composition, so that after a period of significant weight gain, it may no longer be realistic to pursue levels of lightness and leanness that might have been realistic before.

There is some evidence that fat stored above the body's midline is broken down more easily than fat stored below the waist. Therefore, so-called apple-shaped individuals may lose their excess body fat more easily than so-called pear-shaped individuals. Unfortunately, women are more likely than men to be pear-shaped, and studies show that overweight men generally lose weight faster than equivalently overweight women on the same weight-loss program. But there are plenty of men and women who are able to become very lean even after gaining large amounts of excess fat in their hips and thighs. The bottom line is that you just never know what's possible for you until you have trained and fueled your way into peak form.

TRACKING PERFORMANCE, WEIGHT, AND BODY COMPOSITION

So far, we've established that inability to reach optimal performance weight is one of the factors that most commonly prevent endurance athletes from performing better than they do. Furthermore, you can only be certain of your optimal performance weight once you've achieved it. This is why we define optimal performance weight functionally, as the combined body weight and body composition associated with your highest level of performance in your sport.

To determine your optimal performance weight, begin by creating a table that plots your body weight and body composition against your performance during a period of progressive training and carefully controlled diet in pursuit of a peak race performance. Once every four weeks, step on a body-fat scale and note your weight and body-fat percentage. On the same days you weigh in, perform a test workout that provides a good indicator of your race-specific fitness. For example, if you're a runner, go to the track and do a 10K time trial at 95 percent effort.

Create a four-column table with the date in the farthest left column, your performance test time in the next column, your body weight in the next, and your body composition in the rightmost column. After three or four testing days have been completed and recorded, you will begin to notice a clear pattern, demonstrated in the illustration that follows. It is likely that you will achieve your best performance at your lowest body weight and body-fat composition. And if you train and eat right, you will reach your highest performance level at the time of your scheduled peak race.

You're not done yet, however. Your weight at the time of your next peak race is not necessarily your optimal racing weight. If your current body-fat level is too high, you might not have enough time to reach your optimal performance weight by the date of your next peak race. And regardless of your starting weight, any one of a number of common training and dietary errors could prevent you from reaching your optimal racing weight in time for your next peak race. If you're in this situation, you can't rely on your test workout or race performances to tell you what your optimal performance weight is—yet. It may take you two or three full training cycles to arrive at the point where your performance is no longer limited by your weight. In this case your focus should be on consistently practicing the Racing Weight plan presented in Part II, which will eliminate the dietary and training errors that are currently holding you back.

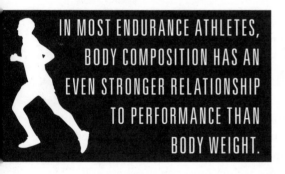

IN MOST ENDURANCE ATHLETES, BODY COMPOSITION HAS AN EVEN STRONGER RELATIONSHIP TO PERFORMANCE THAN BODY WEIGHT.

In the meantime, keep tracking your weight, body-fat percentage, and performance so you can watch and draw motivation from your progress along the way.

As you track your progress, it is important that you measure both your body weight and your body-fat percentage. Again, this is because you can reach any given body weight at more than one body-fat percentage, and in most endurance athletes, body composition has an even stronger relationship to performance than body weight. If you track only body weight, you may be prone to making the all-too-common mistake of approaching performance weight management with a simplistic "lighter is better" mentality, and as a result you may try to slim down in ways that cause you to lose muscle along with fat (most likely by undernourishing your body).

Consequently, while you may eventually reach your optimal body weight through these means, you will do so at a greater-than-optimal body-fat percentage. Your performance at this body weight/body-fat percentage combination will not be as good as it is when you are at your optimal body weight *and* body composition (that is, your true optimal performance weight). Tracking your body-fat percentage along with your body weight can function as a check against making this mistake. Yes, you want to be light (unless, perhaps, you're a swimmer or rower), but you don't want to be light at all costs. You want to be light and lean.

Here's a concrete example of the process I've just outlined. A female runner completes five performance tests at four-week intervals spanning the duration of a full training cycle that begins with base training and culminates in a peak 10K race. Her performance test consists of a 10K run on the track completed at a 95 percent effort level. She measures her body weight and body-fat percentage on the day of each performance test. Her results are seen in Table 2.1.

TABLE 2.1 TRACKING BODY WEIGHT, PERFORMANCE, AND COMPOSITION

Date	Performance Test Time (10K)	Body Weight (lbs.)	Body-Fat Percentage
3/7/09	43:02:00	141	22.1
4/4/09	42:29:00	137	21.0
5/2/09	41:58:00	136	20.7
5/30/09	42:30:00	134	20.2
6/27/09	40:43:00	130	19.7

PERFORMANCE TESTS

The following are suggested performance tests for the most popular endurance sports. Be sure to warm up properly for each of them.

CROSS-COUNTRY SKIING. Because snow conditions are ever changing and have a strong effect on cross-country skiing performance, it is seldom possible to do regular fitness tests outdoors on skis that provide a valid indication of changes in fitness. Therefore I recommend that you use one of the following two alternatives instead.

Option 1. Ski as hard as you can for 20 minutes on a cross-country ski ergometer (and indoor ski machine with power measuring capability). Note your average power output (watts).

Option 2. If you do not have regular access to a cross-country ski ergometer and you use cycling as a cross-training modality, perform the cycling test described below.

CYCLING. Ride 20 minutes at maximum effort on a flat, smooth road course or an indoor trainer. Note your distance covered and use it to calculate your average speed, or, if you use a power meter, note your average power. Whichever options you choose for your ride location and performance measurement variable, use them for every test for maximum validity of comparisons between tests.

MOUNTAIN BIKING. If your sport is mountain biking, you can use the cycling test described above or perform a 20-minute maximum effort on a stretch of trail that is easily accessed from your home. Be sure to ride the same stretch of trail every time you repeat the test.

ROWING. Perform a 5,000-meter time trial at maximum effort on a rowing ergometer. Note your time and calculate your average speed or note your average power output.

RUNNING. Run 10 kilometers at 95 percent of maximum effort on a running track or a smooth, flat road. Note your time and calculate your average pace.

SWIMMING. Swim 5 × 100 yards on a 5:00 interval (with plenty of rest) in your main stroke discipline. Calculate your average time per 100 yards.

SWIMMING (OPEN WATER). If you want to use your performance test to prepare for open-water swimming, try one of the following options.

Option 1. Swim 1,000 yards at maximum effort in a pool. Note your time and calculate your average pace per 100.

Option 2. Swim a marked open-water course that takes roughly 10 minutes to complete at maximum effort. Note your time. Be sure to swim in an area that is easily accessed from your home so you can use it for all of your performance tests.

TRIATHLON. Perform one of the two cycling tests, the running test, and one of the two open-water swimming tests described above once every four weeks. Stagger the cycling and running tests so that you're never doing them in the same week. It's okay to do either the cycling and swimming tests or the running and swimming tests in the same week.

You may find it helpful to estimate your optimal performance weight before you discover it experientially. Many athletes train hard and eat right (or so they think) and yet still have a visible excess of flab on their tummies, hips, and/or thighs even when they are in race shape. If you find yourself at just such an impasse, you may find it helpful to estimate how much more fat you can reasonably expect to lose with further refinements to your training and diet. This estimate might not be completely precise, but it can give you a goal and a target that will encourage you to modify your training and diet in new ways to make you leaner, lighter, and faster.

For that matter, generating an estimated optimal performance weight can be helpful to any endurance athlete who has not yet gone through the process of determining it functionally. After all, it takes many weeks to work your way into peak shape. And since you're reading this book on racing weight *now*, you would probably like to know *now* at least approximately what your racing weight should be, so that you can go after it consciously the same way you consciously go after race performance goals. Numbers are powerful motivators. In all domains of human endeavor, we typically achieve more when we quantify our goals than we do when we just go by feel. For this reason, I encourage all endurance athletes to estimate their optimal performance weight even before they have a chance to determine it functionally, despite the fact that there is no absolutely reliable way to create such an estimate. What the optimal performance weight estimation method I'm about to show you lacks in accuracy it makes up for in practical benefit. It makes you more conscious of the effects of body weight and composition on your performance, more aware of the training methods and dietary habits that affect your weight and fat levels, and more focused on and motivated to achieve your optimal performance weight. Once you have achieved it, you can do away with estimates and use the numbers you arrived at functionally to give you the same benefits in the future.

Generating an estimate of optimal performance weight (which, remember, includes a body-weight number and a body-fat percentage number) really amounts to setting an initial performance weight *goal*. This method is designed to generate realistic goals, but you're just as likely to exceed the target as to fall short of it. Either way you will end up with a lean body that is fit for maximal performance.

To generate an estimate of your optimal performance weight you will need to get an initial body-fat measurement. The easiest and most affordable way to measure your body-fat percentage (but not the most accurate) is to step on a body-fat scale, but there are other methods. I

TABLE 2.2 **BODY-FAT PERCENT POPULATION PROFILES**

Locate the body-fat percentage closest to your own current number.

Percen-tile	MEN					Goal
	20–29	30–39	40–49	50–59	60+	
99	2.4	5.2	6.6	8.8	7.7	
95	5.2	9.1	11.4	12.9	13.1	
90	7.1	11.3	13.6	15.3	16.3	
85	8.3	12.7	15.1	16.9	17.2	
80	9.4	13.9	16.3	17.9	18.4	Improve 10%
75	10.6	14.9	17.3	19.0	19.8	
70	11.8	15.9	18.1	19.8	20.3	
65	12.9	16.6	18.8	20.6	21.1	
60	14.1	17.5	19.6	21.3	22.0	
55	15.0	18.2	20.3	22.1	22.6	Improve to 80%
50	15.9	19.0	21.1	22.7	23.5	
45	16.8	19.7	21.8	23.4	24.3	
40	17.4	20.5	22.5	24.1	25.0	
35	18.3	21.4	23.3	24.9	25.9	
30	19.5	22.3	24.1	25.7	26.7	
25	20.7	23.2	25.0	26.6	27.6	
20	22.4	24.2	26.1	27.5	28.5	Improve 25%
15	23.9	25.5	27.3	28.8	29.7	
10	25.9	27.3	28.9	30.3	31.2	
5	29.1	29.9	31.5	32.4	33.4	
1	36.4	35.6	37.4	38.1	41.3	

Source: Compiled from data collected by Kip Russo, founder of Body Fat Test, Inc.; reproduced here with permission. Russo used a testing method called hydrodensitometry, which is one of the most accurate methods of body-fat measurement.

will briefly discuss all of them in the next chapter. After you conduct an initial body-fat test, go to Table 2.2 and find the column for your gender and age group. Then find the percentile that most closely corresponds to your result. For example, suppose you are a 40-year-old woman and your initial body-fat measurement is 26.5 percent. The closest match in your table is 26.4 percent, which corresponds to the 50th percentile for your gender and age group. This means your body-fat percentage is lower than that of exactly half the people in your gender and age group.

			WOMEN			
Goal	20–29	30–39	40–49	50–59	60+	Percen-tile
	5.4	7.3	11.6	11.6	15.4	99
	10.8	13.4	16.1	18.8	16.8	95
	14.5	15.5	18.5	21.6	21.1	90
	16.0	16.9	20.3	23.6	23.5	85
Improve 10%	17.1	18.0	21.3	25.0	25.1	80
	18.2	19.1	22.4	25.8	25.7	75
	19.0	20.0	23.5	26.6	27.5	70
	19.8	20.8	24.3	27.4	28.5	65
	20.6	21.6	24.9	28.5	29.3	60
Improve to 80%	21.3	22.4	25.5	29.2	29.9	55
	22.1	23.1	26.4	30.1	30.9	50
	22.7	24.0	27.3	30.8	31.8	45
	23.7	24.9	28.1	31.6	32.5	40
	24.4	26.0	29.0	32.6	33.0	35
	25.4	27.0	30.1	33.5	34.3	30
	26.6	28.1	31.1	34.3	35.5	25
Improve 25%	27.7	29.3	32.1	35.6	36.6	20
	29.8	31.0	33.3	36.6	38.0	15
	32.1	32.8	35.0	37.9	39.3	10
	35.4	35.7	37.8	39.6	40.5	5
	40.5	40.0	45.5	50.8	47.0	1

Table 2.2 is based on data collected from thousands of body-fat tests performed on men and women of all ages. These data have been used to create percentile rankings for men and women in various age brackets, and they can show how you compare against a broad population that is skewed toward the athletic. The numbers in Table 2.2 are significantly lower than those in the general population (as we saw earlier in the chapter), because the data come from a self-selected group, and those who volunteer for body-fat testing tend to be much leaner than those who do not. But, of course, this very fact makes the numbers more relevant to athletes like you.

The next step in estimating your optimal performance weight is to use your current body-fat percentage and Table 2.2 to make an estimate of your optimal body-fat percentage. Most endurance athletes, including beginners, are genetically capable of reaching at least the 80th percentile for their gender and age group. In other words, most endurance athletes can sculpt a body that is leaner than those of eight out of ten persons in their reference group. If your current body-fat percentage is

ESTIMATING YOUR OPTIMAL PERFORMANCE WEIGHT

Let's look at an example of estimating optimal body weight. Suppose your current body weight is 170 pounds, your current body-fat percentage is 14.4, and, as a 35-year-old male, your body-fat percentage goal is 12.0 percent (moving you two rows up from halfway between the 75th and 80th percentiles to halfway between the 85th and 90th percentiles). To determine how many pounds of body weight you will lose in lowering your body-fat percentage from 14.4 to 12.0, first calculate your current lean body mass. This is the portion of your body weight that consists of stuff other than fat (muscle, bone, etc.) and it won't change much as you shed body fat to get leaner. Since your current body-fat percentage is 14.4, you know that the other 85.6 percent of your current body weight consists of lean body mass. Multiplying your current body weight by your current lean body mass percentage yields your current lean body mass: 170 lbs. x 85.6 = 145.5 lbs.

When you reach your optimal body-fat percentage of 12.0, your lean body mass will remain approximately 145.5 pounds, because you will not lose any muscle or bone, only fat. But your lean body mass will now account for 88 percent of your total body weight instead of only 85.5 percent. Representing your new body weight as X, use the following equation to calculate its value: 145.5 lbs. = 0.88X, or X = 145.5 lbs. ÷ 0.88. Using a calculator to divide 145.5 by 0.88 we get an estimated optimal body weight of 165.3 pounds.

between the 40th and 70th percentile for your age and gender group, set an initial goal to reach the 80th percentile. For example, if you are a 52-year-old male and your current body-fat percentage is 21.5, placing you in the 60th percentile for men aged 50 to 59, then set a goal of lowering your body-fat percentage to 17.9, which defines the 80th percentile for your group.

If your current body-fat percentage places you between the 1st and 35th percentiles for your age and gender group, you might still be able to reach the 80th percentile eventually, but you might not, so it's best to set a more modest goal. Don't feel bad, though, because in another respect your goal can be more ambitious than those of athletes who are already relatively lean. Because your body carries a greater amount of excess fat, you can expect to sharply lower your body-fat percentage through proper training and diet. Your initial goal, if you are currently between the 1st and 35th percentiles, should be to move up five rows on Table 2.2. So if you're a 26-year-old female and your current body-fat percentage is 28.0, placing you in the 20th percentile for women aged 20 to 29, your

This method of using an estimated optimal body-fat percentage to calculate an estimated optimal body weight will be less accurate for individuals who are likely to gain some lean body mass—namely muscle—in the process of getting in shape. That's because gaining muscle lowers one's body-fat percentage even in the absence of body-fat loss. If you plan to do more weightlifting than you have in the recent past as part of your training, you can expect to gain a pound or two of muscle even as you lose fat and should account for this expected muscle weight gain in your estimated optimal body weight.

The final step in the process of estimating your optimal performance weight is to use your optimal body-fat percentage estimate to calculate an optimal body-weight target. First, step on a scale to get your current body weight. Next, use your current body weight and current body-fat percentage to determine your lean body mass, which will not change much. Finally, use your lean body mass and estimated optimal body-fat percentage to arrive at an estimate of your optimal body weight.

Step	How It's Done	Example
1. Calculate your current lean body mass	Current body weight × current lean body mass percentage	170 × 0.855 = 145.5
2. Calculate your optimal body weight	Lean body mass ÷ optimal lean body mass percentage	145.5 ÷ 0.88 = 165.3

Note: You can calculate lean body mass percentage by subtracting your current body fat percentage from 100%.

initial goal is to move up five rows to the 45th percentile, at 22.7 percent body fat.

Those near the lean end of the body composition continuum, whose current body-fat percentage places them at or above the 75th percentile for their reference group, cannot expect to lose much more body fat, but they can still expect to make big performance gains in losing a little body fat. If your current body-fat percentage is between the 75th and 90th percentiles, set an initial goal to move up just one or two rows on Table 2.2. Two rows represent an acceptable goal if you're currently rather far from peak race shape and/or your diet leaves much to be desired; one row is more realistic if you're already quite fit and eating healthily.

Athletes whose current body-fat percentage places them in the 95th or 99th percentile for their age and gender should not set goals to lose any more of what little body fat they have, although they might become a bit leaner still in the process of becoming race fit. If you are already leaner than 95 out of 100 active persons your age, it is best to determine your optimal body composition using the functional method described earlier in the chapter.

In setting your body-fat percentage goal, it's okay to "split the difference" when your current body-fat percentage places you between rows of Table 2.2. For example, if you're a 35-year-old male whose current body-fat percentage is 14.4, you're almost smack between the 75th percentile (14.9 percent) and the 80th percentile (13.9 percent) for your reference group. The appropriate goal for you is to move up two rows in your column on Table 2.2. To make your goal more accurate, go ahead and set a target to reach a body-fat percentage that is roughly halfway between the body-fat percentage associated with the 85th percentile (12.7) and the body-fat percentage associated with the 90th percentile (11.3). A target of 12.0 percent would be about right in this case.

THE HEISENBERG PRINCIPLE

In physics there is a principle called the Heisenberg uncertainty principle that states that merely observing a phenomenon at the subatomic level changes it. You can think of this principle as the scientific version of the expression "The watched pot never boils." We apply the notion that watching a thing alters its course to many other domains of human endeavor as well. In the corporate world, for example, senior executives are fond of the expression "What gets measured gets managed." I like this expression, too, and I think it applies equally to health, fitness, and endurance performance. It expresses the idea that if you want to gain greater control over some aspect of your business (or your body), one of the best things you can do is to monitor it systematically using some kind of relevant measuring stick. The very effort to do so makes it a higher priority and helps you improve this aspect of your business or your body independently of other efforts.

You will find that estimating and tracking your progress toward your racing weight is similarly effective with respect to your objectives to become leaner and to maximize your race performance. In the following chapter I will give you detailed guidelines for three important components of this tracking process: measuring your body weight and body-fat percentage, keeping a food journal, and calculating the number of calories you burn each day.

THREE

TRACKING YOUR PROGRESS

Endurance athletes are often shocked by what they learn the first time they have their diet analyzed by a sports nutritionist or analyze their own diets with the use of the increasingly sophisticated do-it-yourself diet analysis tools that are available. A typical example is the case of Rafael de la Vega of Miami, Florida. An elite-level swimmer in his teens and early twenties, Rafael later got into triathlons but then stopped training altogether upon becoming a father and suffering some overuse injuries. After four years without exercise he weighed 236 pounds. Disgusted with himself, Rafael started swimming again and then hired triathlon coach Lee Zohlman, who requested that Rafael log his eating for one week using the nutrition tools available on the TrainingPeaks Web site. "One week was more than enough," Rafael says. "The tools showed me that I was overeating and my calorie intake was much higher than I needed."

Zohlman showed Rafael how to modify his diet so that his calorie intake matched the number of calories his body used each day. Over the next six months Rafael lost 46 pounds while working his way back into peak triathlon shape.

Rafael's story is a good illustration of the principle, which I discussed in the previous chapter, that the very act of regularly measuring certain variables that are relevant to your racing weight will help you reach and maintain it. Studies of nonathletic populations have yielded scientific evidence supporting this notion. For example, in a 2008 study by researchers at Minneapolis Heart Research Institute (VanWormer et al. 2009), 100 overweight individuals enrolled in a 12-month weight-loss program were encouraged to weigh themselves frequently at home. The study's authors found that frequency of self-weighing was significantly correlated with weight loss and weight-loss maintenance. Subjects lost approximately one extra pound for every 11 days they weighed themselves.

In this regard, keeping a food journal appears to work just as well as weighing yourself regularly. In a study from the Kaiser Permanente Health Research Center (Hollis et al. 2008), researchers found that overweight individuals participating in an eight-month weight-loss program lost twice as much weight when they kept a daily food diary than when they logged their food intake irregularly or not at all.

There's no magic to these effects. The act of monitoring variables that are relevant to one's goals affects one's pursuit of those goals by increasing awareness. Frequent self-weighing helps the dieter lose weight and maintain weight loss by presenting the dieter with clear, undeniable evidence of weight changes (in either direction). Keeping a food journal, especially a journal that includes calorie counts, helps the dieter lose weight by providing clear, quantitative proof of how much he or she is eating and provides the opportunity to compare this number against the number of calories the dieter needs to eat to lose weight.

In this chapter I will show you how to track three variables that are relevant to your goal of reaching and maintaining your racing weight, which bears a family resemblance but is certainly not identical to the dieter's goal of losing weight. These three variables are: (1) Body weight and body composition (which are two different variables, of course, but for the purposes of tracking I lump them together); (2) Calories consumed in food (or "calories in"); and (3) Calories burned through resting metabolism and activity (or "calories out").

The number of calories you consume daily and the number of calories you burn daily are inputs into an equation whose output is changes in your body weight and body composition. Tracking the number of calories you consume and burn each day is a bit like tracking the daily performance of each stock in your retirement portfolio. Tracking your body weight and body composition (weekly, biweekly, or monthly) is more like tracking the total value of your retirement portfolio on a quarterly basis. In other words, tracking your body weight and body composition provides a global, long-term view of your progress toward your racing weight. Counting calories in and calories out gives you a narrow, immediate glimpse of the primary factors that affect your body weight and body composition over time. Tracking your body weight and body composition is something that you should do consistently year-round, because it provides direct information about how close you are to your racing weight, and because it is easy to do. Tracking your calories in and calories out is something that you need to do only periodically, because it will not tell you anything new during periods when your diet (calories in) and training (calories out) are consistent, and because it's a bit of a hassle.

MEASURING YOUR BODY WEIGHT AND BODY-FAT PERCENTAGE

There's really nothing to weighing yourself, but some people still manage to make a mess of it. Take my wife, for example. Whenever she's trying to lose weight, she weighs herself two or three times a day and drives herself crazy by making too much of any upward fluctuations, which are normal over the course of a day even when you are successfully losing weight. It really doesn't make sense to weigh yourself more often than once a week, as doing so is likely to distract you with arbitrary fluctuations that mask a true upward or downward trend.

Weigh yourself with a minimum frequency of once every four weeks, on the same day you perform your periodic fitness-test workouts as described in the previous chapter. These are your "official weigh-ins" for use in determining your optimal performance weight.

It was once believed that weighing oneself too often could cause anxiety and depression, but the latest research suggests that this is not the case. In fact, the most recent study on this issue found that women who weighed themselves daily were leaner than women who weighed themselves once a week, probably because of the heightened level of awareness that attends more frequent self-monitoring. So if you wish to weigh yourself daily, go ahead; just be sure not to take daily fluctuations too seriously, and do weigh yourself at the same time each day and in the same circumstances for accurate comparisons. Don't weigh yourself first thing in the morning on the upstairs bathroom scale wearing pajamas one day and then weigh yourself after dinner on the downstairs bathroom scale in the nude the next day.

Some scales are better than others. I suggest you invest in the best scale that's within your budget. One feature to look for is automatic zero calibration, which resets the scale to "true zero" weight after each use. You might also want a scale that gives readings to the ounce, or tenth of a pound. Those little less-than-a-pound changes can be surprisingly motivating when you're pursuing your optimal performance weight. Finally, since you are also monitoring your body-fat percentage, it makes a lot of sense to purchase a weight scale with integrated body-fat measurement capability.

Body-Fat Scales

Until fairly recently, there was no convenient, affordable, and accurate way to measure your own body-fat level. The best option available was the skinfold method, which entails pinching skinfolds between calipers and running the measurements through a complex mathematical formula. It was affordable enough, but a hassle to do, and often inaccurate when performed without formal training. Hydrostatic (or underwater) weighing was considered the most accurate method, but it required bulky, expensive equipment that was not widely available. Hydrostatic weighing has been replaced by DEXA scanning as the most accurate way to measure body-fat percentage, and in fact it is the only method that *directly* measures body-fat levels instead of estimating them based on measurements of other things. A DEXA scanner uses advanced imaging technology to "see" the body fat inside you (it is also used to measure bone mineral density). But getting a body-fat analysis from a DEXA scanner requires that you make an appointment with a doctor who has one, so it's no more convenient and affordable than hydrostatic weighing.

Thank goodness for body-fat scales! Body-fat scales using bioelectrical impedance technology are now widely available at department stores, drugstores, sporting goods stores, and elsewhere. These devices are easy to use, affordable, and, while not as accurate as professional body-fat measurement methods such as DEXA scanning, are accurate enough.

A 2007 study published in the journal *Clinical Nutrition* that compared measurements obtained from a Tanita body-fat scale and DEXA scanning reported a better than 96 percent level of agreement between the two methods (Thomson et al. 2007). Body-fat scales with this degree of accuracy are available for as little as $40.

Body-fat scales look just like regular bathroom scales. You step onto them and get a measurement. And they do in fact measure your body weight in addition to estimating your body-fat percentage. Body-fat scales work by sending an electrical signal into your body and measuring the degree of resistance (or impedance) encountered. Electrical signals pass through fat tissue more quickly than they do through muscle tissue, so the less resistance the body-fat scale registers, the higher your body-fat percentage must be.

To ensure accurate results, it is important that you use your device in strict accordance with the instructions included with it. Different units have slightly different requirements. Here are some usage guidelines that apply to most body-fat scales:

- Always measure your body fat at the same time of day, preferably at least two hours after eating.
- Make sure you are well hydrated.
- Use the bathroom before stepping on the scale.
- Moisten a towel and step on it with bare feet before stepping on the scale (to enhance conductivity).
- Make sure the scale is on a flat, hard surface (such as bathroom tiles).
- If you have good reason to believe that your body-fat percentage is already low (e.g., you have visible abdominal musculature), purchase a scale with an "athlete" mode. Scales without this feature are less accurate for lean individuals.

Popular brands of body-fat scales include Conair, Tanita (which also makes scales under the Weight Watchers, Ironman, and Jenny Craig brand names), Oregon Scientific, Phoenix, and Taylor. A company called Omron makes hand-held body-fat analyzers that use bioelectrical impedance as well, but these devices do not measure body weight. The difference between the higher-priced body-fat scales and the cheaper models is mainly in the number of features, not their accuracy. You can find body-fat scales at department stores such as Wal-Mart, drugstores such as Walgreens, and sporting goods stores, including Sport Chalet.

Most of the fancier features on these devices have little or no value. For example, some devices purport to measure your hydration status. It sounds like a useful tool for athletes, who are often dehydrated after workouts and must rehydrate fully to maximize performance in their next workout. But the accuracy of this feature is poor. What's more, the popular notion that endurance athletes commonly fail to properly rehydrate between workouts is false. An interesting study from the University of Glasgow, Scotland (Fudge et al. 2008), looked at the hydration status of elite Kenyan runners in heavy training over a five-day period. Despite becoming significantly dehydrated during their runs, and drinking little or nothing during or immediately after workouts, these runners were found to restore their bodies to normal hydration levels by the evening simply by drinking when thirsty throughout the day.

One fancy feature available in some body-fat scales that I do like is a basal metabolic rate calculator. This tool makes it much easier to calculate the number of calories you burn each day, as you will see in the next section.

If you use a body-fat scale, you might as well measure your body-fat percentage as often as you measure your body weight, since you'll get both measurements from the same device. Note, however, that day-to-day fluctuations in body-fat percentage are perhaps even less meaningful than day-to-day changes in your body weight. The body-fat measurements that really matter are those that you calculate roughly once every four weeks, on the same day you do your fitness-test workouts, in the process of determining your optimal performance weight.

Again, body-fat scales are not the most accurate tools for measuring body-fat percentage. For this reason, it is best not to use them to compare your body composition to that of other people. But when your goal is simply to track changes in your own body-fat percentage, it's more important that your measurements be *consistent* (that is, your scale is measuring the same attribute to the same degree of accuracy on each occasion) than *accurate*, and body-fat scales do give consistent results when used properly. If the highest degree of accuracy is very important to you, there is a way to effectively increase the accuracy of your body-fat scale without taking on a lot of extra hassle or expense. Just make an appointment with a physician for a DEXA scan. Before you leave for that appointment, measure your body-fat percentage on your body-fat scale. Use the difference between the two measurements as the "margin of error" for your body-fat scale and use it to correct its measurements going forward.

For example, suppose your body-fat scale gives you a reading of 17.0 percent and the DEXA scanner gives you a reading of 18.8 percent (the number that the DEXA scanner gives you is almost certain to be higher, by the way). In all of your future body-fat scale measurements, add 1.8 percent to your reading to get your "true" body-fat percentage.

Counting "Calories In"

Counting calories makes sense. A calorie (technically a kilocalorie) is a unit of energy. Specifically, it is energy stored in the bonds of the nutrient molecules we consume in food. To oversimplify a bit, when calories remain stored in molecular bonds, those molecules become part of our bodies (for example, body fat). When our bodies break apart those bonds, the energy is released and used to fuel a biological function such as contracting a muscle. Thus, when you ingest more calories in food than you use for biological functions, you gain weight, and when you burn more than you store, you lose weight.

But what's simple in principle can be difficult in practice. Counting calories for the sake of managing body weight has historically been difficult for two reasons. First, it's a pain in the butt, requiring more time and effort than most people feel it is worth. Second, the do-it-yourself methods of calorie counting are not very accurate.

Recent advances have made calorie counting easier than it used to be, however. In particular, online tools such as those on TrainingPeaks have greatly streamlined the process. Furthermore, researchers have found that do-it-yourself calorie counting does not have to be 100 percent accurate, or even 95 percent accurate, to be helpful. That's because counting calories increases dietary awareness, and when people are more conscious of what they are eating they automatically eat better, even when they don't make a conscious effort to act on their awareness, though it works even better when they do.

Very few people, even among those who succeed in losing excess body fat and keeping it off, count every calorie they consume every day of their lives. It simply isn't necessary. Most people naturally maintain fairly consistent eating habits. Counting calories in the beginning can help you identify those eating habits that are most effective in moving you closer to your optimal weight, and it will be easy to stay close to your optimal weight simply by being consistent with those habits. These habits will involve eating certain types of food regularly and eating others minimally, or not at all, choosing particular portion sizes, and establishing a schedule of meal and snack times. Such habits are easy to re-create from one day to the next without calorie counting.

The tool of calorie counting is sort of like the booster rocket that a space shuttle uses for liftoff. The booster rocket provides the power the shuttle needs to overcome the earth's strong gravitational pull at ground level. But once the shuttle reaches a certain altitude, the force of gravity becomes weaker and the shuttle is able to jettison the booster rocket and orbit the planet unassisted. Similarly, calorie counting can help you identify what you should eat, how much, and how often to reach your racing weight. But once you know what, how much, and when to eat, there's no longer any need to count calories, and you can then maintain your weight by continuing to practice the eating habits that calorie counting helped you create.

There are two ways to count calories: low-tech and high-tech. The low-tech way is to record calorie information from the labels of the foods

CALORIE COUNTING ILLUSTRATED

For the sake of illustrating calorie counting, I logged my nutrition intake and tallied the calories. Here's how it came out:

Food	Calories	Source
Breakfast		
Whole-grain breakfast cereal	360	Product label, adjusted for larger serving
Low-fat milk	195	Product label, adjusted for larger serving
Black coffee	5	Starbucks.com
Orange juice	110	Product label
Fish oil	40	Product label
Snack		
ReadyPac Cool Cuts Carrot sticks with ranch dressing	105	Product label (adjusted because less than half the dressing was used)
Lunch		
Organic multigrain bread	140	Product label (2 servings)
Herb-roasted turkey breast	70	Product label

you eat and to find calorie information on nonlabeled foods in a resource such as *The Complete Book of Food Counts* by Corinne Netzer. To do this accurately you need to get your portions right. For example, suppose you have a bowl of Cheerios with skim milk for breakfast. According to the label, Cheerios contain 110 calories per 1-cup serving, and skim milk contains 86 calories in a 1-cup serving. But if you like a nice big bowl of cereal in the morning, you may eat 1½ cups of Cheerios with 1 cup of skim milk (it's normal to add roughly ¾ cup of milk to 1 cup of cereal). As this example shows, your calorie counting will be more accurate if you measure your food portions whenever appropriate instead of assuming you're eating or drinking one serving.

Calorie counting is most difficult when you prepare meals from scratch and when you eat out at independent (nonchain) restaurants. You could go crazy trying to figure out how many calories are in one portion's worth of every ingredient you add to a homemade chili. Likewise, while virtually all large chain restaurants provide calorie information for all of their menu items, the typical independent restaurant chef has no clue how many calories are in his or her creations.

Food	Calories	Source
Swiss cheese	120	Product label
Mayonnaise	90	Product label
Mustard	3	Product label
Banana	105	Nutritiondata.com
Naked Juice Superfood	140	Product label
Dark chocolate	105	Product label
Snack		
Low-fat yogurt	135	Product label
Dinner		
Cod filet	140	Product label
Seafood marinade	25	Product label
Uncle Ben's Ready Whole Grain Medley	220	Product label
Asparagus with olive oil, salt	165	Nutritiondata.com
Beer	150	Product label
Dark chocolate	105	Product label
Total calories	**2,528**	

You just have to do the best you can. Look up all of the foods you eat (and the beverages you drink) at restaurants by type (e.g., grilled salmon) in a calorie counting resource. Estimate the portion sizes as accurately as you can, and be sure to account for the liberal use of butter and heavy sauces that is the norm in restaurants. When cooking at home, you may tally calories ingredient by ingredient, which is horribly tedious, or you may cook from recipes with calories-per-serving estimates, which are increasingly available in magazines, in books, and online.

If you go online, you might as well take the high-tech approach to counting calories. Various Web sites offer applications that allow you to quickly look up the foods you eat and add them to a personal journal, which automatically tallies caloric information and sometimes also grams and percentages of carbohydrate, fat, and protein. One of the better food journaling tools with calorie counting capability is available at livestrong. com. The best, in my humble opinion, lives at racingweight.com.

The racingweight.com training and nutrition log is powered by Training-Peaks, the leading provider of online training and nutrition tools for endurance athletes. Use it to add up the carbohydrate, fat, protein, and calories in each meal and snack you consume, as well as daily totals. All you have to do is find a particular food you ate in a vast multisource database of fresh, prepared, and restaurant foods, "drag" the item over to your calendar and drop it there, adjusting the portion size if necessary. If a specific item is not present in the library already, you can add it. Save meals you eat often as favorites so you can enter them even faster the next time. There are also nutritionist-designed meal plans that you can purchase and load onto your calendar to follow just as you do with training plans.

Using the nutrition tracking tools on TrainingPeaks gets easier and easier the longer you do it. An initial investment of effort is required to put in the foods and meals you eat most often, but once this work is done, it's done. From that point forward it's just a matter of clicking and dragging. The only headaches you'll have are those complex homemade meals and restaurant meals eaten at non–chain restaurants. But even these headaches may ease over time, because as the library of foods and meals added by other TrainingPeaks users grows, so does the likelihood that you will find foods and meals that are similar to those you make at home and eat at independent restaurants. While it is unlikely that these items will *exactly* match the number of calories per serving in the snacks and meals you eat, I will remind you that calorie counting need not be

100 percent accurate to be exact. And guess what? Testing performed by consumer watchdog groups suggests that even commercial food labels cannot be trusted for perfectly accurate calorie counts.

In your TrainingPeaks account, your meals and workouts sit side-by-side on your calendar, and you can even view charts that compare the calories you take in through food against those you burn at rest and in training to help you achieve and maintain your optimal racing weight.

Counting "Calories Out"

Estimating the number of calories your body burns each day is easy with the help of the right technologies. Your daily "calories-out" total is the sum of the number of calories your body burns at rest (referred to as your basal metabolic rate, or BMR) and the number of extra calories you burn through activity, including workouts and all nonworkout activities such as driving. I suggest you approach this calculation in three steps: calculate your BMR; calculate the number of extra calories above your BMR that you burn each day through activities other than workouts; calculate the number of calories you burn in workouts. Let's take a close look at these three steps. I'll forewarn you that it may seem complicated, but the only part that's really complicated is the second step, and you only need to perform that step once. The number of calories you burn each day through activities other than your workouts is low and likely to be fairly consistent from day to day, so it's sensible to calculate it once and use that number as an approximate value for every day.

STEP 1: CALCULATE YOUR BMR. The easiest way to calculate your BMR is to simply step on a body-fat scale that has a BMR calculator. These calculators work by running your gender, age, and height (all of which you enter when you set up the scale) plus your current weight and body-fat percentage through a formula. For example, my height is 6 feet 1 inch, and, as I write this, I am 38 years old. This morning I stepped on my body-fat scale—which "knows" my gender, height, and age—and I was informed that my weight was 157.3 pounds, my body-fat percentage was 9.8, and my BMR was 1,808 calories/day.

If you don't have a body-fat scale with a built-in BMR calculator, you can get a BMR estimate that is likely to be somewhat less accurate from an online BMR calculator. These calculators are less accurate because they don't factor body-fat percentage into their calculations, as the scales do. Instead, they assume an average level of leanness given the individual's gender, age, and height-weight ratio. Therefore these calculators are likely to slightly underestimate the BMR of endurance athletes, who tend to have more calorie-guzzling muscle and less fat than the average person.

STEP 2: CALCULATE CALORIES BURNED THROUGH ACTIVITIES OTHER THAN WORKOUTS. The simplest way to measure calories burned outside of workouts is to wear or carry a pedometer with a calorie-counting feature throughout the day. The device will generate an estimate of the number of calories you burn based on your weight and the number of steps you take. Another way to get the job done is to record how much time you spend performing various activities throughout the day and then visit a Web site such as my-calorie-counter.com that you can use to calculate how many calories you burned performing

COUNTING CALORIES OUT

Suppose your BMR, as determined by a body-fat scale or an online tool, is 1,347 calories/day. (Note that this is the approximate BMR for a 131-pound female.) According to my-calorie-counter.com, the number of calories a 131-pound person would burn doing deskwork for eight hours is 856. So that eight hours of deskwork would add extra calories to your daily total because your body requires calories above and beyond your BMR for an hour of working, even in a desk job.

Our hypothetical 131-lb. female would burn 595 calories in a one-hour workout consisting of cycling at 15.5 mph. Again, this calculation is from my-calorie-counter.com, which estimates the calories burned based on general

Step	How It's Done
1. Calculate your BMR	Use a body-fat scale or an online BMR calculator.
2. Calculate calories burned through activities (not workouts)	Wear a pedometer or estimate calories for each activity in your day (working, errands, etc.).
3. Calculate calories burned during your workouts	Wear a heart rate monitor with a calorie-counting feature, or use an online calculator
4. Total the calories	Multiply the calories burned in an hour by the number of hours spent in each activity. Use your BMR for the remaining hours in the day.

Note: My-calorie-counter.com can provide you with estimates of calories burned in common activities.

these activities (based on your weight). For example, according to my-calorie-counter.com, a 150-pound person burns a total of 984 calories during eight hours of deskwork.

Only when you're sleeping is your metabolic rate not at least slightly above your BMR, so if you use this method to calculate extra calories burned when awake, be sure to account for the whole day (possibly excluding workouts—see the next section for a full explanation). It takes a little time to get through this process, but you only have to do it once. This will give you the number of calories you burn through non-exercise activities in a typical day. You may then add this number to your BMR when calculating your calories out for any subsequent day.

STEP 3: CALCULATE CALORIES BURNED IN WORKOUTS. You may also use calculators such as the one on my-calorie-counter.com to estimate the number of calories you burn in workouts. For example, according to this

zones of exercise intensity (e.g., "cycling between 15.0 and 16.9 mph"), so it's a little less exact.

The table illustrates the way you can use each calculation or estimate to get an hourly rate of calories burned. By then determining how many hours you spend in each activity, you can determine the number of calories needed each day.

When counting calories, it's important to note that you can't simply add the calories required for each activity to your BMR. This would give you an artificially inflated total. You can substitute appropriate fractions of your BMR with calories burned through activity, but if you have an active lifestyle, it's probably easier to break it down to an average number of calories burned per hour for BMR and each activity, as illustrated in the following table.

Example: 131-lb. female	Calories per Hour	Daily Hours	Total Calories
BMR = ~1,347 calories/day	56	15	840
8 hours of deskwork burns = ~856 calories	107	8	856
1 hour cycling workout at 15.5 mph = ~595 calories	595	1	595
		24	2,291

calculator, our hypothetical 131-pound female would burn 595 calories in a 1-hour workout consisting of cycling at 15.5 mph. The trouble with this method of calculating calories burned during a workout is that it uses general zones of exercise intensity (e.g., "cycling between 15.0 and 16.9 mph) instead of actual intensity data from your workouts, and therefore the results are approximate.

A more accurate way to measure the number of calories burned during workouts is to use a heart-rate monitor with a calorie-counting function. These calculators factor together your weight and heart rate, with a respectable level of accuracy, to estimate the number of calories you burn while training. If you use the training and nutrition log on racingweight.com, you can upload your workout data, including the calorie total, directly onto your calendar.

Like counting calories in, counting calories out is not something you need to do all the time. It is most beneficial to count calories out at the same times you count calories in to monitor your caloric balance— that is, whether you are consuming more calories than you're burning or vice versa. Don't put too much emphasis on any single day, however. In endurance sports training it is normal to train much harder (and thus burn many more calories) on some days than on others, while the diet remains steadier from day to day. You'll get the best sense of whether you are in a state of positive or negative caloric balance by averaging out your calories in and your calories out for a full week.

If you use a body-fat scale with a BMR feature and a heart-rate monitor with calorie counts, it will be very easy for you to informally monitor your calories out as often as daily. It would be as simple as stepping on the scale each morning, wearing the monitor in every workout, and recording your calculated BMR and total workout calories in your training journal. While certainly not necessary to reaching and maintaining your optimal body weight, this habit is one more way to focus your attention on factors that are relevant to your racing weight and perhaps to reach it faster and maintain it more consistently.

FOUR

SEASONAL CONSIDERATIONS

I n the preceding chapters, I have focused on the importance of attaining your optimal performance weight for your most important competitions. But in truth it is neither necessary nor even feasible for most of us to maintain that weight year-round. While your racing weight is your ideal weight for maximum performance, it is not necessarily a better weight for training and general health. Most endurance athletes find that there's a difference of a few pounds between their racing weight and what I will call their training weight, and that they hold their racing weight only briefly when engaging in peak-level training. During a recovery phase after his 3rd-place finish in the 2009 Boston Marathon, half-marathon American record holder Ryan Hall told me, "I intentionally put on 5 to 7 pounds during this time off as I feel it is important to not be too lean for the entire year. I try and time it to where I am at race weight right before the marathon." Many elite athletes find that they don't even have to "try," beyond simply training appropriately for peak performance. That's because peak-level training sends a message to the body telling it to get as lean as possible for the impending competition. But in most cases, sustaining this as-lean-as-possible condition throughout the year is no more possible than sustaining peak-level training year-round.

A recent study by researchers from the University of Glasgow (Fudge et al. 2006) found that during seven days of intense pre-race training, elite Kenyan runners burned more calories than they consumed, despite a very large food intake. These guys just couldn't eat enough to keep up with their muscles' fuel demands, which was not a problem during this brief pre-competitive period. "A negative energy balance would result in a reduction in body mass, which, when combined with a high carbohydrate diet, would have the potential in the short term to enhance endurance running performance by reducing the energy cost of running," wrote the authors of the study. This study did not look at the runners' weight outside of the seven-day study period, but if it had, the researchers probably would have found that, after their race, the runners gained back the weight they lost in the peak training period and remained at that slightly higher weight until the next peak training period came around. The only way these runners could maintain their racing weight year-round would be to train at peak level year-round, which would quickly cause an injury or overtraining sickness, or to drastically cut back on eating, which would leave the body underfueled for even base-level training. And the same is true for all endurance athletes, including you.

Endurance sports are seasonal. Triathletes typically compete in the summer and treat the winter as an off-season. Pool swimmers typically compete in the winter and summer, using the spring and fall to regenerate and rebuild. A majority of athletes in every endurance sport lose weight, if only a little, as they approach their most important race or races, and gain weight in the off-season. In recent years, sports nutritionists have popularized the concept of nutrition *periodization*, which holds that endurance athletes need to modify their diet seasonally to match changes in their training. This concept is certainly valid, but those who promote it sometimes suggest, either implicitly or explicitly, that an objective of nutrition periodization is to prevent any weight gain during the off-season.

I don't believe that you should try to prevent a certain amount of weight gain during the off-season. It's simply not realistic to expect to keep the needle on your bathroom scale from moving to the right a little bit between the height of summer—if you're a summer athlete, for example, and approaching peak fitness—and the height of the holiday season, when you're enjoying downtime from competition and intensive training. Doing so would require that you exercise a very high level of dietary restraint at just the time when you're probably feeling most inclined to reward yourself. Psychologically, most endurance athletes find it easier to eat strictly when they're in peak training and have an overall mind-set of discipline and sacrifice than during the off-season, when it is natural to want to relax that exhausted willpower organ. The pros are no exception. Not long ago I wrote an article on "How to Eat Like a Pro" for *Women's Running* magazine. I interviewed four top American runners about their dietary habits and asked each of them whether she ate more or less strictly during the off-season. All four indulged in more exceptions to their normal healthy eating rules between training cycles than within them.

Instead of trying to prevent off-season weight gain completely, I suggest you try to limit your off-season weight gain to no more than 8 percent of your optimal performance weight. So if your optimal performance weight is 162 pounds, you should avoid gaining more than 13 pounds during the off-season. It so happens that my marathon racing weight is 154 pounds, and my off-season weight naturally peaks at 165 pounds (a difference of just over 7 percent), when I'm doing everything an endurance athlete should do in terms of training and nutrition at this time of year. But this 8 percent rule is not based only on my personal experience. It has been confirmed as a good rule of thumb by a number of other athletes, coaches, and sports nutritionists with whom I have discussed the topic of off-season weight gain.

Understand, however, that this rule is not an allowance to gain 8 percent of your end-of-season weight during the off-season regardless of what your end-of-season weight is. It is only an allowance to gain 8 percent relative to your optimal racing weight. If your weight is above optimum at the end of your competitive season, you should still limit your off-season weight gain to 8 percent relative to your (known or estimated) optimum. Thus, if you are already above your optimal racing weight at the end of the competitive season, you should try to avoid gaining any more weight during the off-season.

All too many endurance athletes gain too much fat in the off-season, however. Cyclist Jan Ullrich was infamous for letting himself go during the winter. His racing weight was 158 pounds, but he routinely showed up for his team's first training camp of the year at 180. He would perform poorly throughout the early season as he scrambled to work his body back into shape in time for July's Tour de France. Many cycling experts believe Ullrich would have won more than the one Tour he claimed at age 24 if he had taken better care of himself during the off-season.

Thanks to favorable genes, a few endurance athletes can slack off as much as they want in the off-season without putting on a whole bunch of fat (although not necessarily without losing a ton of fitness), but most endurance athletes, like most humans in general, have a built-in potential for rapid weight gain. The transition from peak-season training to off-season slacking presents the perfect circumstances for this potential to be unleashed. But there are other circumstances that can encourage this weight gain as well, from very short-term (days) to long-term (months) intervals. Before I give you my tips for avoiding the type of rapid weight gain that most commonly affects endurance athletes—off-season slacking—let me first address the phenomenon of rapid weight gain more broadly.

WEIGHT-GAIN SPURTS

There is a popular conception that the average person gains weight slowly and steadily throughout adulthood, beginning at ages 18 to 20 and continuing into middle age. Some research seems to support this conception. For example, a large observational study, known as the CARDIA Study (Gordon-Larsen et al. 2009), revealed an average weight gain of roughly 2.2 pounds per year for 15 years in a population of men and women who were between the ages of 18 and 30 at the beginning of the observation period.

However, large, long-term studies such as this one mask the hidden reality that weight gain seldom happens slowly and steadily over a long time for any given individual. Other types of studies, with a narrower focus, have shown that most of the weight gain that occurs over the course of a year is concentrated in the few short weeks between Thanksgiving and Christmas (Roberts and Mayer 2000). Rapid weight gain is also known to occur in various other situations, including post-dieting, during pregnancy, and with particular medications. Outside of such situations (and there are others that I will touch upon presently), most adults exist in a state of equilibrium in which body weight fluctuates up and down within a narrow range.

Consider the people in your life who are closest to you and are overweight or have been overweight at some time. How many of them gained all of the excess weight on their bodies at a steady rate of 1, 2, or 3 pounds per year, every year? How many gained the weight in one or more spurts? In my family, the answers to these questions are zero and all, respectively. My elder brother, Josh, was always skinny until his sophomore year of college, when he put on 30 pounds. (In middle age he's now closer to his freshman-year weight, thanks to running.) Both my mother and my wife experienced rapid weight gain caused by medications (and, thankfully, lost the weight after changing medications).

My own experience was even more extreme. Between infancy and the age of just over 17 years, I was the skinniest boy I knew. When I entered my senior year in high school, I stood 6 feet 1 inch (my current height) and weighed all of 138 pounds. But in the middle of my senior year I stopped running. In the first 10 weeks after I quit the track team I gained 34 pounds, and within another two years I tipped the scales at 206 pounds. I lost most of this extra weight when I returned to endurance sports in my mid-20s. An abrupt switch from burning perhaps 400 calories per day through weightlifting to burning 1,000 or more calories a day through swimming, cycling, and running caused my gut and love handles to shrink very quickly.

Why does weight gain tend to occur rapidly over short periods rather than slowly over long periods? I believe that it is because our bodies are designed to gain weight rapidly in response to messages directing our bodies to gain weight. It's as if the body contains a switch with three settings: gain weight, hold steady, or lose weight. When we flip the switch into the "gain weight" setting by eating more and/or becoming less active, our bodies do the best they can to obey. Fortunately, the same is true of the "lose weight" setting.

The following is an annotated list of the seven most common causes of weight-gain spurts, with information about how to avoid and overcome those that may affect you.

Weekends

Studies have shown that Americans typically eat more and are less active on the weekends, and that consequently we gain more weight on the weekends than during the week (Racette et al. 2008). As an endurance athlete, you are probably at least as active on the weekends as between

PRACTICAL TIPS FOR THE HOLIDAY SEASON

- Do your holiday shopping at the largest indoor shopping mall in your area and walk the entire length of it—twice. Park at the opposite end from the first store you plan to visit, walk to it, and work your way back toward your vehicle.

- Learn simple ways to trim calories from any traditional holiday foods you may cook. For example, use fat-free chicken broth instead of cream in mashed potatoes; substitute butter or shortening with apple sauce in cookies and other baked goods; and prepare turkey dressing outside the turkey so it doesn't absorb the bird's fat drippings.

- Be aware of how drinking alcohol can affect your plans for healthy eating. Alcohol both lowers inhibitions and stimulates appetite. It also makes you less aware of how much you're eating. To reduce your alcohol consumption at gatherings, drink one nonalcoholic, calorie-free beverage, such as tonic water or diet soda, after each alcoholic beverage.

- Spoil your appetite by having a bowl of soup before you head out to a party or sit down to a feast. Research has shown that eating a broth-based soup before a meal substantially reduces the number of calories consumed in the meal and later in the day (Flood and Rolls 2007).

Monday and Friday, but your eating habits may change for the worse. Research involving a large pool of individuals who had lost a significant amount of weight found that those whose weekend eating habits were most similar to their weekday eating habits were least likely to regain weight (Gorin et al. 2004). Be aware of poor weekend eating habits as a potential obstacle to progress toward your racing weight, and try your best to eat consistently seven days a week without taking all the fun out of your weekends.

Holidays

It's often said that the average person gains five pounds during the six-week period from Thanksgiving week to New Year's Day. Actually, according to a study in the *New England Journal of Medicine* (Yanovski et al. 2000), the average person gains only one pound over the holidays—but then never loses it. So, for the typical American, 20 years' worth of turkey dinners, office holiday parties, and New Year's Eve toasts add up to 20 pounds of lard around the middle. You don't want that!

The holiday season coincides with the off-season for most endurance athletes except cross-country skiers and pool swimmers. So the means to avoid holiday weight gain are by and large identical to the means for avoiding any off-season weight gain, which I will share in the final section of this chapter.

Periods of Stress

Rapid weight gain during periods of unusual stress is common. Stress causes weight gain in two ways. First, the primary stress hormone cortisol promotes fat storage, particularly in the abdominal region. Second, some but not all individuals respond to stress by eating more and by seeking out "comforting" high-calorie foods such as potato chips and candy. Such foods briefly increase the brain concentration of neurotransmitters that counteract some of the negative feelings associated with stress, but they do so at the cost of weight gain.

If you're a stress eater, the first step you can take to avoid stress-related weight gain is simply to increase your awareness of stress eating. Pay closer attention to your urges to eat and learn to distinguish true physical hunger from emotionally based impulse. Find effective substitutes for stress eating such as talking to friends, walking, playing with your pet, surfing the Internet—whatever is healthy and practical.

The "Freshman 15"

The average college freshman does not gain 15 pounds. It's more like 5 pounds, but that's still 5 pounds too many for most young men and women. The main cause of the freshman 5 appears to be the transition from structured eating at home to free eating at college dining centers, in dormitories, fraternities and sororities, and elsewhere. The most straightforward way to avoid gaining weight in one's first year of college is to re-create one's at-home eating habits (provided they were healthy) as closely as possible in the college environment. This is easier said than done for many 18-year-olds. The most realistic way to minimize early-college weight gain for many endurance athletes is through training. Another way—realistic for some, less so for others—is to minimize sleep deprivation (caused by too much studying, of course).

Pregnancy

Weight gain during pregnancy is normal, natural, and necessary. This weight gain should be limited, however, to the amount necessary for the health of the mother and the healthy development of the fetus. Unfortunately, there is evidence that many women gain significantly more weight during pregnancy today than in the past (Rasmussen and Yaktine 2009) and are less likely to return to their pre-pregnancy weight (Walker 2007). Excess gestational weight gain has serious health consequences not only for mothers but also for their children. Women who gain excessive weight during pregnancy tend to become or remain overweight or obese for the rest of their lives (Amorim et al. 2007) and to raise overweight and obese children (Olson et al. 2008).

Although it is not always easy in today's society, there is no magic to avoiding excess weight gain during pregnancy and returning to an appropriate body weight after childbirth. Research has demonstrated that women who are at a healthy weight before pregnancy and maintain a healthy diet and exercise regularly throughout pregnancy and after childbirth are generally able to avoid excess gestational weight gain and return to their pre-pregnancy weight after giving birth (Stuebe et al. 2009).

Menstruation and Menopause

Eighty percent of women exhibit symptoms of premenstrual syndrome (PMS). In some cases they can be quite severe. Although the most prevalent PMS symptoms are bloating and water retention, one of the most common ones is food cravings and increased appetite. Menopause provides no relief. Studies show increases of appetite (up to 60 percent) in women after they reach menopause. Researchers have shown that in postmenopausal women there is a decrease in certain appetite regulatory proteins (Ritland et al. 2008).

Happily, the available evidence suggests that being an athlete provides nearly full protection against menstrual and menopausal weight gain. For example, while the average woman gains 2 to 5 pounds during the menopausal period, female runners typically gain no more than this amount of weight throughout their entire adulthood. Indeed, a 1998 study found that postmenopausal female runners were no heavier than female runners in their late 20s, and their body-fat percentages were still significantly lower than those of sedentary young women (Van Pelt et al. 1998). If this finding is surprising to you, it is because we have become all too accustomed to the idea that gaining weight through adulthood is natural and unavoidable. In fact it is not. While staying active will not entirely prevent an age-related decline in muscle mass and increase in body fat, it will slow these processes and can keep actual weight gain minimal between early adulthood and the golden years.

Individual genetic makeup determines just how much protection against age-related weight gain a person (whether male or female) will get. A 2007 study out of Lawrence Berkeley National Laboratory (Williams 2007) followed adult runners over seven years. While both men and women who ran more than 30 miles per week gained less than half as much weight as those who ran fewer than 15 miles per week, the average runner in the 30-plus-miles-per-week group still gained weight. Yet many individuals within this group—far more than in the lower-mileage groups—gained no weight at all over seven years.

Post-Diet Rebound

Weight gain tends to be most rapid in men and women who have just lost weight through dieting, exercise, or both, and then returned to their old habits—a phenomenon often referred to as the "yo-yo effect." A person's body weight is largely a function of his or her activity level and caloric intake. Regardless of your starting weight, you will eventually end up at the body weight that is determined by a specific level of activity and caloric intake. Suppose you eat 2,800 calories per day, don't exercise, and weigh 200 pounds. You then start exercising 30 minutes a day, cut your caloric intake, and drop down to 175 pounds. What will happen if you then return to not exercising and eating 2,800 calories a day? You are certain to gain back those 25 pounds.

And that's exactly what happens to most people who lose weight. Researchers at UCLA found that two-thirds of men and women who lose weight through dieting regain all of the lost weight, or more, within a few years (Mann et al. 2007). One reason why some gain more than they lose in the first place is that weight loss reduces the metabolic rate. It is expected that the metabolic rate will decrease in those who lose substantial amounts of weight because the metabolic rate is largely a function of total body mass. However, research has consistently shown that metabolism decreases more than would be expected based on loss of body mass alone. But is this exaggerated metabolic slowdown transient or more or less permanent?

Researchers from Columbia University recently answered this question through a study in which they compared the metabolic rates of age- and weight-matched subjects who had not lost weight, subjects who had recently lost weight, and subjects who had succeeded in maintaining weight loss for a long time (Rosenbaum et al. 2008). They found that resting energy expenditure was significantly lower in both the recent weight loss and the long-term weight loss subjects than among the group of subjects of the same body weight who had not lost weight.

Fortunately for endurance athletes like us, exercise tends to prevent weight regain. A recent study (MacLean et al. 2009) involving laboratory animals showed why. Rats that exercised regularly after significant weight loss regained less weight than rats that did not; the same rats exhibited less appetite and a greater rate of fat burning at rest. This is another good example of how the body can adapt in response to the messages you send it through your lifestyle. Exercise tells the body of the individual who has lost weight, "Stay lean." The body responds by inhibiting the normal increase in appetite that comes with dieting and also by increasing fat burning at rest to conserve muscle glycogen for workouts.

MANAGING OFF-SEASON WEIGHT GAIN

Weight gain of any kind can sabotage the quest to reach your highest level of performance as an endurance athlete. Excessive off-season weight gain is the type that affects endurance athletes most commonly. As I suggested above, you need not burden yourself by trying to prevent *any* weight gain during a break between training cycles. But it is important to limit your weight gain to no more than 8 percent of your optimal performance weight. The following are five proven tactics that will help you meet this objective.

Set a Weight-Gain Limit

You will probably gain less body fat during the off-season if you replace your vague intention to stay trim with a definite goal—specifically, a maximum weight limit. Use the 8 percent rule described above to calculate your limit. For example, suppose your racing weight is 133 pounds. Eight percent of 133 is 10.6 pounds. So in this case you'll want to set a goal not to exceed 143.6 pounds. Once your weight limit is established, weigh yourself once a week to track any movement toward it and make changes as necessary (e.g., lay off the eggnog) if you find yourself getting too close, too quickly.

Gain Muscle Instead of Fat

The off-season is a good time to focus on strength training. Functional strength is important in every endurance sport, but for most endurance athletes the development of functional strength necessarily takes a back seat to race-focused endurance training during periods of peak training. When the off-season arrives, you can take advantage of the time freed up by your de-emphasis of endurance training to increase your commitment to functional strength development and create a reserve of strength that will carry you through the next competitive season. A side benefit of this tactic is that it will add muscle mass to your body and thereby reduce off-season fat accumulation.

Gaining muscle mass reduces fat accumulation in a couple of ways. Building muscle requires calories, and as more of your food calories are channeled into making muscle, fewer are left over to be channeled into your fat stores. Also, a lot of energy is required to maintain muscle tissue once it's been created. It takes 30 to 50 calories a day to maintain a pound of muscle, compared to only 2 calories per day for a pound of fat. So if you gain 2 pounds of muscle during the off-season, there will be 60 to 100 fewer food calories available for storage as body fat.

Even if you do commit to strength training during the off-season, and embrace the muscle weight gain that is likely to result from this commitment, you should still avoid gaining more than 8 percent of your racing weight. Muscle weight gain happens very slowly. Even a previously untrained young man who throws himself headlong into weight-lifting is unlikely to gain more than 5 pounds of muscle in an entire year, so you shouldn't expect to gain more than 2 pounds of muscle during a typical off-season, and you should not use a commitment to strength training as an excuse to allow yourself to gain more weight than you would otherwise. The point is to use strength training to ensure that more of whatever weight you do gain is "good weight" instead of "bad weight" (although you'll most likely want even that good muscle weight to gradually come off as you train toward your next competitive peak).

Be Consistent

The thing that really throws endurance athletes off-track during the off-season is reducing their exercise frequency—going from working out every day, perhaps more than once a day oftentimes, to working out just a few times per week. It's okay to take a week or two off of training after a peak race for physical and mental regeneration, but after that you should return to daily exercise. Returning to daily exercise need not equal returning to progressive, race-focused training. If you have time before you need to begin your next formal training cycle, and you still need a break from hard training, you can train lightly or in non-sport-specific ways with a focus on fun, but you need to do something at least 6 days a week or you're likely to experience damaging off-season weight gain.

Too many endurance athletes approach training with an all-or-nothing mentality. If they normally train hard for 60 minutes a day, they assume that 30 minutes of light exercise are no better than staying on the couch. Thus, if they are not motivated to train hard for 60 minutes during the off-season, they do nothing. But in fact, short, easy workouts are much better than nothing. You can burn 300 to 400 calories during a comfortable 30-minute spin on the bike. If you do that on each of the 2 days per week when you might otherwise skip exercise altogether during an 8-week off-season, then you will prevent nearly 2 pounds of fat gain.

> YOU CAN BURN 300 TO 400 CALORIES DURING A COMFORTABLE 30-MINUTE SPIN ON THE BIKE.

In addition to the mistake of equating exercise with hard training, endurance athletes often make the mistake of equating exercise with their competitive sport. But there are lots of effective ways to exercise. If as a cyclist you don't feel like riding, you might still enjoy a run or a workout on one of the cardio machines at the gym. Crosstraining outside your primary sport is a great way to give yourself a break from your sport without missing workouts altogether and experiencing the resulting fat gain. Expand your repertoire during the off-season. Do whatever motivates you to get off the couch.

Keep Counting

If you count calories in and calories out during the competitive season, you might be tempted to stop doing so in the off-season as part of the general relaxation you indulge in at that time. But while it is appropriate to reduce your training and even acceptable to allow yourself a few more dietary indulgences in the off-season, it is as important as ever to track calories in and calories out between training cycles. As I suggested in the previous chapter, it is not necessary to count calories in and calories out all the time. Rather, it is sufficient to do so periodically as a way of auditing your diet and training. At times when your diet and training are consistent, one quick audit will cover you until your diet or training changes. But when either of these factors does change, it's a good idea to perform another audit to quantify the change and keep it within acceptable parameters.

At the very least your training does change as you move into the off-season, and your eating habits will likely change, too, so be sure to count your calories in and calories out early in each off-season and perhaps also periodically throughout it. This measure will help keep you from relaxing too much! Also, as I've suggested a number of times, the very act of recording your eating heightens your awareness and steers you away from the worst excesses.

Shift from Carbohydrate to Protein

Unlike fat and protein, which are used structurally in the body, carbohydrate is strictly an energy source, and it is the main energy source for high-intensity muscle work. Therefore the amount of carbohydrate in your diet should vary

INCREASING DIETARY PROTEIN

The typical American diet is 18 percent protein. Getting 30 percent of your calories from protein requires some effort. The healthiest and most efficient way to increase your protein intake is to consume whey protein shakes as snacks. A study from the University of Oklahoma (Lockwood et al. 2008) investigated the effects of whey protein–based shakes and exercise on body composition and fitness. Thirty-eight overweight, sedentary subjects participated in the study. Eighteen of them engaged in a 10-week aerobic and resistance exercise program. Nine of these 18 also consumed a high-protein shake once a day for the first two weeks of the study period and twice a day for the last eight weeks. The remaining 10 subjects did not exercise or consume shakes. The increase in protein intake appeared to reduce the appetite of the subjects receiving shakes, as their average daily caloric intake decreased by 14.4 percent. Fat mass decreased by 4.6 percent in the exercise-only group and by 9.3 percent in the exercise-plus-shakes group.

We'll take a closer look at the use of whey protein supplements in Chapter 14. While I have long used them and consistently recommend them to endurance athletes looking for new ways to get leaner, I would never suggest that they be considered mandatory during the off-season or at any other time. Nor is it imperative to switch to a high-protein diet to avoid off-season weight gain. It's just one effective option.

with your training workload. During peak training you may need anywhere from 7 to 10 grams of carbohydrate per kilogram of body weight, depending on your size and exactly how much you're training. (I'll have much more to say about meeting your body's carbohydrate needs in Chapter 8.) But during the off-season you need less—as little as 4 grams of carbohydrate per kilogram of body weight.

DURING THE OFF-SEASON YOU NEED AS LITTLE AS 4 GRAMS OF CARBOHYDRATE PER KILOGRAM OF BODY WEIGHT.

In addition to reducing your carbohydrate intake, you may wish to increase your protein intake during the off-season. The reason is not that increased protein intake will support your off-season efforts to increase muscle mass and strength, but rather that it will help you avoid gaining fat despite your reduced activity level. The notion that increased protein intake is required for muscle growth is a myth. Research by Mike Rennie, one of the world's foremost researchers on protein and muscle growth, determined that whole-body protein synthesis achieves its maximum rate at a protein intake level of 1.4 grams per kilogram of body weight daily (Rennie and Tipton 2000). This is higher than the government's recommended daily allowance but not higher than the protein intake level of the average American. Other research by Rennie showed that a single dose of 10 grams of essential amino acids is sufficient to maximize acute muscle protein synthesis. That's the amount of essential amino acids in a glass of skim milk. Based on this evidence, protein researcher Stuart Phillips of McMaster University in Canada concluded, "At present there is no evidence to suggest that supplements are required for optimal muscle growth or strength gain. Strength-trained athletes should consume protein consistent with general population guidelines, or 12 percent to 15 percent of energy from protein" (2004).

However, a higher level of protein intake—as high as 30 percent of total calories—does offer other benefits: it reduces appetite, eating, and fat storage, thereby promoting weight loss in those who maintain or increase their exercise level and limiting weight gain in those who have reduced their exercise level, such as endurance athletes entering the off-season. Calorie for calorie, gram for gram, protein provides more satiety (i.e., appetite satisfaction) than carbohydrate or fat, so when you switch to a high-protein diet, you feel fuller and eat less. For example, in a study performed at the University of Washington (Weigle et al. 2005), overweight women spontaneously began to consume 441 fewer calories per day, on average, when their protein intake was increased to 30 percent of total calories. As a result, they lost weight despite not making any conscious effort to eat less.

SPORT-SPECIFIC RACING
WEIGHT CONSIDERATIONS

Managing one's body weight and body composition to maximize performance is challenging in every endurance sport, but the nature of the challenge is different across the various individual endurance sports. The special demands of your chosen endurance sport, and sometimes your specialization within the sport, determine whether you will have to work harder to keep fat off, put muscle on, balance weight and power, or meet some other challenge in achieving your optimal racing weight.

As you might expect, the specific form that the struggle takes to reach and maintain racing weight depends not only on the sport but also on the athlete's genetic predispositions. For example, one marathon runner might struggle to maintain adequate muscle mass and power while another struggles more to shed excess body fat. However, there are particular weight management challenges that are typical of each sport. Of course, being lean is critical in every endurance sport and is the primary weight management concern of most athletes. Fundamentally, the best eating and training practices to achieve this objective are the same for all athletes in all sports, and they are the five steps of the Racing Weight plan that you will encounter in Part II of this book.

CROSS-COUNTRY SKIING

The cross-country ski season is short in most climates. Thus the primary weight management challenge experienced by these athletes is to stay relatively close to their optimal performance weight through a long off-season. Because it's necessary not only to stay lean over the summer but also to stay fit, the best approach to weight management in the cross-country skiing off-season is to maintain a high volume of training in one or more alternative endurance activities with a high degree of fitness carryover to skiing, such as cycling and running.

It can be hard to sustain motivation to train hard in alternative modalities for a long stretch of time without a competitive outlet. Thus I recommend that cross-country skiers devote the summer to competing in another endurance sport such as mountain biking or triathlon. Sprinkling the warmer months with a few races will make your off-season training more immediately rewarding and enjoyable and will probably motivate you to work harder and consequently enter the cross-country season at a higher fitness level. Too much racing will burn you out, though, so it's best to divide the year into quarters as follows, as suggested in Table 5.1.

TABLE 5.1 SEASONAL TRAINING FOR CROSS-COUNTRY SKIERS

Winter	Peak training for cross-country skiing Cross-country ski racing
Spring	Preparatory training for summer endurance sport (no racing)
Summer	Peak training for summer endurance sport Summer endurance sport racing
Fall	Base training for cross-country skiing (roller skiing, indoor Nordic skiing, strength training, cycling) (no racing)

CYCLING

Power-to-weight ratio is one of the best predictors of cycling performance. The more power you can generate at race intensities, the faster you will reach the finish line. But the most powerful cyclist does not always win. That's because when cyclists are climbing hills and accelerating, some of the power they generate must overcome the resistance imposed by their own body weight, and the more they weigh, the more power is lost to the fight against inertia and gravity. Understanding the negative effect of weight on performance, many cyclists are fanatical about minimizing the weight of their bodies and bikes alike. But the wrong approach to minimizing body weight—namely, severe calorie restriction or endless moderate-intensity riding or a combination of both—will sap power even as it annihilates excess body-fat stores. So the greatest weight management challenge for cyclists is to train and nourish themselves in a way that increases sustainable power output while also minimizing body weight.

With regard to training, increasing your power capacity requires that you consistently perform a small amount of training at very high power-output levels. This type of training sends a message to your body that it needs to let the muscles adapt in ways that will enable them to meet the stress imposed by maximal and near-maximal efforts. A little high-power training goes a long way. Moderate-intensity riding below the lactate threshold (the exercise intensity at which blood lactate begins to rise exponentially) should account for at least 80 percent of your weekly riding time. It's this type of training that does the most to develop your aerobic capacity, raw endurance, and pedaling efficiency. But close to 20 percent of your training should be done at lactate threshold intensity and above. Threshold rides (e.g., 2 x 20 minutes at threshold intensity), intervals at the maximum rate of oxygen uptake, or VO_2max intensity (e.g., 5 x 4 minutes at VO_2max power with 3-minute spinning recoveries), hill repetitions (e.g., 4 x 5 minutes uphill at VO_2max intensity with downhill coasting recoveries), speed intervals (e.g., 12 x 1 minute at maximum effort relative to interval duration with 2-minute spinning recoveries), and power intervals (e.g., 10 x 20 seconds at maximum power with 1-minute spinning recoveries) will boost your maximum and sustainable power while further increasing your aerobic capacity and pedaling efficiency above the levels achieved through moderate-intensity training.

High-intensity training will only increase your power capacity if you support it with a diet that allows your muscles to fully adapt to it. If you're currently above your racing weight, this objective is best achieved with a slight caloric deficit. Anything more than a slight deficit will deprive your muscles of adequate fat and protein to maintain themselves and adapt to training and adequate carbohydrate to fuel optimal performance. A slight deficit will reduce your body-fat percentage and perhaps also your body weight without affecting your average power output in performance tests such as a 40K time trial. A daily caloric deficit of 100 to 300 calories per day is most likely to yield these results. Track calories in and calories out according to the guidelines presented in Chapter 3 to achieve this deficit. Also track your body weight, fat percentage, and performance to ensure that this deficit is in fact yielding the desired result of making you leaner without making you less powerful.

The primary weight management challenge in mountain biking is the same as that in road cycling, which is increasing power output while minimizing body weight. The best means of addressing this challenge are also the same.

ROWING

The most common weight management challenge in rowing is a consequence of its partition into separate lightweight and heavyweight competitive divisions. The reason for this partition is the significant competitive advantage associated with above-average height, which is, of course, linked to weight. Because of the reality of this advantage, rowers who compete in the lightweight divisions tend to be right at the maximum weight limit. Indeed, they are naturally heavier and must make special efforts to "make weight" as do athletes in other sports with separate weight classifications, such as boxing.

Many lightweight rowers prefer to compete at a natural weight above their limit and lose weight rapidly in the final weeks, days, and even hours before a competition. This pattern would not be the norm if it didn't often work, but it carries risks and may just as often backfire. Athletes who lose too much weight too quickly may sabotage their performance by depleting their muscle-fuel stores, compromising their recovery from and adaptation to training, weakening the immune system, and becoming dehydrated.

A better strategy for lightweight rowers is to carefully control their diet throughout the year and maintain a high activity level in the off-season to keep their body weight within easy reach of their limit and to drop weight gradually over a fairly long period of time prior to competition. The superiority of this approach was demonstrated in a 1994 study by researchers at the University of Wolverhampton, England (Koutedakis et al. 1994). Six members of the British Women's Lightweight Rowing Team were separated into two groups. Members of one group used a reduced-calorie diet to lose 6 to 7 percent of their body weight in order to reach their weight limit over a four-month period. The other group used a more aggressive diet to drop an equal amount of weight over a two-month period. Members of both groups experienced a decline in anaerobic threshold power and peak torque of the knee flexors over the dieting period, but the declines were much milder in the group that completed the more gradual, four-month weight-loss program.

Lightweight rowers also commonly use fasting and fluid restriction to shed as much as 5 percent of their weight in the 48 hours before racing, hoping to recover their performance capacity by consuming large amounts of fluid and calories in the 1 to 2 hours between the official weigh-in and the race start time. Research suggests that this method is also self-defeating. A 2007 study at the Australian Institute of Sport (Slater et al. 2007) found that performance in a 2,000-meter ergometer test declined by an average of 1.25 percent in rowers who dropped 5.2 percent of their

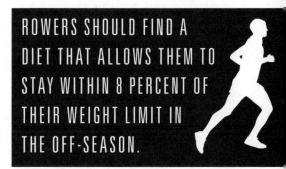

ROWERS SHOULD FIND A DIET THAT ALLOWS THEM TO STAY WITHIN 8 PERCENT OF THEIR WEIGHT LIMIT IN THE OFF-SEASON.

body weight through fasting and fluid restriction in 48 hours and then guzzled fluid and carbohydrate for 2 hours before repeating the test.

It's a problem of psychology. A majority of lightweight rowers find it easier to follow a nonrestrictive diet most of the time, and then restrict it severely for short periods prior to competition, than to maintain moderate restrictions consistently. But it's better to do the latter. You might find it difficult initially to limit your calories at times when the next race is far away, but it will get easier, and when you see the results you won't want to go back to that old feast-or-starve approach. Count calories, monitor your body weight and body composition, and track your performance until you find a diet that allows you to stay within 8 percent of your weight limit in the off-season and within 5 percent whenever a race is fewer than four months out. Limit weight loss in the final 48 hours before competition to no more than 2 percent of your body weight.

RUNNING

In no other sport is a low body weight more beneficial than it is in running. Without a doubt, getting as lean and light as possible without undernourishing their bodies is the greatest weight management challenge runners face. The secret to overcoming this challenge is maintaining consistently high running mileage, which sends a message to the body that all excess fat stores and even muscle tissue must be thrown overboard for the sake of maximizing running economy. Maintaining a high running volume is more difficult than maintaining a high training volume in other endurance sports, however. The human body simply can't absorb as much running as it can cycling or swimming without breaking down. For this reason, elite runners typically train only 10 to 15 hours per week, whereas elite cyclists and swimmers train upward of 25 hours per week. One consequence of this disparity, especially at the sub-elite level where genes favoring lightness and leanness are less predominant, is that it's more difficult for runners to shed excess fat stores (and muscle mass).

Yet most runners simply don't train as much as they could. Cyclists, swimmers, and triathletes are typically willing to commit substantially more time to training. True, this is the case in part because they can train more without getting injured, but it's also more than that—a matter of sport culture. With a careful approach, you can increase your running mileage without greatly increasing your risk of injury. First, increase your mileage very gradually, by roughly 10 percent per week with 20 to 30 percent mileage reductions every third or fourth week for recovery. Second, once your running volume is high, keep it high. Injuries are most likely to occur during periods when you are aggressively increasing your running mileage; if you keep your mileage high, these periods will be minimized. For example, if your peak weekly running volume is 60 miles, don't let your volume drop below 35 miles per week except during brief off-season breaks. Third, listen to your body and reduce your running volume briefly or crosstrain instead of running whenever your body sends you a warning signal of a developing injury. These cautious short-term reductions in running will enable you to run more in the long term by keeping you healthy.

FOR RUNNERS, HIGH MILEAGE IS A BETTER WAY TO GET LEAN THAN CALORIE RESTRICTION.

For runners, high mileage is a better way to get lean than calorie restriction because calorie restriction does not send the same message. Calorie restriction tells your body to conserve energy, which it will do by reducing its metabolic rate to retain fat stores, dismantling more muscle tissue than it otherwise would, and making you feel sluggish in workouts so you go slower, quit sooner, and thereby burn fewer precious calories.

Female runners—especially young female runners—are more likely than male runners to make the mistake of trying to achieve optimal leanness and lightness through calorie restriction. This may be so in part because being lean and light is as much a culturally imposed aesthetic expectation for young female runners as a matter of performance. In any case, the dietary restrictions that young female runners often impose on themselves are as likely to sabotage their performance as enhance it and cause significant health consequences including irregular menstrual cycles and low bone mineral density (BMD). A 2008 study (Barrack et al. 2008) of female adolescent runners found that 28 percent had BMD levels more than one standard deviation below the norm and another 11.8 percent were found to have BMD levels more than two standard deviations below the norm. Low BMD values were strongly correlated with menstrual irregularity, which was reported by 25.8 percent of the runners. More experienced runners were also more likely to have low BMD. The authors of the study concluded, "Female adolescent endurance runners may represent a population with an increased risk of low bone mass. Future studies are necessary to further understand the factors contributing to low bone mass in young runners and to identify behavioral strategies that will promote optimal bone mineral accumulation during the adolescent years" (Barrack et al. 2008, 36).

Coincidentally, a study addressing these very issues was published the next day. In this study, researchers from the Norwegian School of Sport Sciences sought to identify nutritional correlations with menstrual irregularity in runners, with a special focus on vitamin E (Tomten et al. 2009). Ten runners with menstrual irregularity and 10 runners with normal menstrual cycles submitted three-day dietary recalls. Analysis of these data revealed that women with menstrual irregularity consumed significantly less fat than the others. Both groups consumed inadequate amounts of vitamin E, but blood analysis revealed that the women with menstrual irregularity had low levels of vitamin E, while vitamin E levels in the others were normal. The authors of the study wrote, "Our results indicate that irregular menstrual function in athletes on a low-fat diet is associated with low concentrations of circulating alpha-tocopherol [vitamin E], rendering the red blood cells more susceptible to haemolysis in connection with physical activity" (Tomten et al. 2009, 69).

While this study focused on vitamin E and dietary fat, I believe that deficiency in these nutrients in the diets of young female runners is a consequence of general undereating, motivated by a desire to be lean and light. Being lean and light is beneficial for all runners, but the idea is to be lean and light in a way that maximizes running performance. The best strategy to achieve this objective is to increase running volume sensibly while fueling the body adequately to support consistent high-mileage training.

SWIMMING

When you think about managing body weight and composition for endurance performance, you probably think primarily about reducing body-fat levels. But there are some circumstances in which individual athletes also need to gain muscle to perform better. It's not muscle growth per se that they need; rather, it's increased muscle strength and power. But muscle strength and power are closely correlated with muscle cross-sectional area. Thus, muscle growth and increased strength and power go hand-in-hand.

Because swimmers are able to succeed with higher body-fat levels than athletes in other endurance sports, I believe that the greatest weight management challenge that competitive swimmers face is that of increasing swim-specific strength and power, which typically requires gaining some muscle mass. While strength and power are also important in the other endurance sports, only in swimming do they often represent the key to optimizing body composition for performance. Cyclists and runners especially must scrupulously avoid gaining weight through strength training, whereas swimmers are not hindered by adding a few

> THE GREATEST WEIGHT MANAGEMENT CHALLENGE FOR COMPETITIVE SWIMMERS IS INCREASING SWIM-SPECIFIC STRENGTH AND POWER.

pounds of lean muscle to their frame in the gym. And the benefits of pure muscle strength and power are greater in swimming than in every other endurance sport except rowing, which also entails movement through water, which is more resistant than air.

Research has shown that muscle mass and strength have a significant impact on performance in swimming. In a 1997 study, anthropometric measurements were correlated with performance in members of the Greek National Swim Team (Avlonitou et al. 1997). The authors of the study reported that there was a positive relationship between lean body mass and performance, and that lean body mass in the arms was particularly beneficial.

An extreme example is my friend and colleague Brad Culp, editor of *Triathlete*, who was a butterfly specialist in high school and college. Brad's high school coach identified strength as the key to his continued improvement, and Brad took his advice seriously. Through a serious commitment to weight training and anabolic eating (described in Chapter 11), he gained 40 pounds of muscle in four months and lowered his 100-meter butterfly time by 4 seconds. Again, Brad is an extreme case. Most swimmers could not gain 40 pounds of muscle no matter how hard they tried, and would not swim better if they did. But every swimmer can benefit from an effort to maximize his or her muscle strength and power in ways that do not negatively affect other performance-relevant variables such as hydrodynamics and flexibility.

At the elite level, every sport evolves in the direction of effective innovations, and within the past decade one of the most significant innovations in elite swimming (which has trickled down to the college and high school levels), is a much greater commitment to strength training. Swimmer Dara Torres is the poster girl of this trend, but the poster boy of the sport is an equally good example. Between the 2004 and 2008 Olympics, Michael Phelps added 5 hours per week of strength training to his routine and successfully addressed the key weight management challenge in swimming by adding 14 pounds of muscle—and a corresponding amount of strength and power—to his body.

While building muscle and strength represents the key weight management challenge for most swimmers, it is also beneficial for some individuals in other endurance sports. There are two main requirements for muscle growth: resistance training and eating habits that support muscle protein synthesis (or "anabolic eating"). Chapter 11 will include more instruction on strength training and anabolic eating.

TRIATHLON

Two common weight management issues affect triathletes. One is specific to those athletes who come to the sport from a single-sport swimming, cycling, or running background. While these individuals are typically leaner than those who come to triathlon without prior experience as endurance athletes, their bodies are highly adapted to their background sport and must transform to become customized to multisport performance. Swimmers most often need to lose weight, cyclists need to shift muscle mass from their legs to their upper body, and runners need to develop muscle mass in their legs and upper body.

Consider the example of Andy Potts. A swimmer throughout his youth, Potts just barely missed qualifying for the 2000 U.S. Olympic Team in the 400 individual medley (IM). Throughout his years at the University of Michigan he maintained a fairly steady weight of 183 pounds that seemed optimal and did not require any special weight management efforts on his part. Potts quit swimming after the Olympic Trials and ballooned up to 218 pounds over the next two and a half years. Then he decided to become a triathlete—and not just *a* triathlete, but a professional.

To become a strong enough cyclist and runner to qualify for the 2004 U.S. Olympic Triathlon Team—Potts's first major goal—Potts needed to lose more than the 35 pounds he had gained above his swim racing weight. Smartly, he pursued the goal of optimizing his body weight for triathlon initially through balanced, intensive training. "The first 20 pounds came off easily. The next 20 came off more slowly," he recalls. Unlike in his days as a competitive swimmer, Potts paid careful attention to the relationship between his weight and his performance, and found that his cycling and running performance continued to improve as his weight dropped until it naturally leveled off at roughly 176 pounds at his peak training workload.

Potts realized his goal of making the Olympic Team, but was not satisfied. In 2004 he set a goal to take his running to the next level, in part by losing even more weight. This is where he went off track. In addition to running more, Potts ate less, reducing his consumption of some favorite high-calorie fuels and imposing a seven o'clock eating curfew in the evening. As a result, his weight dropped to 167 pounds, but he developed symptoms of overtraining that included a flu he could not shake and declining workout performance. Having learned his lesson, Potts stopped starving himself, gained back a few pounds, and reclaimed his performance edge.

Every triathlete who comes to the sport from a single-sport swimming, cycling, or running background must negotiate some kind of physiological transformation that yields a hybrid body more or less equally suited to all three disciplines. There is a right way and a wrong way to go about it. In terms of training, the right way to proceed is to maintain a balanced training regimen with a slight emphasis on your weaker discipline(s). This will send a message to your body that it needs to transform to better support performance in those disciplines. In terms of nutrition, the right way to proceed depends on whether you need to gain muscle, lose fat, or both. To lose fat, simply follow the Racing Weight plan presented in Part II of this book. In particular, increase your diet quality so that you get more nutrition from fewer calories, balance your energy sources to support muscle maintenance and muscle work while "starving" your excess body-fat stores, use nutrient timing to your advantage, and learn how to manage your appetite effectively. Don't try to simply "diet" your way to a leaner physique. More than likely you will face the same consequences Andy Potts did. To gain muscle, follow the "anabolic eating" tips presented in Chapter 11.

A second weight management challenge that is common especially among long-distance triathletes is avoiding excessive weight loss during periods of especially high-volume training. Andy Potts is familiar with this one as well. "In heavy training it's all I can do to keep my weight at 171 or 172 pounds, which is a pound or two below my racing weight," he says.

In many cases, the body responds to inadequate caloric intake during periods of heavy training not by shedding more and more weight but by reducing its metabolic rate and imposing fatigue during training to conserve weight. These maladaptations to undereating wreak havoc on performance. A 1997 study by researchers at Xavier and Dayton Universities provided evidence that the phenomenon is quite common in long-distance triathletes (Baer and Frentsos 1997). The subject pool was a group of triathletes preparing for the Hawaii Ironman®. At the beginning of the study, all of the athletes participated in a test sprint triathlon, and their daily caloric intake and expenditure levels were estimated. After completing the test race, the subjects met with the researchers to discuss ways of improving their diet for better performance. On average, their daily caloric intake was increased by a massive 72 percent, with most of the extra calories coming from carbohydrate. After four weeks, during which the subjects' training was standardized, the sprint triathlon test was repeated. On average, their performance improved by 8 percent. While it's possible that changes in fitness accounted for a portion of the improvement, it's probable that improved fueling accounted for the bulk of it.

Andy Potts keeps from becoming too lean during periods of heavy training by adding what he calls "cheap calories," such as gourmet pretzels, to his diet that he generally restricts at other times. The same qualities that make these foods cause weight gain in other circumstances (caloric-density and lack of satiating power) make them ideal tools to prevent excess weight loss in triathletes during heavy training. If you're burning upward of 3,000 calories a day in workouts, as even many age-group triathletes are wont to do, you will find it difficult to satisfy your body's energy needs with greens, beans, and the like. As long as these foods continue to be the foundation of your diet, there is no harm and clear benefit in getting the extra calories you need from gourmet pretzels, breakfast cereals, and other reasonably wholesome carbohydrate bombs.

You will probably find yourself craving such foods if you need them. Research has shown that appetite and cravings naturally adjust to ensure that energy needs are met at times of extreme energy expenditure. It's when we're sedentary that these instincts can't be trusted. But in high-volume endurance trainers, a well-heeded appetite can guide you toward energy balance so reliably it's almost creepy. In a famous case study, scientists estimated the energy expenditure and energy intake of the Greek ultrarunning legend Yiannis Kouros as he completed a five-day, 1,000K race (McArdle et al. 2005). They found that he burned nearly 12,000 calories a day (more than five times the amount needed to maintain his body weight without exercise) and consumed a nearly identical number of calories "by feel." When you're training especially hard, you simply stay hungry until you have taken in enough calories to keep your muscles structurally sound and

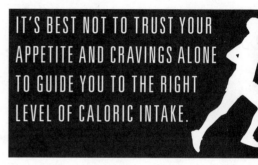

IT'S BEST NOT TO TRUST YOUR APPETITE AND CRAVINGS ALONE TO GUIDE YOU TO THE RIGHT LEVEL OF CALORIC INTAKE.

fully fueled, and when the job is done your hunger vanishes. It's your job not to second-guess your appetite and cravings in such circumstances.

But be honest with yourself, and don't just use your training as an excuse to pig out on your favorite treats. If you're swimming, cycling, and running a total of 6 hours a week, weight gain is still more likely to be your problem than excess weight loss. Only at the level of roughly 20 hours of training per week or more do athletes need to work to keep the meat on their bones with measures such as second helpings at every meal and snacking on gourmet pretzels between meals.

Regardless of your level of training as a triathlete, it's best not to trust your appetite and cravings alone to guide you to the right level of caloric intake. Many of us (like the Ironman triathletes in the study described above) are too out of touch with our bodies to interpret their messages appropriately. Periodically counting calories in and calories out, as the researchers did for the triathletes in that study, will help you determine whether you really are eating enough (or too much) and make an appropriate adjustment.

GUIDELINES FOR BEGINNERS

T ypically, endurance athletes manage their weight in order to perform better. They do not participate in endurance sports to lose weight. While endurance activities such as running are excellent ways to lose weight, those men and women who take up such activities primarily to lose weight seldom stick with them. An American College of Sports Medicine Study (Havenar and Lochbaum 2007) of individuals participating in a group training program for first-time marathoners found that those whose primary motivation was weight loss were significantly more likely to drop out than were those whose primary motivation was to achieve personal goals.

Overwhelmingly, the men and women who stick with an endurance activity long enough to become full-fledged endurance athletes cite simple enjoyment of the activity as their primary motivator for pursuing it. In the Montana State University study on endurance athletes' weight-related beliefs, attitudes, and practices mentioned in the introduction, respondents were asked to select their top three reasons for exercising from a list of ten options. Enjoyment ranked number one. Weight loss ranked dead last (Stults-Kolehmainen et al. 2009).

The poster child of these principles is Natascha Badmann, a six-time winner of the Hawaii Ironman. In her early 20s Badmann, who is Swiss, was an overweight and depressed single mother who loathed the very idea of exercise. A coworker at her office (Badmann was employed as a secretary at a computer company) noticed Badmann nibbling on

MEN AND WOMEN WHO TAKE UP ENDURANCE ACTIVITIES PRIMARILY TO LOSE WEIGHT SELDOM STICK WITH THEM.

tiny lunches at noon and then gorging on chocolate later in the day. He kindly explained to her that if she wanted to lose weight, she needed to eat more lunch and less chocolate, and that she needed to exercise.

Although she had no interest in working out, Badmann was determined to lose weight, and she thought her coworker, Tony Hausler, now her husband, was kind of cute, so she accepted his offer to take her running and cycling. In the beginning she could not even run a mile, and suffered through every step. A triathlete, Hausler understood the psychology of exercise, and thus steered Badmann's attention away from weight loss and toward developing competence and enjoying a feeling of accomplishment on the bike and on her two feet.

Hausler talked Badmann into participating in a short duathlon only six months after she started training with him. Upon crossing the finish line, she was hooked. And it did not hurt that, thanks to her one-in-a-million endurance genes, she took 3rd place.

Duathlon, and later triathlon, gave Badmann a sense of identity and purpose and made her feel good about herself. Endurance sports also made her lose weight, but after a few months she had lost all the weight she needed to lose, and maintaining her losses was the last motivation to keep going. Five years after completing her first half-mile run, Badmann became the duathlon world champion, and a year after that she took 2nd place behind the legendary Paula Newby-Fraser in the Hawaii Ironman.

Affectionately nicknamed the "Swiss Miss," Badmann is a favorite of triathlon fans because she wears a smile throughout every race, win or lose. What started as a reluctant means to weight loss has become for her a source of the greatest happiness.

So that's the fairytale version of the phenomenon. But there are millions of less extreme cases that are no less meaningful in the lives of everyday folks. Consider the case of Wesley Howarth, a 40-year-old IT professional from Liverpool, England. Wes had been a competitive Olympic weightlifter in his youth, but downshifted from competitive to recreational training at age 17 and then let himself go altogether in his early 30s. At age 35 he was hospitalized for three months with a condition that was eventually diagnosed as chronic myofascial pain. His weight ballooned to 342 pounds.

One day, after his release from the hospital, Wes stepped on a scale and it registered an error message because his weight exceeded its measurement capacity.

"I decided to change my life right then," he says.

Wes had always hated aerobic exercise but knew he had to bite the bullet and do it to lose weight. He was so out of shape that he began with 10-minute walks. But while he couldn't exercise long he could exercise often and consistently, and by doing so he was able to make rapid progress, advancing from longer walks to walk-jog workouts to real running. And as he made progress, something magical happened: He started to enjoy running.

Inevitably, Wes began participating in races. His first event was a 5K. He has since moved up to the half-marathon distance and is currently training for his first marathon. Wes's headlong leap into endurance sports has resulted in a most welcome and unexpected side effect: He no longer has to take medication for his once burdensome pain condition. He's also lost 124 pounds and hopes to lose 20 more. However, "Weight loss has become secondary," he says. It's pure enjoyment that keeps Wes running (and swimming, biking, and strength-training). "As much as I used to hate running, that's how much I love it now," Wes confirms.

Beginning endurance athletes often need to change their mind-set before they can fully enjoy the many benefits (including weight loss) of staying involved in it over the long term. Too often, they are motivated primarily by a goal to lose weight. Ironically, they will lose more weight if they replace this goal with performance goals and with a focus on simply "getting hooked" on their new sport. Enjoyment and the desire to perform better are the only motivations that can keep endurance athletes involved in their sport, and loss of motivation is the greatest barrier that prevents beginning endurance athletes from getting lean and light and enjoying the other benefits their sport offers. So in this chapter I will provide a set of guidelines to help beginning endurance athletes build and maintain motivation to participate in their sport. (If you're not a beginner, feel free to skip this chapter!)

AN ACQUIRED TASTE

Endurance training is an acquired taste. Learning to love an endurance sport involves learning to love physical straining, extreme fatigue, and

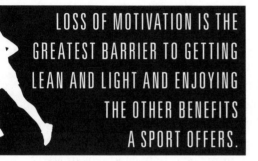

LOSS OF MOTIVATION IS THE GREATEST BARRIER TO GETTING LEAN AND LIGHT AND ENJOYING THE OTHER BENEFITS A SPORT OFFERS.

sore muscles. Granted, pain and suffering may not be what endurance athletes love most about training and racing, but they are inseparable from the greatest joys of training and racing, such as the joy of getting faster. So it's not surprising that most passionate adult endurance athletes first fell in love with exercise as children, when the physical straining of exercise is introduced as play.

In this regard my story is utterly typical. I took up running at age 11 after watching my dad run the Boston Marathon. He never told me to run or even encouraged me to run. He just ran and enjoyed it, so I thought I might enjoy it too. I did not seek weight loss, fitness, approval, glory, or any other reward from running—just enjoyment. And enjoy it I did.

I wish every child could be so fortunate as to experience an early, positive introduction to exercise. Yet while the story of my early affinity for exercise may be the norm, and while it may be easiest to develop a passion for endurance sports as a youth, previously exercise-averse adults catch the endurance bug every day.

I meet such folks all the time in the course of my work. For example, on a flight to Bermuda to cover the Escape to Bermuda Triathlon, I met Bryan Lee, a 46-year-old furniture store owner from Seattle, Washington. In conversing with Bryan over the Atlantic Ocean I learned that he had taken up triathlon the previous spring, having been a non-exerciser his whole life. It started when a cousin, who happened to be a Navy SEAL, invited Bryan to his wedding, and Bryan decided to try to get in shape so that he did not make his cousin "look bad" at the big event. (Bryan was roughly 40 pounds above his college weight.) So he joined a triathlon training class, confident that all the swimming, cycling, and running involved would quickly trim him down and tone him up, but having no intention of actually completing a triathlon ("because those people are crazy," he recalled thinking).

Unexpectedly, Bryan discovered that he actually liked the class, and he signed up to participate in a local sprint triathlon after all. Self-admittedly obsessive-compulsive, he developed an instant endorphin addiction, began looking for races to do every weekend, and was soon traveling all over the world (Chile, South Africa, Monaco, and so forth) for fixes. Escape to Bermuda was to be his thirty-fifth triathlon in 18 months. He had lost 35 pounds along the way, but losing weight had long since ceased to be his main motivator for swimming, cycling, and running. "I just love the whole lifestyle," he said.

Bryan Lee's story contains some important cues about how best to develop a love for endurance sports, which should be every beginning endurance athlete's first objective. Weight loss can be a goal, as well—indeed, if you need to lose weight, it should be a goal—but understand that you are unlikely to still be exercising one year from now if you don't learn to enjoy your training.

HOW TO LEARN TO ENJOY EXERCISE

There are four key steps in the process of learning to enjoy exercise.

Choose a Sport That Feels Right

In our society, exercise is promoted as a means to achieve desired results. Exercise product manufacturers and service providers compete by promising better results through more efficient means. It is assumed that you cannot possibly enjoy exercise; therefore fitness solutions are marketed on claims of minimizing the amount of time the consumer is required to suffer through them to achieve the results he or she wants. This phenomenon is epitomized in the best-selling fitness book *8 Minutes in the Morning*, which promises a body like that of author Jorge Cruise, with a commitment to exercise not exceeding that which is described in the title, and in the infomercials for the BowFlex exercise machine, which promise bodies like those of the fitness models they show using the machine "in just minutes a day."

Such marketing encourages consumers to choose modes of exercise utterly without regard for any possible affinity for the activities themselves. It teaches us to view working out strictly as a chore to get through as quickly as possible, and hence to choose the particular form of exercise that will yield the desired results in the least amount of time. But there is no form of exercise that yields the results we really want in just minutes a day. It takes hours a week, every week, to sculpt and maintain a fitness model's body, and it is nearly impossible to sustain that level of commitment unless exercise is enjoyable.

Despite their efforts to make us believe that some forms of exercise are more effective than others, the truth is that all forms of exercise are more or less equally effective—if you keep doing them. But you're unlikely to keep doing any form of exercise that you view as a chore to be gotten over with as quickly as possible. Only if you truly enjoy the actual experience of performing a given form of exercise is it probable that it will become a permanent part of your lifestyle.

So if there's a particular endurance sports activity that you've tried in the past and kind of liked, make it your primary form of exercise going forward. If you haven't yet found a favorite, try them all and choose the one that feels most "right" as you do it.

Set a Big Goal

I encourage every beginning endurance athlete to set his or her sights on finishing a race. Establishing such a "big" initial goal seems counterintuitive to many, but it's actually a much surer way to cultivate enjoyment of exercise than setting a small goal, such as losing 10 pounds. The reason is that big goals are more consonant with human psychology.

First, any goal tends to be most motivating when it is quite challenging. Small, easy-to-achieve goals don't always excite or, frankly, frighten us enough to inspire consistent hard work toward their fulfillment. Setting a goal to finish a first race—whether it's a sprint triathlon, a century ride, a half-marathon or something else—will make exercise a "bigger deal" in your daily life and encourage you to invest more in it, thereby accelerating the process of coming to enjoy it.

Secondly, psychological research has shown that human beings are natural game players. Almost any sort of hard work becomes more enjoyable when it is structured as a game, with a clear objective and clear means of "counting points" or measuring progress toward that goal. When I was a child, my mother cleverly made a game of the chore of putting away my toys before bedtime—a chore that my two brothers and I loathed. She would put a fun song on the record player and challenge us to put all of our toys away before it ended. We raced around giggling and screaming instead of moping and pouting as we had always done when tidying up in the past. More to the point, studies in exercise psychology have demonstrated that men, women, and children have more fun playing sports than they do exerting themselves at the same intensity in mere fitness activities (Bakshi et al. 1991). By establishing a goal to finish a race, you transform an activity, such as bicycling, that could be a mere fitness activity into a sport.

Thirdly, research has also shown that self-efficacy, or a feeling of activity-specific competence, is the single best predictor of enjoyment in a given activity, and pursuing and achieving the goal of completing a race is a great way to develop a sense of self-efficacy in your chosen endurance sport (Lewis et al. 2002). The first distance-running race I ever completed was a roughly 1-mile run against my fellow fifth graders on our school's annual field day. It hurt like hell, but I won, and the winning made me want to race again, despite the suffering that racing entailed. Studies in sports and exercise psychology indicate that my experience was quite typical. The naturally fittest kids (and adults, for that matter) tend to most enjoy fitness activities, while the naturally most coordinated kids and adults most enjoy motor skill sports, such as basketball. In short, we most enjoy doing what we do well.

Does this mean you have to be capable of winning races to enjoy an endurance sport? Fortunately, it does not. Research suggests that exercise enjoyment increases as fitness does. Thus, as long as you enjoy your chosen sport well enough to continue doing it until you get that first race under your belt, you will gain so much fitness and self-efficacy along the way that you will enjoy it much more by the time you have achieved that initial goal. Also, crossing your first finish line has a magical effect on self-efficacy. It's transformative in many cases, such as that of furniture-salesman-turned-triathlete Bryan Lee. Something about stopping the clock at the end of an official event puts a hook in you, such that no sooner have you showered off your race sweat than you are already plotting your next race goal.

Go Overboard

A change of lifestyle is also a change of identity. One's self-definition is transformed in the process of making significant modifications to one's daily routines and rituals. It's a big deal. Major lifestyle changes are often disruptive and are not completed without a certain rallying of one's entire personality around the lifestyle change. This is why a honeymoon period of intense absorption in one's new lifestyle is often seen when a new lifestyle is assumed. We see the phenomenon played out in every sphere of life. Perhaps you know someone who found religion as an adult and couldn't stop talking about God for a while. You can probably think of at least one person who found a career and threw himself into it head-long, suddenly dressing the way people in that profession dress, talking the way they talk, and so forth.

The same pattern is normal in endurance sports. Running, triathlon, or whatever it is, becomes the biggest thing in the beginner's life for a time as he or she develops a new sense of identity as an athlete that is essential to learning to enjoy sport and establish it as a permanent lifestyle component. Bryan Lee is once again an extreme case in point, completing 35 triathlons in his first 18 months as a triathlete. He'll want to slow down sooner or later, of course, as one needs to be balanced in the long run. But in the novice endurance athlete, a short-term imbalance in the direction of obsession with one's new hobby is normal and healthy.

I am not quite instructing you to become obsessed with your newly chosen endurance sport, because one cannot force such a thing. Either it happens on its own or it doesn't happen at all. I will only advise you not to try to stop this process through misguided self-doubt, conscience, or sense of propriety should it begin. If you find yourself feeling compelled to read all the books and magazines on your sport, pass time on related Web sites, purchase new gear every week, seek out new friends in your sport, and so forth, let it happen. Go ahead. Go overboard!

Remove Barriers

If you are not currently a regular exerciser, then there are barriers between you and exercise. They are the very reasons you have not exercised consistently to this point. As such, these barriers, which may be logistical, psychological, social, and perhaps even physical in nature, must be dismantled if you are to succeed in becoming a bona fide endurance athlete who enjoys exercise.

The primary logistical barrier to exercise is time. Lack of time is the most commonly cited excuse for not exercising. But surveys suggest that those who exercise regularly are just as busy with their jobs, families, and other responsibilities as those who don't work out. So the time excuse is just that: an excuse. We're all pressed for time, yet we all have time for our highest priorities. If exercise is important to you, you will find the time to do it. Consider the case of David Morken, an age-group triathlete whom I had the pleasure of profiling for Ironman.com a few years ago. Morken is a husband, an involved father of six children, and the CEO of a high-tech company, and yet still he finds enough time to train for triathlons. If David Morken can do it, anybody can!

Creative ways that endurance athletes find to fit training into their schedules include working out early in the morning and late in the evening, commuting to and from work on foot or by bicycle, working out on their lunch break, packing most of their training into weekends, working out indoors at home (for example, cycling on an indoor trainer) and combining workouts with other responsibilities (for example, running laps around a soccer field while your child's team practices on it). You might be amazed to see how creative you become after you drop the time excuse!

Perhaps the greatest psychological barrier to exercise, after lack of exercise enjoyment itself, is lack of self-esteem, and the attending demons of self-doubt, pessimism, and fear of failure. Lifelong non-exercisers are often ashamed of their bodies and convinced they cannot accomplish anything positive with them. There are many effective methods of battling these internal barriers. Recognizing that they exist is the first. Once you recognize that your expectation of failure in exercise is a self-fulfilling symptom of low self-esteem, instead of a rational deduction based on solid evidence, it will suddenly seem worthwhile to make every effort to destroy this illusion. Other methods to employ in this effort include seeking your family's support and encouragement, exercising with a friend or a group of like-minded individuals, speaking encouragement to yourself (possibly in the form of inspirational notes left in key locations, such as on your car steering wheel), and even seeking professional counseling if you feel you could benefit from it. Remember, you really are worth every effort made to learn to enjoy exercise and become an endurance athlete (who just happens to be lean and look great)!

SEVEN

IMPROVING YOUR DIET QUALITY

T he single most important characteristic of your diet is its quality. A high-quality diet is made up of a balance of different foods containing high concentrations of a variety of nutrients. With a high-quality diet you can rest assured that you are optimizing your body weight, minimizing chronic disease risk, slowing the aging process, maximizing your endurance performance, and much more. That's why improving your diet quality is the first step of the Racing Weight plan.

Society has lost sight of the importance of diet quality. Science and the weight-loss and health-food industries that science informs have tended to overcomplicate the subject of diet by creating fancier metrics by which to evaluate diet. All of these metrics are just awkward stand-ins for quality. The most notorious pseudometric of diet quality is the glycemic index (GI).

Twenty years ago, most Americans had never heard of the glycemic index, which is, of course, a measure of how quickly the blood glucose level rises after carbohydrate-containing foods are consumed. Researchers began to focus on the glycemic index in the early 1980s. They found that the body processes equal amounts of high-GI and low-GI carbs quite differently, and that these differences might have important implications for health. Their excitement gradually made its way out of the laboratory and into society at large.

In 2002, with the publication of *The New Glucose Revolution*, the glycemic index burst into the collective consciousness as the low-carb diet craze (which did not distinguish between high-GI and low-GI carbs) sank toward its inevitable demise. In the United States, diet trends trumpeted the glycemic index as the new skeleton key of weight management. *The New Glucose Revolution* and the many similar books that followed it taught us that high-glycemic foods increase appetite, cause carbohydrate cravings and sugar addiction, promote fat storage, and lead to the development of diabetes.

There was never much proof that any of this was true, but subsequent research has made it quite clear that the glycemic index is a nearly useless tool for weight management or general health promotion. The essential problem with the glycemic index is that it isolates one characteristic of food, pulls it out of context, and blows it completely out of proportion. Notwithstanding the fact that key tenets of the GI philosophy (such as the notion that high-GI foods promote cravings for more high-GI foods) have been exposed as myths, the key weakness of the GI philosophy is that there's a lot more to food than its effect on blood glucose.

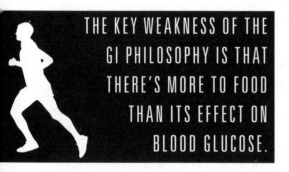

THE KEY WEAKNESS OF THE GI PHILOSOPHY IS THAT THERE'S MORE TO FOOD THAN ITS EFFECT ON BLOOD GLUCOSE.

To draw an exercise analogy, using the glycemic index to guide your diet is a bit like using blood lactate measurements to control the intensity of your workouts. While there is a correlation between blood lactate levels and fatigue, recent studies have determined that there is no causal connection. Blood lactate levels just happen to increase in parallel to other muscle chemistry events that do cause fatigue. And since blood lactate is not only unconnected to fatigue but tedious to measure, there's really no point in doing so.

Similarly, many of the low-quality, processed foods we eat today have high GI values, while most of the high-quality natural foods we are meant to eat have low GI values. Consequently, the average GI value of one's diet is, in fact, a somewhat reliable indicator of a diet's healthfulness. However, foods are not high- or low-quality *because of* their glycemic index. There is merely an association between properties that make certain foods high- or low-quality, such as fiber content, and their effect on blood glucose levels.

While the glycemic index is the metric that has distracted the most people from diet quality, there are many other examples, including the inflammatory index, which makes too much of the effects of various foods on systemic inflammation, and pH value (a measure of the acidity or alkalinity of a substance), which makes too much of the effects of various foods on body acidity. All such metrics suffer from the fact that they are too narrow. The only truly useful measure of a food's value is its total concentration and balance of nutrients. So how do we measure food and diet quality?

MEASURING DIET QUALITY

Before the last years of the twentieth century, scientists focused primarily on the health effects of individual nutrients in their research. The value of such studies is limited, however, because the health effects of individual nutrients depend heavily on the total dietary context in which they are consumed. Thus it became apparent that there was a need to quantify the overall quality of a diet to reflect how people really eat.

Various diet-quality indices, including the Healthy Eating Index and the Diet Quality Index, have since been created. The Diet Quality Index has been described as "a dietary assessment instrument based on 10 dietary recommendations reflecting dietary guidelines and policy in the United States." The original Diet Quality Index assigned scores in a range of 0 to 16 (where the lowest score was the best) based on the amount of eight different food and nutrient types present in the diet. These nutrients are total fat, saturated fat, cholesterol, fruit and vegetables, grains and legumes, protein, sodium, and calcium. Testing of the original index revealed that its effectiveness as a predictor of disease risk was limited by the fact that it did not consider dietary *variety* (a more varied diet tends to reduce disease risk), *proportionality* (it's not just the absolute amount of various nutrients and foods in the diet that matters, but their proportions relative to one another), and *moderation* (a diet that provides more calories than needed tends to increase disease risk regardless of where the calories come from). Hence a revised index that incorporated these factors was created and has been used ever since.

TABLE 7.1 NUVAL SCORING BY FOOD GROUP

Foods	Scoring Range	Median Score
Bread	2–81	25
Canned vegetables	2–100	46
Cereal	4–100	25
Cookies	1–40	3
Crackers	2–87	14
Eggs & egg products	26–67	33
Frozen potatoes and onions	5–96	25
Frozen vegetables	22–100	91
Fruits & vegetables	24–100	100
Meat & poultry	24–53	28
Milk	12–91	54
Pasta	11–91	52
Refrigerated juices	1–82	31
Salty snacks	1–52	17
Seafood	36–89	81
Shelf-stable juices	1–82	9
Shortening/oils	2–34	11
Snack/granola bars	1–42	14
Yogurt	22–99	28

While the Diet Quality Index is a useful tool in nutritional epidemiological studies, it is far too complex for the average layperson to use to monitor and control the quality of his or her own diet. Within the past decade, nutrition scientists who recognized the potential value of a dietary-quality measurement tool for individual consumers, and the inadequacy of existing scientific tools for this purpose, have proposed various new metrics that do not require a doctorate to implement. Among these metrics is NuVal, a nutritional scoring system devised by David Katz, a professor of public health at Yale University. NuVal uses an algorithm to assign a score of 1 to 100 to individual foods (where the highest score is the best) based on a weighted consideration of 30 different nutrient factors. Table 7.1 shows the NuVal categories and the range of scores and median score for each group of foods. Figure 7.1 presents a sample listing of NuVal scores for a variety of specific foods. You'll notice that the scores vary significantly from one brand to the next. And just because a food is organic doesn't mean it scores high; in fact, the opposite can be true, and fortified foods often score highest.

FIGURE 7.1 EXAMPLES OF NUVAL SCORES FOR VARIOUS FOODS

Left	Score	Right
Spinach	100	Green beans (canned, frozen, or fresh)
Blueberries		Asparagus (fresh)
Carrots	99	
Corn	91	McCann's Steel-Cut Irish Oatmeal
Fat-free skim milk		
Barilla Whole-Grain Penne Pasta	89	
Codfish	87	Silk Soy Milk, plain
Frozen mixed vegetables		
	82	Tropicana Ruby Red Grapefruit Juice with Calcium
Kellogg's Special K Protein Plus	60	
Quaker Instant Oatmeal Original		Yoplait Light Fat-Free Yogurt
Creamette Spaghetti Pasta	58	
	56	Asparagus (canned)
	52	Natural Oven's Bakery 100% Whole Grain Bread
Turkey breast (skinless)	48	
	40	V8 100% Vegetable Juice
Chicken breast	39	
	34	Activia plain yogurt
Eggs, brown or white (all sizes)	33	
	30	Lean ground beef
Kashi 7 Whole Grain Flakes	29	Frozen potatoes
Nabisco Wheat Thins Multi Grain	28	
Ham	27	POM Wonderful Pomegranate Juice
Potato chips	24	
	11	Bertoli Extra-Virgin Olive Oil
Nabisco Oreo "Double Stuf" cookies	5	
	1	Soda

A number of supermarket chains have signed on to provide NuVal scores in their stores to help customers make healthier food buying decisions. But while NuVal has some value in enabling consumers to compare the quality of individual foods, it falls far short of being an adequate tool for total diet-quality management. Its first major shortcoming is that it simply provides no standard for overall diet quality. How many total NuVal points should one aim for each day? The system has no answer to this question. The second major shortcoming of NuVal as a tool for diet-quality management is that it does not incorporate the macrofactors of variety, proportionality, and moderation that are as essential to dietary quality as the microfactors of the amount of individual nutrients within specific foods.

Thus, ratings of individual foods in the NuVal system cannot serve as guides to their usefulness in contributing to a varied and healthy overall diet. For example, Figure 7.1 shows that the NuVal score for broccoli is much higher than that for chicken, which might suggest that a diet with lots of broccoli and no chicken is of higher quality than a diet with both. But because the nutrient profiles of broccoli and chicken are complementary, meaning each food is richest in nutrients in which the other is poorest, there is a much stronger case to be made in favor of a diet that includes both. Variety in the diet is important precisely because no single food contains all of the nutrients we need. Neither can the NuVal system be used to encourage moderation because scores are not intended to be totaled. A high NuVal score in an individual food is good, but a high composite NuVal score for an entire day is not necessarily good, because one way to achieve it is by eating vast quantities of junk.

THE DIET QUALITY SCORE

Not satisfied with any of the existing tools that individuals might use to manage their own dietary quality, I created the Diet Quality Score (DQS) a couple of years ago (see Table 7.2). It works by assigning a score to your total eating for one day that is the sum of point values assigned to the individual items you eat throughout the day. The higher your DQS score, the healthier your diet is. As such, the DQS represents a simple, practical, realistic, and holistic approach to measuring diet quality. It is a tool you can use as often as every day to generate an accurate picture of how healthily you're eating without making a significant commitment of time and energy.

TABLE 7.2 DQS SCORING BY FOOD TYPE

Food	SERVINGS					
	1st	2nd	3rd	4th	5th	6th
Fruit	2	2	2	1	0	0
Vegetable	2	2	2	1	0	0
Lean protein	2	2	1	0	0	−1
Whole grain	2	2	1	0	0	−1
Lowfat dairy	1	1	1	0	−1	−2
Essential fats	2	0	0	0	−1	−1
Refined grain	−1	−1	−2	−2	−2	−2
Sweet	−2	−2	−2	−2	−2	−2
Fried food	−2	−2	−2	−2	−2	−2
Full-fat dairy	−1	−1	−2	−2	−2	−2
Fatty protein	−1	−1	−2	−2	−2	−2

The Diet Quality Score considers the intrinsic wholesomeness of foods as well as the factors of balance and moderation that also contribute to overall diet quality. Foods are divided into the following 11 categories: fruits, vegetables, lean proteins, whole grains, low-fat dairy, essential fats, refined grains, sweets, fried foods, full-fat dairy foods, and fatty proteins. Foods in the first six of these categories are considered "high-quality" and therefore add points to your daily DQS. The foods in the last five categories are considered "low-quality" and therefore subtract points from your daily DQS. To determine your DQS for any given day, all you have to do is identify the category for each item you've eaten, find the point total assigned to that category, and tally the points.

The DQS encourages balanced eating through its use of six separate high-quality food categories. To maximize your daily DQS, you need to eat foods in all six of these categories, in part because the point value assigned to foods within any given category declines as you consume more servings of them throughout any single day. For example, your first, second, and third daily servings of low-fat dairy add one point each to your score, but your fourth serving adds none, your fifth serving subtracts one and your sixth serving subtracts two. This feature of the DQS reflects the fact that it is possible to consume too much of any food, no matter how nutritious. The declining point value of high-quality foods with multiple servings also encourages moderation, because it ensures that you cannot indefinitely increase your DQS simply by eating more.

The DQS approach to diet-quality assessment has been indirectly validated by a large study conducted by Swedish researchers (Michels and Wolk 2002). The authors of this study divided foods into "healthy" and "unhealthy" categories very much like the "high-quality" and "low-quality" categories of the DQS. The diets of more than 58,000 women were analyzed for the variety of healthy and unhealthy foods they contained. It was discovered that those women who ate the greatest variety of healthy foods had the lowest mortality rate over a 10-year period, while those who ate the greatest variety of unhealthy foods had the highest mortality rate.

FOOD CATEGORIES

Before I give you specific guidelines on using the Diet Quality Score, let me first define and explain the 11 food categories. I will be the first to admit that strictly defining some food categories as "high-quality" and others as "low-quality" is somewhat artificial. In truth, I don't think it's quite accurate to classify any food category as low-quality. A can of soda could save your life in the right circumstances, for example. Going a step further, I don't even like the nearly universal practice of distinguishing some nutrients as "good" and others as "bad." By definition, a nutrient is a chemical compound that the body can use to keep itself functioning. Therefore all nutrients are good in one sense. Consider the example of saturated fat. This nutrient is widely considered to be bad, but the human body uses saturated fats in all kinds of helpful ways. Saturated fat is good. It just so happens that the modern diet contains too much of it. In most cases, what we really mean when we label a certain nutrient bad is that we tend to consume it in excess.

The logic by which I developed the high-quality and low-quality food categories of the Diet Quality Score was this: I wanted a set of categories that would, in a practical if not a scientifically rigorous way, encourage individuals to consume enough of the nutrients (such as fiber) that most of us do not consume enough of and to consume fewer of the nutrients (such as sugar) that we typically consume in excess. I don't really believe that whole-milk dairy foods are low-quality and that low-fat dairy foods are high-quality in any rigorous sense. I do, however, believe that designating them as such is a helpful way to promote more balanced nutrition.

In order to use the DQS effectively, you need to know how to count servings for the various food types listed on the DQS table. With high-quality foods, I believe in using commonsense guidelines for serving sizes that are based on the amounts we typically eat. While it is often said that we tend to eat excessively large portions these days, this is typically not the case with high-quality foods such as vegetables and whole grains. The thing to watch out for is counting too small a portion of a high-quality food as a serving. A packet of ketchup does not count as a vegetable serving (and not because it's technically a fruit)! In the following sections I present commonsense serving-size guidelines for each of the 11 food categories. While I do define serving sizes for low-quality foods, any amount of an unhealthy food (within reason—you don't have to count a single sip of soda or two french fries) counts as a serving. The primary reason I define serving sizes for low-quality foods is so that you will be sure to count your portions of such foods as *two* servings when you consume more than one serving's worth of them!

HIGH-QUALITY FOODS

Here's the basic information you need to know about the six high-quality food categories.

Fruit

The fruit category includes whole fresh fruits, canned and frozen fruits, and 100 percent fruit juices. Commonsense fruit serving sizes include one medium-size piece of whole fruit (e.g., one whole banana), a big handful of berries, and a medium-size glass of 100 percent fruit juice. Fruits are considered high-quality because they are rich in a variety of essential vitamins and minerals. In addition, fruits are packed with technically non-essential nutrients, known as phytonutrients, that function as antioxidants in the body. Until recently it was believed that phytonutrients functioned in the same way as the body's endogenous antioxidants, such as glutathione, which directly neutralize free radicals. Now it is believed that they are actually weak toxins that stimulate the body's endogenous antioxidants through a stress reaction, much as other positive stressors such as exercise strengthen various systems of the body. In any case, we know that men and women who consume high levels of fruits exhibit higher antioxidant capacities, are less prone to chronic diseases, and live longer.

Fruits also contain a lot of fiber and water and relatively few calories. The effect of a food on hunger is determined primarily by its volume and only secondarily by the calories within it. Fiber and water add volume to foods without adding calories. Consequently, they have a high-satiety index, which means that they provide a relatively large degree of hunger satisfaction per calorie and promote a lean body composition. The health benefits of fruit consumption are optimized at an intake level of three to four servings per day, as reflected in the Diet Quality Score.

Note that fruit juice counts as fruit in government and other official dietary guidelines. This is controversial, though, because fruit juices do not contain all of the nutrients in the whole fruits they come from. For example, most of the flavonoids (antioxidants) in oranges are contained in the pulp, very little of which makes its way into orange juice. Thus, while 100 percent fruit juices are more nutritious than most beverages, I do not recommend that you rely on them too heavily to meet your daily fruit requirements.

Vegetables

The vegetable category of the DQS includes whole, fresh vegetables eaten cooked or raw, canned and frozen vegetables, and pureed or liquefied vegetables used in soups, sauces, and such. Commonsense vegetable serving sizes are a fist-sized portion of solid veggies, a half-cup of tomato sauce, and a medium-size bowl of vegetable soup or salad.

Like fruit, vegetables are loaded with vitamins, minerals, and phyto-nutrients, contain large amounts of fiber and water, and are relatively low in calories, so they provide nearly everything your body needs to function healthily and promote a lean body composition. The benefits of eating vegetables, like those of fruit, are maximized at an intake level of three to four servings per day.

Lean Proteins

Included in the lean protein category are all types of fish, meats that are 10 percent fat or less, and nuts and seeds. Count your first serving of low-fat dairy as a lean protein as well. A commonsense serving of meat or fish is the size of your open hand. A commonsense serving of nuts is a palmful.

Fish and lean meats support a lean body composition because they are the best sources of protein and are low in fat. Again, fat is not inherently unhealthy, as many people believe, but is a type of nutrient that we tend to consume in excess. Fish and lean meats are also good sources of a variety of vitamins and minerals including vitamin B12 and iron. The very highest-quality fish is wild fish, as opposed to farm-raised, and the highest-quality meats are organic meats.

We are often advised to moderate our consumption of nuts because they are high in fat and calories, but unlike the typical American diet, nuts have a nice balance of saturated and unsaturated fats. They are also quite filling and not the type of thing many people eat in excess. Honestly, I don't think anyone ever got fat by eating nuts. Indeed, some research (Bes-Rastrollo et al. 2009) suggests that persons who eat a lot of nuts tend to have slightly *lower* than average body weights.

Whole Grains

The whole-grain category includes brown rice and breakfast cereals, breads, and pastas made with 100 percent whole grains. Commonsense servings of whole grains are a fist-size portion of brown rice, a medium-size bowl of cereal or pasta, and two slices of bread.

While some nutrition experts encourage minimal consumption of any and all grains, because they are less nutrient-dense and more calorie-dense than vegetables, I believe that whole grains have a place in the endurance athlete's diet because they are rich sources of carbohydrate, which is the energy source that endurance athletes need most. Whole grains have more fiber, vitamins, and minerals than refined grains

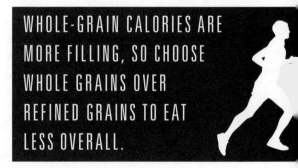

WHOLE-GRAIN CALORIES ARE MORE FILLING, SO CHOOSE WHOLE GRAINS OVER REFINED GRAINS TO EAT LESS OVERALL.

such as white rice. Whole grains also support a lean body composition. Studies have shown that the individuals who consume the greatest amount of whole grains are less likely to be overweight than those who

VITAMIN D

The vitamin D found in milk is not naturally occurring but added. Recent research indicates that vitamin D is even more important than it was previously believed to be and that vitamin D deficiency is very widespread in American society. Research out of Harvard University suggests that between 24 and 40 percent of Americans have low levels of vitamin D, which is needed to maintain healthy bones and a strong immune system (Gordon et al. 2004). Vitamin D deficiency weakens the bones and muscles and increases the risk of cancer by as much as 30 percent. The primary source of vitamin D is actually the sun. The skin naturally produces vitamin D when exposed to ultraviolet radiation. Some experts now believe that it is not possible to get enough vitamin D for optimal health without regular sun exposure.

eat fewer whole grains (Good et al. 2008). This is the case in part because whole-grain calories are more filling, so those who tend to choose whole grains over refined grains eat less overall, and because the body uses more energy to digest whole grains than refined grains.

Low-Fat Dairy

Low-fat dairy foods encompass all foods made with low-fat or skim milk, including milk itself. Goat and sheep's milk count as well as cow's milk. Commonsense servings of low-fat dairy include a glass of milk or the amount of milk you'd normally use in a bowl of breakfast cereal, two slices of deli cheese, and a single-serving tub of yogurt.

Low-fat dairy foods support a lean body composition by providing substantial amounts of protein for muscle support, carbohydrate to fuel activity, and substantially less fat than whole-milk dairy foods. In addition, low-fat dairy foods are a good source of calcium and vitamin D. Calcium also supports a lean body composition by reducing the activity of a hormone called calcitriol that promotes fat storage.

Essential Fats

There are several types of fat, known as essential fats, that the human body cannot synthesize from other fats (and so must obtain them from the diet) and cannot survive without. Some essential fats are classified as omega-6 fatty acids and others as omega-3 fatty acids. Omega-6 fatty acids are abundant in commonly eaten foods but omega-3 fatty acids are not, and omega-3 fatty acid deficiency is widespread in our society. Omega-3 fatty acids play vital roles in the formation of healthy cell membranes, nerve cell function, and the formation of anti-inflammatory compounds in the body.

Preliminary research also suggests that omega-3 fatty acids may promote a lean body composition by enhancing the fat-burning effect of exercise (Hill et al. 2007). What's more, they may even boost aerobic exercise performance. A solid body of scientific research has shown that omega-3 fats increase the elasticity of the blood vessels, which improves circulation and lowers blood pressure. Omega-3 fats may boost cardiac efficiency during exercise through the same mechanism (Peoples et al. 2008).

The best food sources of omega-3 fats are certain types of fatty fish (wild salmon, herring, anchovies), flaxseeds, and flaxseed oil. Experts recommend consuming omega-3-rich fish at least twice a week to avoid deficiency. I recommend that everyone, regardless of how much fish he or she eats, take a daily essential fat supplement. Chapter 14 will explain this recommendation in more detail.

LOW-QUALITY FOODS

Here's the basic information you need to know about the five low-quality food categories.

Refined Grains

The category of refined grains includes white rice, processed flours, and all breakfast cereals, pastas, breads, and other baked goods made with less than 100 percent whole grains. Commonsense servings are the same as they are for the whole-grains category—a fist-size portion of white rice, a medium-size bowl of cereal or pasta, and two slices of bread.

Refined grains are classified as low-quality foods in the Diet Quality Score because they contain more calories and provide less satiety than whole grains. There are 100 percent whole-grain varieties of every grain-based food you might care to eat, from bagels to ziti, so it just makes sense to choose them instead of varieties made with refined grains whenever possible.

Sweets

This category includes all foods and beverages containing large amounts of refined sugars, including soft drinks, candy, pastries, and other desserts. If you're unsure about whether a certain food or beverage should be counted as a sweet, use the second-ingredient rule: If any type of refined sugar is the second or first ingredient, it's a sweet. Commonsense serving sizes of sweets include one small cookie, 12 ounces of soft drink, one label-defined serving of candy or chocolate, one regular-size slice of pie or cake, and a scoop or bowl of ice cream.

Sweets are classified as low-quality foods because they are a major source of excess calories in the American diet. Seventeen percent of the average American's calories come from sugars. That's ridiculous. Sweets promote body-fat accumulation more than any other type of food because they are extremely calorie-dense and provide relatively little satiety.

Fried Foods

This category includes all deep-fried foods, including potato chips, fried chicken, fried meats, and donuts. It does not include pan-fried foods such as stir fries and fried eggs. Commonsense servings of fried foods include one small bag of potato chips, one fried hamburger patty, three or four buffalo wings, one small bag of chips, one small order of french fries, and one donut.

A BAKED POTATO CONTAINS 145 CALORIES, WHEREAS A MEDIUM SERVING OF FRENCH FRIES CONTAINS 387 CALORIES.

Deep frying adds a ton of calories to the base foods being fried. For example, a 156-gram baked potato contains roughly 145 calories, whereas a medium serving of french fries (117 grams) contains 387 calories. The oils used in frying are some of the most calorie-dense foods that exist. Including fried foods in your diet is a surefire way to gain excess body fat. Eat as few of them as your cravings will allow!

Whole-Milk Dairy

Dairy foods made with whole milk contain all of the good stuff that low-fat dairy foods contain plus a lot more fat, hence a lot more calories.

While fat, too, is good in moderation, most of us do not eat fat in moderation; therefore it is sensible to remove it from the diet in ways that are convenient. Substituting whole-milk dairy foods with low-fat alternatives is a convenient way to trim excess fat and calories from your diet. Commonsense servings of whole-milk dairy foods are the same as they are for low-fat dairy foods.

Fatty Proteins

Fatty proteins are meats containing more than 10 percent fat. Eggs are an exception to this rule. Research has shown that, despite their high fat content and caloric density, eggs tend to support a lean body composition. For example, one study by researchers at St. Louis University found that two eggs eaten for breakfast resulted in significantly greater satiety and less eating through the remainder of the day than a bagel containing equal calories (Vander Wal et al. 2005). So count your first two eggs of any given day as lean proteins. Fatty-meat serving sizes are the same as low-fat meat serving sizes—enough meat to fit in your open hand.

USING THE DIET QUALITY SCORE

Now that you know how to calculate a one-day Diet Quality Score, it's time to use the DQS to improve your diet. The first step is to calculate an initial score to establish a baseline. Write down everything you eat over the course of one day, determine the food types and the number of servings represented, and add up your positive and negative points. Having established your baseline, find ways to increase your DQS.

There are three ways to increase your DQS: (1) eliminate low-quality foods from your diet, (2) add high-quality foods, and (3) replace low-quality foods with high-quality substitutes. I recommend that you start by making substitutions. Eliminating low-quality foods is not the best way to start in most cases because it tends to reduce dietary satisfaction. By replacing low-quality foods with high-quality alternatives you maintain a steady level of eating while reducing excesses in sugar, fat, and total calories. It's the least disruptive way to improve your diet quality. Table 7.3 illustrates that there are several types of substitution that almost suggest themselves.

TABLE 7.3 FOOD SUBSTITUTIONS TO INCREASE YOUR DQS

Instead of	Eat (or drink)
Refined-grain food (e.g., white rice)	Whole-grain food (e.g., brown rice)
Fatty protein (e.g., 80% lean ground beef)	Lean protein (e.g., 95% lean ground beef)
Whole-milk dairy (e.g., ice cream)	Low-fat dairy (e.g., fat-free yogurt)
Sweet (e.g., ice cream)	Fruit (e.g., mixed berries)
Fried food (e.g., fried chicken)	Nonfried alternative (e.g., boneless, skinless chicken breast)

The next way to improve your DQS is to add high-quality foods. I recommend that you add fruits and vegetables first, as it is probable that these are the high-quality foods your diet is most lacking. Add servings until you are consuming at least three and preferably four servings of each. Easy ways to add fruits and vegetables to your diet include adding fruits as midmorning and midafternoon snacks and simply doubling vegetable portion sizes at meals. Don't be concerned that adding high-quality foods to your diet will promote weight gain. These foods provide more satiety than they do calories, so when you add them you will naturally eat slightly less of other stuff. Perhaps the simplest addition you can make to your diet is that of adding a serving of healthy fats in the form of a fish oil or flaxseed oil supplement.

There are different strategies you can use to improve your diet quality. If change is not difficult for you, it might be best for you to make a bunch of changes simultaneously. Other personalities might find it more effective to make one or two changes at a time. Naturally, the first approach will give you faster results whereas the second is likely to feel less disruptive and overwhelming. Neither option is inherently better than the other, but each is better for some people. Consider your psychological makeup and choose the option that will work best for you. Regardless of how you decide to begin improving your diet quality, be sure to calculate your daily DQS as long as the process of improving your diet lasts so that you can quantify your improvement and create a new personal target score.

FOCUS ON IMPROVING YOUR EXISTING SCORE UNTIL YOU ARE SATISFIED WITH THE RESULTS YOU GET.

The maximum possible score on the DQS is 29. You will achieve this score by eating four servings of fruits and vegetables, three servings of lean proteins, whole grains, and low-fat dairy, and one serving of essential fats, and by eating no low-quality foods whatsoever. You don't need to hit a DQS of 29 every day—or ever, for that matter—to reach your racing weight and maximize your endurance performance and overall health. Instead of trying to achieve a perfect DQS, I recommend that you focus on improving your existing score until you are satisfied with the results you get. Once you have arrived at that point there is no need to improve it any further. Continue to calculate your DQS every once in a while to make sure you are hitting your personal target, whatever it is.

EIGHT

BALANCING YOUR ENERGY SOURCES

I n the last years of the twentieth century and the first years of the twenty-first, our nation was gripped by a positive mania for weight-loss diets based on ratios of carbohydrate, fat, and protein—the three major sources of energy (calories) in the diet—which are known collectively as macronutrients. Every new diet that came along touted a new and supposedly better way of balancing your energy sources—a certain magical macronutrient ratio—as the key to rapid and permanent weight loss.

First, the low-fat diets gained ascendancy. These diets were based on the belief that reducing fat consumption is the best way to shed excess body fat because, after all, the problem of fatness is that there is too much *fat* in the body. Among the most popular low-fat diets was that of Dean Ornish, MD, which was explicated in his best-selling book *Eat More, Weigh Less*. The magical macronutrient ratio recommended in the Ornish diet and other low-fat diets is 80 percent carbohydrate (compared to 48 percent in the average American's diet), 10 percent protein (compared to 18 percent), and 10 percent fat (compared to 34 percent), making the low-fat diet a de facto high-carbohydrate diet as well.

After the low-fat diets (which, of course, have not gone away entirely) came the low-carbohydrate diets. Advocates of low-carb diets argue that carbohydrate contributes to weight gain more than fat does because carbohydrate is not very satiating and is essentially addictive and therefore causes overeating. The king of the low-carb diets is Robert Atkins, whose manifesto, *Dr. Atkins' New Diet Revolution*, became the bestselling diet book in history. Atkins advocated a carbohydrate intake of no more than 40 grams per day, which is equivalent to less than 10 percent of total calories for most people. That's extreme when you consider that mainstream nutrition experts believe that the nervous and immune systems of the average person cannot function properly on a diet that provides fewer than 150 grams of carbohydrate per day. Less zealous low-carb diets, such as the Zone Diet of Barry Sears, recommended more realistic carbohydrate intake levels. The magical macronutrient ratio of the Zone Diet is 40 percent carbohydrate, 30 percent fat, and 30 percent protein.

It was probably inevitable that the low-carb diet fad would give way to a high-protein diet era, and the latter did indeed rise from the ashes of the demise of Atkins and friends, although it has arguably never really taken off. Most low-carb diets are de facto high-protein diets, but true-blue high-protein diet advocates tend to emphasize the benefits of protein instead of vilifying carbohydrates, and they prescribe macronutrient ratios accordingly. The typical high-protein diet calls for a protein target of 30 to 40 percent of total calories, or three to four times the generally accepted minimum requirement for protein. The rationale for adopting a high-protein diet is that protein is the most satiating macronutrient, so people tend to eat less overall when they eat a lot of protein.

So which is truly the best weight-loss diet: low-fat, low-carb, or high-protein? Research suggests that none of them is clearly superior. Epidemiological studies have found no relationship between the relative proportions of carbs, fats, and protein in the diet and body weight. It appears that the human body is able to adapt to a wide range of macronutrient ratios. There is no magic ratio—no single best way to balance your energy sources. We can point to historical and present-day examples of high-carbohydrate, high-fat, and high-protein diets that are associated with both low and high rates of overweight. What does matter is not the ratio of macronutrients but the total amount of calories consumed, which is heavily influenced by the sources of calories. Processed foods (or low-quality foods) tend to be much more calorically dense than natural foods; therefore people who eat a lot of processed foods tend to eat more total calories and to be heavier than people who don't. It is possible to eat a natural food–based (or high-quality) diet that is relatively high in carbohydrate, or in fat, or in protein. All are likely to promote a lean body composition, whereas a diet packed with low-quality foods is likely to make one fat regardless of its macronutrient ratio.

As an endurance athlete, you want a diet that not only promotes a lean body composition but also maximizes your performance in training. Endurance sports nutrition has been largely unaffected by macronutrient ratio–based diet fads. Mainstream experts on endurance sports nutrition have consistently advised athletes to maintain a high-carbohydrate, low-fat diet for more than half a century. There have been some voices supporting high-fat and high-protein diets in endurance sports, but they have remained a minority. The most commonly touted magical macronutrient ratio for endurance athletes is 60 percent carbohydrate, 20 percent fat, and 20 percent protein. The high-carb part of this formula is intended to maximize workout performance, as muscle glycogen, derived from dietary carbohydrate, is the limiting energy source for endurance exercise. The low-fat part of the formula is intended to minimize excess body-fat stores. Clearly this approach is informed by the old idea that eating fat makes us fat.

Is the 60-20-20 formula the optimal macronutrient ratio to maximize workout performance and promote a lean body composition? If not, is there a better ratio, or can endurance athletes achieve their goals with a variety of different macronutrient ratios, just as dieters can achieve their goals with a low-fat diet, a low-carb diet, or a high-protein diet, as long as it's a high-quality diet?

There has not been much research on the effects of different macronutrient proportions on body weight and/or body composition in endurance athletes. There is a lot more research on the effects of different macronutrient proportions on endurance performance. This research tells us all we really need to know, however, because, as I have mentioned previously, any dietary or training influence that benefits performance is almost certain to make you leaner, and for that matter, any dietary or training influence that benefits performance is good, regardless of how it affects your body weight and body composition. A close look at the available research and real-world evidence suggests that endurance athletes are able to have equal success on diets featuring various proportions of carbohydrates, fats, and proteins. There is no magic to the 60-20-20 macronutrient ratio nor is there any other magical macronutrient ratio for all endurance athletes. There are certainly minimum amounts of each macronutrient that athletes need to perform optimally, but there's quite a bit of flexibility to exceed the minimum requirement for any of the three macronutrients without negative consequences.

While neither the scientific research nor the real-world evidence supports the notion that every endurance athlete needs to maintain a high-carbohydrate diet, both sources of evidence suggest that carbohydrate intake should vary with training load. The less you train, the less carbohydrate you need to perform optimally (and, by extension, to reach your racing weight). The more you train, the more carbohydrate you need. Training does increase protein and fat needs too, but not to the same degree

> SHAPE YOUR DIET TO MEET A DAILY CARBOHYDRATE TARGET WITHOUT FAILING TO GET ADEQUATE AMOUNTS OF FAT AND PROTEIN.

that it increases carbohydrate needs. So the 15-miles-a-week runner might perform optimally on a diet that's significantly less than 60 percent carbohydrate, while the triathlete who trains 15 hours a week might perform best on a diet that's significantly more than 60 percent carbohydrate. Put another way, it's not carbohydrate as a percentage of total calories that you need to worry about. Rather, it's the absolute amount of carbohydrate (that is, the total number of carbohydrate grams you eat). Therefore my primary recommendation for balancing your energy sources as an endurance athlete—for the sake of maximum performance and optimal performance weight—is that you select a daily carbohydrate intake target that is appropriate to your training workload and shape your diet to meet or exceed this target without failing to get adequate amounts of fat and protein.

In the last section of this chapter, I will show you how to tailor your carbohydrate intake to meet the needs imposed by your training volume. But first let's look at what science says about the carbohydrate, fat, and protein needs of endurance athletes individually. This will establish the (fairly broad) ranges within which you should try to stay.

CARBOHYDRATE: COUNT ON IT

The 60 percent carbohydrate intake guideline for endurance athletes dates back to the late 1960s, when exercise scientists discovered that higher muscle-glycogen levels were associated with greater fatigue resistance in exhaustive endurance tests, and that high-carbohydrate diets increased muscle-glycogen levels (Kreider et al. 2009). The problem with most of the studies that have shown performance benefits associated with high-carbohydrate diets is that they have really been designed to produce the very result that was sought. In the typical study of this sort, athletes are required to train harder than they normally do for a certain period of time and then perform a long time trial or exhaustive endurance test after an overnight fast. The fact that athletes tend to perform better in these tests of high-carbohydrate diets is taken as proof that endurance athletes will tend to perform better in real-world training on such diets.

Among the most recent studies of this sort was one performed by researchers at the University of Birmingham, England, in 2004. This study compared the effects of a high-carb diet (8.5 grams of carbohydrate per kilogram of body weight per day, or 65 percent of total calories) and a low-carb diet (5.4 grams of carbohydrate per kilogram per day, or 41 percent of total calories) on running performance during a period of intensified training. Seven high-level runners spent 11 days on each diet. Their training load was substantially increased for the last week of each 11-day period. At the beginning and again at the end of each heavy training period, the runners completed an 8-km time trial on the treadmill and a 16-km time trial outdoors. On both diets, the runners ran worse in the 8-km time trial after heavy training, but performance in the 16-km time trial worsened after heavy training only on the low-carb diet (Achten et al. 2004).

On the surface, this study provides compelling evidence that competitive runners should maintain a high-carbohydrate diet, period. However, the study design was flawed in key ways. First, endurance athletes seldom increase their training load as suddenly and drastically as did the runners in this study, and they almost never race or perform time trials without a buffer of rest or recovery days separating such efforts from their most recent hard training days. And only the craziest runners would run a race or perform a time trial more than 10 hours after their last meal or snack, as the runners in this study were required to do.

In the real world, endurance athletes increase their training workload gradually, they alternate heavier and lighter training days, they rest up for races and important fitness tests, and they do not train or race in a fasted state. All of these practices, I believe, enable many if not most endurance athletes to train effectively on diets that contain less carbohydrate than the high-carbohydrate diet used in the University of Birmingham study. In fact, simply inserting lighter training days between heavier training days—which every endurance athlete, no matter how great his or her carbohydrate intake, must do—enables the endurance athlete who eats moderate amounts of carbohydrate to replenish muscle-glycogen stores. Because less muscle glycogen is used on lighter training days, there is still sufficient muscle glycogen available on the heavier training days. In addition, the normal practice of consuming some carbohydrate in a pre-exercise meal or snack (not to mention consuming carbohydrate in sports drinks or energy gels during exercise) effectively supplements muscle-glycogen stores and acts to adequately maintain the day-to-day workout performance of the endurance athlete on a moderate-carbohydrate diet.

In 1991, William Sherman, of Ohio State University, conducted a review of the accumulated scientific literature on carbohydrate intake, glycogen levels, and endurance performance and concluded that there was no solid evidence that either short-term or long-term reductions in carbo-hydrate intake significantly impairs performance (Sherman and Wimer 1991). This assessment was based in part on the fatal biases I've already identified in much of the research in this area and in part on Sherman's own, better-designed research. One of Sherman's studies showed that runners and cyclists performed just as well in exhaustive exercise tests after 7 days on a moderate-carbohydrate diet as they did after 7 days on a high-carbohydrate diet, despite the fact that the moderate-carb diet reduced their muscle-glycogen stores by 30 to 36 percent compared to the high-carbohydrate diet (Sherman et al. 1993).

Nevertheless, Sherman now recommends that endurance athletes consume a high-carbohydrate diet on the grounds that, while the evidence suggests that a high-carbohydrate diet is better than a moderate-carbohydrate diet only in the most extreme circumstances, there's no evidence that a moderate-carbohydrate diet is better than a high-carbohydrate diet in any circumstance. My own view is that the evidence indicates that carbohydrate intake should be proportional to the individual athlete's training load, and that one should err on the side of eating more carbohydrate than might be necessary rather than less.

After all, studies such as those at the University of Birmingham do clearly demonstrate that in extreme circumstances, a high level of carbohydrate intake is necessary to support optimal performance. So it stands to reason that the more extreme your own training is, the more carbohydrate you should eat. A good illustration of this principle is to be found in the diet of the Greek ultrarunner Yiannis Kouros during a 5-day, 600-mile race, as mentioned in Chapter 5. To get through that event, Kouros had to eat and drink a tremendous number of calories—almost 12,000 per day—and nearly all of these calories—95.3 percent—came from carbohydrate. Kouros was wise to fuel his body in this seemingly unbalanced manner, as the body of a trained endurance athlete cannot store more than about 800 grams of carbohydrate yet burns carbs at a rate of nearly 1 gram per minute even during moderate-intensity exercise such as ultrarunning. Thus if Kouros had consumed "only" 60 percent of his 12,000 daily calories in the form of carbohydrate, his glycogen stores would have been depleted long before he reached the finish line (even despite the fact that the body can convert a certain amount of dietary fat into carbohydrate).

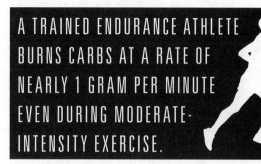

A TRAINED ENDURANCE ATHLETE BURNS CARBS AT A RATE OF NEARLY 1 GRAM PER MINUTE EVEN DURING MODERATE-INTENSITY EXERCISE.

Nobody runs 120 miles a day routinely, of course, and therefore nobody needs to maintain a diet that's 95 percent carbohydrate. But other real-world evidence suggests that endurance athletes who maintain high but sustainable training loads are able to thrive on a diet that is substantially more than 60 percent carbohydrate. Indeed, the diet of the world's best runners—the East Africans—is exceedingly high in carbohydrate. One analysis of the diet of seven elite male Kenyan runners (Onywera et al. 2004) found that they consumed extremely high amounts of carbohydrate—76.5 percent of calories—and very low amounts of fat (13.4 percent of calories) and protein (10.1 percent of calories). While we cannot rule out the possibility that these athletes would run better if their carbohydrate intake were lowered to 60 percent and their fat and protein intake increased, the fact that these runners were already world-class performers makes it far more likely that they were not held back in any way by their diet.

To summarize, we know that although classic studies on the effects of different chronic carbohydrate intake levels on endurance performance in single sessions after periods of heavy training do not match real-world circumstances, they do demonstrate that at very high training loads, carbohydrate intake limits performance. We also know that whereas low levels of carbohydrate intake hinder endurance performance during heavy training, very high levels of carbohydrate do not. The natural conclusion to draw from these facts is that endurance athletes should take pains to ensure that they are consuming enough carbohydrate to meet the demands imposed by their training load.

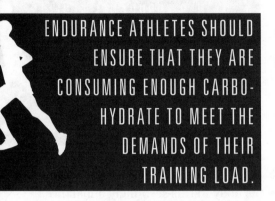

ENDURANCE ATHLETES SHOULD ENSURE THAT THEY ARE CONSUMING ENOUGH CARBOHYDRATE TO MEET THE DEMANDS OF THEIR TRAINING LOAD.

Based on my review of the scientific literature, I suggest that you aim for a daily carbohydrate intake target that is based on your training workload as indicated by Table 8.1.

TABLE 8.1 RECOMMENDED DAILY CARBOHYDRATE INTAKE FOR ATHLETES

Weekly Training Hours	Carbohydrate Intake (g/kg of body weight)
≤4	5–6
5–6	6–7
7–10	7–8
11–14	8–9
15–19	9–10
20–24	10–11
≥25	11–12

Note: 1 kilogram is equal to 2.2 pounds.

One obvious implication of these recommendations is that not only should some endurance athletes eat more carbohydrate than others, but any single endurance athlete's carbohydrate intake should vary as his or her training workload changes. If your training load increases, your carbohydrate intake should rise, and if your training load drops, your carbohydrate intake should also come down. The proportions of carbohydrates, fats, and proteins that nonathletes eat are as irrelevant to your body-weight management as an endurance athlete as they are to nonathletes' efforts to lose weight and prevent weight gain. All that matters in this regard is the total number of calories consumed daily.

In Chapter 6, I explained that your total caloric intake should vary seasonally with your training. Your carbohydrate intake will naturally fluctuate appropriately as your total caloric intake increases or decreases. Periodically tracking your calories in and calories out and adjusting your calories in, as necessary, will suffice to ensure that you don't gain excess fat. It is not necessary to count carbohydrate grams and reduce your carbohydrate intake specifically to prevent fat gain if you find that it is above the minimum recommended level for your current training load. It is a good idea to count carbohydrate grams occasionally, however, to ensure that you are always getting enough to maximize your training performance. After all, simply maximizing your training performance will make you leaner.

On the practical level of food selection, what does it take to meet your daily carbohydrate requirements? If your training load is moderate, it requires only that you include a few high-quality high-carbohydrate foods in your daily nutrition regimen. If your training load is high, it may require such foods in every meal and snack throughout the day. Table 8.2 presents a selection of high-quality high-carbohydrate foods that you can rely on to meet your needs and the amount of carbs in each. Generally, the richest sources of carbohydrate are grains, dairy foods, legumes, and certain fruits (especially fruit juices).

TABLE 8.2 HIGH-QUALITY, HIGH-CARBOHYDRATE FOODS

Food	Carbohydrate Content (g)
Bagel, whole wheat	57
Banana	25
Bread, whole wheat (2 slices)	36
Breakfast cereal, whole grain (1 cup)	45
Brown rice (1 cup)	45
Lentils, cooked (1 cup)	40
Oatmeal, old-fashioned (1 cup)	25
Orange juice (1 cup)	25
Potato, baked	50
Spaghetti, whole wheat (1 cup)	40
Tomato sauce (½ cup)	22
Yogurt, low-fat with fruit (1 cup)	50

As we discussed, it is possible for an endurance athlete to consume too much carbohydrate. Some athletes simply overeat, creating an excessive daily caloric intake. Other athletes maintain the right caloric intake, but too many of those calories are carbohydrates, creating a deficit of fat and/or protein calories.

FAT: DON'T WORRY ABOUT IT

The conventional recommended fat intake level for endurance athletes is 20 percent of total calories. But research suggests that this standard should be viewed as closer to a minimum than an optimum.

The typical endurance athlete gets 30 to 35 percent of her daily calories from fat—substantially more than the minimum. Indeed, even most elite American endurance athletes maintain relatively high-fat diets. The fact that our most gifted runners, cyclists, rowers, and others are routinely able to win national championships on a high-fat diet is the best possible proof that a high-fat diet is not inimical to endurance performance.

Some believe that endurance athletes should actually go out of their way to maintain a high-fat diet. After all, fat is the muscles' primary fuel for low- to moderate-intensity exercise. Carbohydrate, which is the muscles' primary fuel for moderately high- to high-intensity exercise, is stored only in small amounts in the body. Consequently, carbohydrate fuel depletion is a major cause of fatigue during prolonged exercise at higher intensities, such as triathlons. Fat fuel supplies, by contrast, are virtually unlimited in the body. Thus, by increasing their reliance on fat fuel and decreasing their reliance on carbohydrate fuel during race-intensity exercise, athletes could theoretically delay fatigue and perform better (and by performing better, get leaner). Can you achieve this effect by maintaining a high-fat diet? If so, is there a downside?

Several years ago, researchers from the University of Buffalo published a study on the performance effects of various levels of fat consumption in men and women (Horvath et al. 2000). Endurance and VO_2max tests (the criterion measure of aerobic power in athletes) were completed at the end of four-week periods in which runners consumed diets of 16 percent, 31 percent, and 44 percent fat. Athletes on the 31 percent fat diet saw more favorable results on the endurance test. Their time to exhaustion was 14 percent longer than the times for athletes on the low-fat diet. However, there was no change in VO_2max.

These results would seem to suggest that increasing fat intake increases endurance, perhaps by boosting fat burning during exercise. One major limitation of this study, however, was that the order of the diets was not random; therefore we cannot rule out the possibility that the runners performed better in the second endurance test simply because they were more familiar with it, or in better shape, not because

> THE TYPICAL ENDURANCE ATHLETE GETS 30 TO 35 PERCENT OF HER DAILY CALORIES FROM FAT.

of their diet. In addition, there was no difference in the rate of fat burning in the second endurance test versus the first. If higher fat intake was the cause of superior endurance, we would expect increased fat burning during exercise to be the mechanism.

Other studies have found that increased fat intake does result in greater fat oxidation during exercise. Researchers from New Zealand compared the effects of a 14-day high-carbohydrate diet, a 14-day high-fat diet, and an 11.5-day high-fat diet followed by a 2.5-day carbo-loading diet on fat oxidation and performance in a 15-minute cycling test and a 100-km cycling test (Rowlands and Hopkins 2002). Performance in the 15-minute test was slightly better after the high-carb diet, but not to a statistically significant degree, while performance in the 100-km test was slightly better, but again not to a statistically significant degree, following the high-fat diet. Fat oxidation was significantly greater during the 100-km test following the high-fat diet.

Like this study, other studies have also suggested that, while increased fat intake may increase endurance, it may also reduce performance in shorter, higher intensity races. This was shown in a study from the University of Connecticut (Fleming et al. 2003). Twenty volunteers were divided into two groups and placed on either an endurance training program and a high-fat diet (61 percent fat) or an endurance training program and a moderate-fat diet (25 percent fat) for 6 weeks. They performed a VO_2max test and a 45-minute time trial before and after the study period. Members of the high-fat diet group exhibited a marked increase in fat burning during the 45-minute time trial, but their work output dropped by 18 percent relative to the moderate-fat group.

In a recent review of the existing literature on this topic, researchers from Kansas State University concluded, "We and others have observed that although fat oxidation may be increased [with a high-fat diet], the ability to maintain high-intensity exercise (above the lactate threshold) seems to be compromised or at least indifferent when compared with consumption of more carbohydrate" (Erlenbusch et al. 2005). Perhaps, however, athletes could have it both ways by eating a high-fat base diet followed by short carbohydrate-loading periods before competition, as the New Zealand researchers had subjects do in their study. The rationale for this approach is that an extended period of time (2 weeks or more) on a high-fat diet will stimulate increases in fat oxidation capacity during exercise, and that following this adaptation period with a couple of days of carbo-loading immediately preceding a race or other maximal endurance effort will maximize muscle-glycogen stores. The athlete could have the best of both worlds.

A recent study from University of Cape Town, South Africa (Lambert et al. 2001), suggests that this strategy just might work. Researchers examined the effects of a high-fat diet versus a habitual diet prior to carbohydrate loading on fuel metabolism and cycling time-trial performance. Five trained cyclists participated in two 14-day randomized crossover trials during which they consumed either a 65 percent fat diet or their habitual 30 percent fat diet for 10 days, before switching to a 70 percent carbohydrate diet for 3 days.

All subjects then performed a cycling test consisting of 2.5 hours at 70 percent of peak oxygen uptake followed immediately by a 20-km time trial. The high-fat, carbohydrate-loading diet resulted in increased total fat oxidation and reduced total carbohydrate oxidation during exercise. Most noteworthy, the high-fat, carbohydrate-loading treatment was also associated with improved time trial performance. On average, the cyclists completed the 20-kilometer time trial 4.5 percent faster after the high-fat, carbohydrate-loading diet.

The problem with this study is that the design of the exercise test was biased to take advantage of improved fat burning. The initial 2.5-hour ride at a moderately high intensity ensured that the cyclists' muscles were significantly glycogen depleted before they even started the time trial, forcing a greater reliance on fat, of which the cyclists were more capable after the high-fat diet. But if this study had instead involved a time trial after a standard warm-up, it is unlikely that the high-fat diet would have been seen to result in better performance. Indeed, other studies, including the University of Connecticut study cited above (Fleming et al. 2003), have found that a high-fat diet followed by a carbohydrate-loading phase impairs performance in high-intensity time trials that are not immediately preceded by long endurance efforts.

On the whole, research tells us that most endurance athletes can function equally well on a diet that is anywhere from 20 to 40 percent fat, provided you're also getting enough carbohydrate to support your training load and neither too few nor too many total calories. It is not necessary to keep your fat intake close to the minimum level of 20 percent to get leaner or stay lean. Fat does not make us fat.

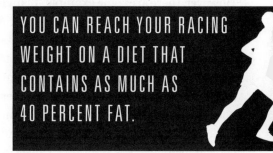

YOU CAN REACH YOUR RACING WEIGHT ON A DIET THAT CONTAINS AS MUCH AS 40 PERCENT FAT.

Again, as long as you are getting the right amount of carbohydrate and the right number of total calories, you can reach your racing weight on a diet that contains as much as 40 percent fat.

I am happy to report that I am not alone in advocating such flexibility in fat intake. In 2009, the American Dietetic Association and the American College of Sports Medicine changed their dietary fat intake recommendation for athletes to a broad range of 20 to 35 percent of total calories. Gone is the notion, codified in their past guidelines, that the minimal adequate level of fat intake is also the optimal or even the maximum acceptable level of fat intake. It is now recognized that many athletes can perform equally well at a range of fat intake levels and that some individual athletes may need to experiment before they find their personal "sweet spot" within that range.

PROTEIN: A LITTLE GOES A LONG WAY

The recommended protein intake level for endurance athletes has been set conventionally at 20 percent of total calories. But this number is arbitrary, having been arrived at indirectly after subtracting the high, 60 percent recommended carbohydrate intake and the low, 20 percent recommended fat intake from 100 percent. As mentioned above, the world's best runners, the East Africans, get only approximately

10 percent of their calories from protein, and it clearly does them no harm. The average American endurance athlete gets roughly 18 percent of his or her calories from protein, and there is no evidence that this amount is either too little or too much. But what about even higher levels of protein intake?

Few endurance athletes consciously maintain a high-protein diet. However, there are some examples of high-performing endurance athletes who eat a relatively high-protein diet. Among them is Dean Karnazes, winner of the 2004 Badwater Ultramarathon, who claims to follow a classic Zone Diet comprising roughly 40 percent carbohydrate, 30 percent fat, and 30 percent protein. Six-time Hawaii Ironman winner Mark Allen followed the same diet in the latter part of his career. There is some question about whether the intent of these athletes matches reality. It is difficult to maintain such a diet with anything resembling normal meal choices, which gives doubters cause for speculation that runners and other athletes on Zone-type diets eat less protein and more carbohydrate than they think they do.

Very little research exists on the effects of high-protein intake on endurance performance. In one short-term study (Macdermid and Stannard 2006), New Zealand researchers found that cycling time-trial performance was significantly impaired after 7 days on a high-protein diet. The high-protein diet in this study was 30 percent of calories, which is three times the minimum daily requirement of 10 percent. Again, the average American gets 18 percent of his calories from protein. In other words, the average American, including the average American runner, is already on a high-protein diet.

While increasing protein intake to 30 percent of calories might have a negative effect on endurance performance, it's also possible that increasing protein intake from the minimum recommended level of 10 percent of calories to the 18 percent level of the typical American might enhance performance in some athletes. A 2006 study from the University of Connecticut (Gaine et al. 2007) suggests that this could be the case. Researchers placed trained runners on each of three diets in random order: a low-protein diet providing 0.8 grams of protein per kilogram of body weight; a moderate-protein diet (1.2 g/kg); and a high-protein diet (1.8 g/kg). Only runners on the low-protein diet exhibited a negative nitrogen balance, meaning they were excreting more nitrogen in urine than they were taking in through dietary protein (carbs and fats do not contain nitrogen), which indicates that muscle mass is being lost. On the basis of this observation, the study's authors concluded that runners need to consume at least 1.2 grams of protein per kilogram of bodyweight daily, which is more than the recommended amount (the low-protein diet aligns with recommendations for the general public) but still less than the average person consumes. However, this was only a short-term study. It's possible that over the long term, the body is able to adapt to a low-protein diet in such a way as to preserve muscle mass. Also, this study did not look at performance, and performance clearly takes precedence for athletes. If the runners in this study were still able to run well on a low-protein diet despite having a (short-term) negative nitrogen balance, then they would have had no cause to be concerned about the negative nitrogen balance. There is simply no scientific evidence that the habitual diets of endurance athletes, including vegetarians, sabotages their performance through inadequate protein provision.

The balance of scientific and real-world evidence suggests that, in general, endurance athletes should not go out of their way to eat a lot of protein. You're almost certainly eating enough for optimal performance already, so increasing your protein intake will either have no effect on your performance or will decrease it. An exception to this guideline should be permitted to athletes who have substantial excess fat stores and who are not currently engaged in a high level of training (such that their

ENDURANCE ATHLETES SHOULD NOT GO OUT OF THEIR WAY TO EAT A LOT OF PROTEIN.

carbohydrate needs are moderate). These athletes may choose to get as much as 30 percent of their daily calories from protein, as protein is highly satiating and studies show that individuals on such high-protein diets voluntarily eat less and lose excess body fat.

RECOMMENDED MACRONUTRIENT INTAKE RANGES

The scientific and real-world data presented thus far demonstrate that any notion of a magical macronutrient ratio for endurance athletes should be jettisoned and replaced with broad recommended macronutrient intake ranges. Most endurance athletes will find that they can perform well and maintain their racing weight on a diet that falls

FIGURE 8.1 OPTIMAL MACRONUTRIENT RANGES

anywhere within the broad ranges shown in Figure 8.1, provided that the overall quality of the calorie sources is high and the diet provides enough carbohydrate to meet the energy need imposed by their training load.

The average American's diet is 48 percent carbohydrate, 34 percent fat, and 18 percent protein. Since each of these percentages falls within the range that appears to be neither too little nor too much for optimal endurance performance, it is unlikely that you will benefit from systematically manipulating your macronutrient breakdown—for example, increasing your carbohydrate intake and reducing your fat intake—unless your carbohydrate intake level is too low for your training load.

FINDING YOUR MACRONUTRIENT BREAKDOWN

Suppose you eat an average of 350 grams of carbohydrate, 85 grams of fat, and 60 grams of protein daily. The table below shows that you are therefore consuming 1,400 carbohydrate calories, 765 fat calories, and 240 protein calories daily, and a total of 2,405 calories. By individually dividing the number of carbohydrate, fat, and protein calories in your daily diet by the total calories, you discover that your diet is 58 percent carbohydrate, 32 percent fat, and 10 percent protein.

All of these percentages fall within the recommended ranges. Your protein intake is at the very bottom of the recommended range, so you might want to consider bumping it up slightly. Whether you need to make any other changes to your energy balance depends on whether your carbohydrate intake is appropriate for your weight and training load and whether your total caloric intake is in balance with your total daily calories out. Let's suppose that your calories in and calories out are in balance and that you weigh 125 pounds, or 56.8 kilograms. By dividing your average daily grams of carbohydrate intake (350) by your body weight in kilograms (56.8) you discover that you are consuming 6.16 grams of carbohydrate per kilogram of body weight per day. According to Table 8.1, this is adequate for a training load of 5 to 6 hours per week.

If your current training load is higher than 6 hours per week, you'll want to increase your carbohydrate intake slightly and reduce your fat intake by an equal number of

To ensure that your energy sources are properly balanced, perform a "dietary audit" to determine how much carbohydrate, fat, and protein you currently consume in your habitual diet. Record everything you eat for 3 days and use resources such as food labels and the nutrition tracker on racingweight.com to determine the average number of grams of carbohydrate, fat, and protein you consume per day. To find out whether your absolute level of carbohydrate intake is adequate, multiply the average number of carbohydrate grams you eat daily by your weight in kilograms (1 kilogram = 2.2 pounds) and look up the result on Table 8.1. If your current level of carbohydrate intake matches your training load, then leave it alone. If it is too low, then add more carbohydrate to your diet and continue to record and analyze your daily nutrition intake until you reach your target. If you are consuming more than the recommended amount of carbohydrate for your training load, reduce your carbohydrate intake only if you are also consuming more calories than you are burning daily (refer to the instructions for tracking calories in and calories out in Chapter 3) or if your fat or protein intake level is below the recommended minimum level.

calories. Since you're already in caloric balance, you won't want to increase your total caloric intake, and since your protein intake is already minimal, you won't want to maintain caloric balance by eating less protein. If your current training load is 6 hours per week or less, there's no need to shuffle your energy balance.

Macronutrient	Calories in 1 g	Daily Diet	Daily Calories	Breakdown
CARBOHYDRATE	4	350g	1,400	58
FAT	9	85g	765	32
PROTEIN	4	60g	240	10
Total Calories			2,405	

Step 1: Multiply your daily average for each macronutrient by the respective number of calories in 1 gram.

Step 2: In this example, the total calories add up to 2,405. Divide each macronutrient total by this number.

To determine the percentage of calories in your diet that comes from each macronutrient, multiply the average number of each macronutrient by the number of calories in one gram:

1 g carbohydrate = 4 calories

1 g fat = 9 calories

1 g protein = 4 calories

Then divide each product by the total number of calories you consume daily. See the sidebar "Finding Your Macronutrient Breakdown" for an illustration of this calculation.

It is impossible to definitively diagnose inadequate intake of a macronutrient through the signs and symptoms it may produce, because each of these signs and symptoms may have other causes. Nevertheless, they can provide helpful clues of a possible insufficiency that you can then confirm through a dietary audit and appropriate dietary modifications. Table 8.3 shows some of those clues.

TABLE 8.3 POSSIBLE WARNING SIGNS OF INADEQUATE MACRONUTRIENT INTAKE

Macronutrient	Warning Sign
Carbohydrate	Poor performance in workouts/competitions
	Slow recovery from workouts
	Slower-than-expected fitness gains
	Persistent fatigue
	Difficulty losing excess body fat
	Burnout/loss of motivation to train
	Frequent illness
Fat	Frequent injury
	Poor performance in workouts/competitions
	Slow recovery from workouts
	Persistent fatigue
Protein	Loss of muscle mass despite training
	Increasing body-fat percentage without weight gain
	Slow recovery from workouts
	Frequent injury
	Slow healing from injury
	Poor performance in workouts/competitions

You will notice that some of the warning signs, such as poor performance in workouts and competitions, can indicate that intake of any or all three of the macronutrients is lacking. Consider your current macronutrient breakdown and do some trial and error to find the changes that are needed for better performance. Be aware of stigmas that you might attach to carbohydrate, fat, or protein that could be preventing you from seeing the changes you need to make to your diet. When you begin to see your performance improve you will be glad you took the time to re-evaluate your diet.

NUTRIENT TIMING

T he effects of nutrients on the body are usually ascribed to properties intrinsic to specific nutrients. Protein builds muscle, sugar causes an energy rush followed by an energy crash, and so forth. But this view is overly simplistic. The effects of nutrients on the body are actually determined as much by the context in which they are consumed as by their intrinsic properties. For example, protein is much more likely to become incorporated into muscle tissue in one who regularly lifts weights as opposed to someone who is inactive. And in one who lifts weights regularly, protein is much more likely to be incorporated into muscle tissue when consumed immediately after a workout than at any other time. And in one who lifts weights regularly *and* has just completed a workout, protein is more likely to be incorporated into muscle tissue if it is consumed with carbohydrate than if it is consumed alone. (I'll explain why later in this chapter.)

As our example shows, there are three major contextual factors that influence the effects of specific nutrients on our bodies: the status of the body in which they are absorbed (weightlifter versus couch potato), the timing of their intake (after a workout versus at any other time), and other nutrients that are ingested with them (protein with carbohydrate versus protein alone). In this chapter we will focus on timing. The timing of nutrient intake is so important with respect to optimizing body weight and body composition that it represents the next step in realizing your racing weight. The first two steps, improving your diet quality and balancing your energy sources, are all about consuming the right nutrients to reach your racing weight. The third step is about taking in the right nutrients at the best possible times to get this desired result.

In simple terms, nutrient timing has a significant impact on *energy partitioning*. You may recall from the introduction that energy partitioning refers to the ultimate fate of the calories your body absorbs from food. There are a few primary destinations for food calories:

- Fat may be stored in *adipose tissue*, making you fatter.
- Protein, carbohydrate, and fat may be stored within *muscle cells* to power muscle work.
- Carbohydrate, fat, and, to a lesser extent, protein, may be used immediately to supply present energy needs.

Naturally, you become leaner by shifting the balance of energy partitioning away from fat storage and toward muscle storage and immediate use. If you time your nutrient intake well, you will store less fat in your fat cells, store more protein and carbohydrate in your muscle cells, and use more calories to supply immediate energy needs than you would if you ate precisely the same nutrients but timed their intake poorly.

Effective nutrient timing is a matter of pairing your intake of calories to your body's usage of calories throughout the day. Your body will tend to store body fat and lose muscle mass when you habitually eat more calories than your body needs to meet its energy demands for the next few hours and also—counterintuitively—when you take in *fewer* calories than you need to meet short-term energy requirements. On the one hand, when you take in too much, your body stores most of the excess as fat in adipose tissue. On the other hand, when you habitually consume too little at certain times of the day, your metabolism will slow, so that more of the calories you consume at other times are stored as body fat, and your body will break down muscle tissue to make up for the deficit of food energy. This negative effect of short-term food-energy deficits on body composition was shown in a study involving elite female gymnasts and distance runners, which found a strong inverse relationship between the number and size of energy deficits throughout the day (that is, periods when the body's calorie needs exceeded the calorie supply from foods) and body-fat percentage (Deutz et al. 2000). In other words, the athletes who did the best job of matching their calorie intake with their calorie needs throughout the day were leaner than those who tended to fall behind.

> ATHLETES WHO DID THE BEST JOB OF MATCHING CALORIE INTAKE WITH CALORIE NEEDS WERE LEANER THAN THOSE WHO TENDED TO FALL BEHIND.

Your body's energy requirements are not consistent throughout the day. They are much greater at some times than at others. To practice nutrient timing effectively, you must maintain an eating schedule that anticipates and responds to these fluctuations in energy needs. Here are five rules of nutrient timing that you can use to match your calorie intake with your body's calorie needs throughout the day.

EAT EARLY

Numerous studies have shown that regular breakfast eaters tend to be leaner than regular breakfast skippers, but the reasons may surprise you. You have probably heard and read a thousand times that you should eat a good breakfast because doing so will rev up your metabolism so that you burn more calories throughout the day. In fact, though, there is very little scientific evidence for such an effect. A 2008 review published in the *Journal of International Medical Research* (Giovannini et al. 2008) did not include increased metabolism on a list of three possible mechanisms by which eating breakfast may promote a healthy body weight. The researchers did, however, identify three mechanisms other than metabolic increase that may explain why starting the day with breakfast is a good idea.

Overall reduced appetite and reduced eating throughout the day (really just two facets of a single mechanism) are both outcomes of eating breakfast. Less overall appetite is experienced throughout the day when one eats early in the day compared to when one waits longer to eat one's first meal. Men and women who eat little or not at all in the morning wind up very hungry in the afternoon and evening, and as a result they overeat, more than making up for the "fasting" they did earlier in the day. A study from the University of Texas–El Paso (De Castro 2007) found that the fewer calories subjects ate early in the day, the more total calories they ate during the day as a whole.

Improved diet quality is another potential mechanism connecting breakfast with leaner body composition. Research has shown that regular breakfast eaters typically eat more high-quality foods and fewer low-quality foods than regular breakfast skippers. This is harder to explain. More than likely, regular breakfast eaters are more conscientious eaters generally, and both their breakfast eating habit and their selection of quality foods are manifestations of their conscientiousness. In my own experience I have found that eating breakfast promotes a higher-quality diet by giving me another opportunity to work toward eating my daily quota of high-quality foods (my typical breakfast is whole-grain cereal with fresh berries and low-fat milk, orange juice, and black unsweetened coffee) and by keeping my appetite under control throughout the morning so I am less likely to eat low-quality foods later, as the hungrier I am, the harder it is for me to resist the temptation of junk food.

Another benefit of eating early that is specific to endurance athletes who train in the morning is that it boosts performance and thereby enhances the training effects of the workout, including its overall fat-burning effect. When you wake up in the morning your liver is approximately 50 percent glycogen depleted due to having powered your nervous system as you slept. Endurance capacity is related to liver glycogen content, so your endurance capacity is reduced after the overnight fast. This is no big deal if you are doing a light workout; you won't be limited even if you eat or drink nothing before starting it. But if your morning workout

EATING FOR EARLY WORKOUTS

If you plan to work out more or less immediately after waking, as I routinely do, your pre-workout nutrition should consist of a small dose of easily absorbed carbs and little else. Eight ounces of sports drink, an energy gel, or a banana will do the trick. If you have an hour or so to get ready, something more substantial—but still high in carbs and low in protein and fat—will give you an even greater lift. Consider a 12- to 16-ounce fruit smoothie, 6 to 8 ounces of low-fat yogurt, or a small bowl of oatmeal.

will be taxing, you will perform at a higher level by consuming some calories before starting.

EAT OFTEN

Although dieters are often encouraged to eat small meals and snacks frequently, under the assumption that frequency promotes metabolic increase and therefore weight loss, research does not support such a mechanism. A 2008 study by Dutch researchers compared the outcomes of normal-weight women who spent 36 hours in a metabolic chamber under two different conditions. In one session they consumed two meals per 24-hour period and in the other they consumed three meals. Measurements taken in the two sessions revealed no differences in either resting metabolic rate or in the amount of energy subjects expended through voluntary activity.

This study was limited by its short duration and the small difference in the number of meals eaten. It does not rule out the possibility that the metabolic rate increases as a long-term adaptation to greater eating frequency or that those who habitually eat six times a day have a higher resting metabolic rate than those who eat just 2.7 times per day, as the average person does. But other studies have addressed the limitations of the Dutch study. For example, an interesting study by undergraduate researchers at the University of Wisconsin–La Crosse (Goodman-Larson et al. 2003) compared the resting metabolic rate and eating frequency of 22 women on their habitual diets. Statistical analysis revealed no correlation between the two variables.

While eating frequently appears not to increase metabolism, it does, however, reduce appetite. Indeed, in the same Dutch study that found no difference in metabolic rate or energy expenditure on three meals a day compared to two meals, subjects reported feeling less hungry throughout the day when they ate three meals (Smeets and Westerterp-Plantenga 2008). Total calories were fixed in this particular study, but other studies have shown that when individuals are allowed to eat as much as they want, they voluntarily eat fewer calories when they eat more meals.

The typical explanation for the effectiveness of frequent eating in suppressing the appetite has to do with blood glucose. The idea is that when meals are separated by long intervals, the blood glucose level declines, triggering intense hunger that in turn causes overeating. However, declining blood glucose levels are not really the primary cause of hunger. There is actually little evidence of a causal relationship between declining blood glucose levels and hunger. True, there is solid evidence of a *correlation* between declining blood glucose levels and hunger. That is, people do tend to become hungry at the same time their blood glucose level is decreasing. But they do not appear to become hungry *because* their blood glucose levels are declining. Rather, other factors that just happen to coincide with blood glucose decline (such as the simple emptying of the stomach) are in fact responsible for causing hunger.

It is important to bear in mind that the point of eating frequently is not simply to eat frequently but to avoid *overeating* at meals. Individuals who eat only two or three times during the day often eat huge numbers of calories in those two or three meals, and as I pointed out above, when we consume more calories in a sitting than we need to supply our short-term energy needs, most of the excess is stored as body fat. According to John Berardi, Ph.D., president of Precision Nutrition, a measurable amount of fat storage is observable in the average person when more than 750 calories are consumed in a meal. Large meals also shift the source of immediate energy supply away from fat and toward carbohydrate—just the opposite of what you want, especially as an athlete trying to get lean and maximize carbohydrate storage between workouts. Fortunately, at least, there is some evidence that endurance training blunts this effect of overeating. Athletes appear to store more carbohydrate and burn more fat after overeating than nonathletes.

There are also apparent genetic differences in the response to overeating. Research has shown that naturally lean people actually burn most of the excess calories consumed in large meals through spontaneous increases in nonexercise activity (fidgeting, restlessness), whereas those who gain weight easily experience much smaller increases in activity and instead store almost all of the excess calories as fat. So if you are among those who struggle to stay lean, it is especially important that you eat often enough that you can supply your body with all of the calories it needs without eating very large meals.

Eating frequently may be advantageous for athletes for a separate reason. There is some evidence that athletes are able to replenish muscle glycogen stores more fully between workouts when they consume carbohydrate frequently, and that muscle repair and growth are enhanced by more frequent protein intake. And athletes with especially heavy training loads often find that eating frequently enables them to meet their elevated caloric requirements without uncomfortably gorging themselves at meals.

EAT BEFORE EXERCISE

Eating before exercise is a nutrient timing method that will help you reach and maintain your racing weight in two ways. First, it will enhance your workout performance and thereby enhance the results you get from workouts, including that of fat burning. Second, eating before exercise will directly affect your body composition by increasing the number of food calories you burn and decreasing the number of calories you store.

It is not a good idea to eat a full meal immediately before working out, of course. The jostling that a full stomach undergoes during vigorous exercise may cause gastrointestinal distress. And even if it doesn't, your workout performance is likely to be compromised by the shunting of blood flow to the gut, and away from the extremities, which normally occurs after a meal. The ideal time for a pre-exercise meal to maximize workout performance is two to four hours out. Four hours allows enough time for a large meal to clear the stomach but not so much that liver glycogen and blood sugar levels begin to drop. Two hours allows enough time for a medium-size meal to clear the stomach.

Carbohydrate is the most important nutrient to consume in a pre-exercise meal. To maximize performance, aim to consume at least 100 grams of carbohydrate within the four hours preceding a hard workout. It does not matter whether these carbs come from high-glycemic (i.e., rapidly absorbed) food sources or low-glycemic (i.e., slowly absorbed) food sources. Studies indicate that there is no difference in their effects on subsequent exercise performance. That said, most or all of your carbs should come from high-quality foods for the simple reason that eating high-quality foods generally will help you get lean and stay lean.

Within these parameters, the precise timing and composition of the pre-exercise meal that works best is an individual matter. Most athletes naturally find a routine that suits them. To find the routine that works best for you, pay attention to how your gastrointestinal system feels and to your energy level and performance after meals of different sizes and compositions eaten at different times before exercise and heed your body's messages.

Research from the 1980s suggests that exercise burns more calories when performed after a meal than at other times. These findings are consistent with the nutrient timing principle that the body uses food calories more effectively when their intake is timed to coincide with periods of increased bodily energy needs. In this case, when you train shortly after fueling, you train harder and burn more fuel, leaving less leftover fuel to be added to your long-term energy stockpile (body fat). The studies I have referred to entailed exercise just 30 minutes after consumption of a 750-calorie meal, but there is other evidence (Davis et al. 1989) that the beneficial energy-partitioning effect of working out after eating extends to at least 1 hour and possibly even 2 hours.

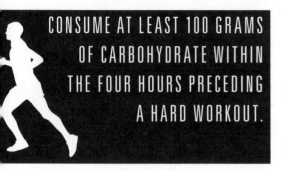

CONSUME AT LEAST 100 GRAMS OF CARBOHYDRATE WITHIN THE FOUR HOURS PRECEDING A HARD WORKOUT.

EAT DURING EXERCISE

It is seldom necessary or practical to eat solid food during exercise, but it is beneficial to drink and consume semisolids such as energy gels. Scores of studies have demonstrated that performance in harder workouts and races is enhanced by the consumption of water, carbohydrate, and, to a lesser extent, protein or amino acids. Consuming these nutrients regularly in your harder workouts will help you become leaner by enhancing the training effects that you derive from them, including that of fat burning.

Water consumed during endurance exercise prevents the blood volume from declining as quickly as it otherwise would as a consequence of sweating. It is the blood, of course, that transports oxygen to the working muscles. Thus as the blood volume declines, the heart has to work progressively harder to pump enough blood to the working muscles to keep up with their oxygen demands, until eventually performance declines, because your brain will only allow your heart to work so hard. Drinking sufficient quantities of water during exercise will significantly delay this point of performance decline. Carbohydrate consumed during exercise enables athletes to perform a fixed amount of work (e.g., cover a set distance) at a slightly faster rate or sustain a given intensity of exercise longer by providing an extra source of energy to the muscles. And when consumed in small quantities with carbohydrate, protein provides yet more energy and further delays fatigue by reducing exercise-induced muscle damage, which is an underappreciated cause of performance decline during prolonged exercise.

A study from the University of Chester, England (Marcora et al. 2008), provides solid proof that muscle damage causes fatigue independently of dehydration and muscle-glycogen depletion. Seven subjects completed an exercise bout consisting of moderate-intensity pedaling on a stationary bike followed by a 5-minute time trial, on two separate occasions. One session was performed in a normal, rested state and the other session was performed 48 hours after a drop-jump session designed to cause muscle damage in the legs without depleting muscle-glycogen stores. The subjects reported a significantly higher rating of perceived exertion during the exercise bout following the drop-jump test and also covered significantly less distance at a lower power output during the time-trial portion of that bout. This study establishes a clear link between exercise-induced muscle damage and reduced endurance performance and helps explain why other studies have shown that consuming carbohydrate and protein together during exercise increases endurance and reduces muscle damage compared to consuming carbohydrate alone.

What remains to be determined is the physiological link between the two effects. It has been proposed that the protein content of carbohydrate-protein sports drinks increases blood amino acid levels, and this increase acts as a signal to the brain to reduce the release of cortisol, a hormone that breaks down muscle proteins to make their constituent amino acids available as fuels.

There are other advantages to carbohydrate-protein sports drinks. Research has shown that consuming carbohydrate and protein together during exercise not only reduces muscle protein breakdown but even promotes muscle protein synthesis during the workout. Therefore it is possible that regular use of a carbohydrate-protein sports drink in training will preserve muscle mass more effectively than use of a conventional carbohydrate-only sports drink and thereby promote a slightly leaner body composition. For example, researchers from the University of Maastricht, the Netherlands, investigated the effects of carbohydrate and protein consumption during a combined strength and endurance workout on muscle protein synthesis during the workout and over a 9-hour period afterward (Beelen et al. 2008). Twenty men completed a 2-hour evening workout after having eaten normally during the day. They consumed either a carb-protein supplement or water during the workout and early recovery period. Muscle protein synthesis was found to increase by 48 percent during the workout in the subjects given the carb-protein supplement. During the nine-hour recovery period, muscle protein synthesis rates were the same in both groups. While this study compared a carb-protein supplement with water, there is no evidence nor any reason to believe that a conventional sports drink containing no protein would stimulate muscle protein synthesis during exercise.

REGULAR USE OF A SPORTS DRINK IN TRAINING MAY PRESERVE MUSCLE MASS AND PROMOTE A SLIGHTLY LEANER BODY COMPOSITION.

Most sports drinks do not contain protein, but the number of carbohydrate-protein sports drinks available on the market is steadily growing, and there are also sports drinks containing carbohydrate and amino acids, which may be equally effective. There are also nonliquid ergogenic aids, including energy gels, chews, and bars, that contain carbohydrate and protein. These products should perform similarly to carbohydrate-protein sports drinks when consumed with water. Because sports drinks provide both the fluid and nutrients you need during exercise in one source and are easily absorbed, I recommend that you use them in all workouts and races except in those very long workouts and races in which you may become hungry. In these circumstances, supplement your sports drink with semisolids and solids plus water.

Regardless of which ergogenic product you choose, I recommend that you use it during all of your "key workouts," or training sessions that are challenging enough to leave you more than moderately fatigued. Doing so will enhance your performance in these workouts and strengthen the benefits that you derive from them. During easier workouts you may drink water or nothing at all. Don't worry about drinking precisely calculated amounts on a rigid schedule to perfectly match your measured sweat rate. Research has shown that performance is optimized when athletes simply drink according to their thirst. Contrary to what is often taught, there is no advantage to be gained by drinking more than thirst dictates.

Many endurance athletes avoid using sports drinks in workouts (when they would, in fact, enhance performance), or water them down to a degree that reduces their performance benefit, because they fear that the calories they contain will sabotage their weight management efforts. This reasoning is understandable but lacks a factual foundation. The extra calories you burn by performing at a higher level, preserving muscle tissue, and so forth will more than outweigh the calories you consume in sports drinks.

A recent innovation in carbohydrate-protein sports drinks allows athletes who are concerned about the calories in sports drinks to have their cake and eat it too, so to speak. This innovation was inspired by a study performed by Michael Saunders at James Madison University, who found that a carbohydrate-protein sports drink increased cycling endurance more than a carbohydrate-only sports drink of equal calories (Saunders et al. 2004). Upon learning of this research finding, the scientists who formulated the original carbohydrate-protein sports drink reasoned that if a carbohydrate-protein sports drink providing a certain number of calories could increase endurance more than a carbohydrate-only sports drink of equal calories, then a reduced-calorie carbohydrate-protein sports drink might still increase endurance as much as a regular-strength carbohydrate sports drink of greater calories. The result would be a lighter sports drink that promoted leanness both by boosting performance and by providing fewer calories.

Testing proved this speculation to be correct. A regular-strength carbohydrate sports drink (Gatorade) was compared against three other options: a carbohydrate-protein sports drink containing 55 percent fewer calories (Accelerade Hydro), a regular-strength carbohydrate-protein sports drink containing 20 percent more calories than Gatorade (Accelerade), and water. Twelve trained cyclists completed an exercise test consisting of 2.5 hours of ergometer riding at 55 percent VO_2max followed immediately by a ride to exhaustion at 80 percent VO_2max on four separate occasions: once with water, once with Gatorade, once with Accelerade, and once with Accelerade Hydro. Average time to exhaustion at 80 percent VO_2max was 14.7 minutes with water, 26.9 minutes with Gatorade, 28.9 minutes with Accelerade Hydro, and 30.5 minutes with Accelerade (Martinez-Lagunas et al. 2009). The differences among the three sports drinks were not statistically significant. The study's authors concluded that the addition of protein to a low-carbohydrate sports drink had similar effects on performance as high-carbohydrate sports drinks despite containing far fewer total calories. This makes it a good choice for athletes who want to limit calorie consumption in ergogenic aids without sacrificing performance.

EAT AFTER EXERCISE

Eating soon after exercise is completed also promotes leanness both directly and indirectly. It promotes leanness directly by shifting energy partitioning toward muscle protein and glycogen synthesis and away from body-fat storage. It does so indirectly by accelerating muscle recovery so the athlete can perform at a higher level in the next work-out and derive a stronger training effect from it. How soon is soon? Research has identified a two-hour post-exercise nutritional recovery window. What this means is that recovery proceeds significantly faster if the right nutrients are consumed less than two hours after exercise than if precisely the same nutrients are consumed more than two hours after exercise. But it is generally agreed that even within this window, the sooner you eat or drink, the better.

The most important nutrients to consume after exercise are carbo-hydrate to replenish muscle and liver glycogen stores, protein for muscle repair and remodeling, and water for rehydration. For the best results, aim to consume at least 1.2 grams of carbohydrate per kilogram of body weight in the first several hours after exercise, along with roughly 1 gram of protein per 4 grams of carbohydrate and enough water (or other fluid) so that your urine is pale yellow or clear within a few hours after the workout is completed. Again, timing is important. In a study conducted by Berardi, cyclists were found to have synthesized 55 per-cent more muscle glycogen 6 hours post-exercise when they consumed a carbohydrate-protein supplement immediately, 1 hour, and 2 hours after exercise, and then ate a small meal 4 hours after exercise, than when they consumed the same total number and types of calories in a larger meal consumed 4 hours after exercise (Berardi et al. 2006).

In this particular study, the different nutritional protocols and their disparate effects on muscle glycogen replenishment had no effect on per-formance in a subsequent 1-hour time trial, but in other, similar studies, better post-exercise nutrient timing and muscle glycogen replenishment have boosted subsequent exercise performance (Williams et al. 2003). Habitually consuming carbs, protein, and fluid soon after completing workouts will generally lift your performance and accelerate your fitness gains, which, again, occur primarily through the recovery process.

Proper post-exercise nutrition also promotes fat burning. A meal eaten after exercise has a very different effect on the body than a meal eaten at any other time. No matter when you eat, your metabolism increases, because your body has to burn calories to digest and absorb food. But this "thermic effect of food" is greater when the food is consumed after exercise. More important, however, is the type of calories your body burns. When a meal is not preceded by exercise, it's carbohydrate burning that increases most. But when a meal does follow exercise, fat burning increases while carbohydrate is spared so that it can be delivered to the muscles to replenish depleted glycogen stores. Thus an athlete who routinely eats within an hour after working out will burn a little more fat and store a little more glycogen each day, and eventually wind up a little leaner, than an athlete who routinely waits 2 hours after working out to chow down.

Not only is more fat burned, but also more muscle is built or preserved when a meal is consumed soon after exercise, as long as that meal includes both carbohydrate and protein. Several studies have shown that individuals engaged in strength-training programs gain significantly more muscle when they consume carbohydrate and protein immediately after exercise instead of waiting to eat. While most endurance athletes have no interest in adding weight of any kind to their bodies, every endurance athlete benefits from maximizing his or her muscle-to-fat ratio at any given weight. Studies showing that endurance athletes build more new muscle proteins when they consume carbohydrate and protein immediately after exercise offer reason to believe that this nutrient timing practice helps endurance athletes maximize their muscle-to-fat ratio.

NUTRIENT TIMING TURNED UPSIDE DOWN

Finally, I want to mention a different approach to nutrient timing that is very nearly the opposite of the Racing Weight approach I've described in this chapter and has gained some converts among endurance athletes in recent years. I'm talking about *intermittent fasting*, or alternating periods of normal or condensed eating with periods of not eating. Intermittent fasting has existed in various forms forever, but it was popularized in its newest form as a body-weight and body-composition optimization tool for athletes and fitness enthusiasts in 2005 by Robb Wolf, a research biochemist and devotee of the CrossFit fitness movement. Since then it has spread into various other gym-based fitness subcultures and even into endurance sports to a limited extent. Indeed, I first learned about intermittent fasting from Ysbrand Visser, editor in chief of the Dutch *Runner's World*.

The rationale behind intermittent fasting is that the practice results in metabolic adaptations that reduce body-fat levels and improve cardiovascular and brain health.

ABUNDANT RESEARCH SHOWS ENDURANCE PERFORMANCE IS COMPROMISED IN THE FASTED STATE.

There is some solid scientific evidence that intermittent fasting does indeed have these effects in certain animals. A 2005 review by researchers from the National Institute on Aging (Mattson and Wan 2005) reported that intermittent fasting had been shown to reduce blood pressure, increase insulin sensitivity, and increase neural plasticity (growth of new brain cells) in rodents. However, most of the human studies on intermittent fasting have failed to duplicate these results. Nevertheless, there is plenty of anecdotal evidence from intermittent fasters who swear by it. Among them are even some hardcore weightlifters, who are just about the last folks you might imagine going for this sort of thing.

The two major intermittent fasting protocols are 24-on/24-off, where fasting and eating days are alternated, and the condensed window or modified Ramadan fast (Ramadan is a Muslim holy month during which its observers eat only after sundown), where one eats only in the evening each day. For the athlete who trains every day, both protocols require that workouts be performed regularly in a fasted state. There is abundant research showing that endurance performance is compromised in the fasted state (more than 12 hours after the last meal). Consequently, performance in these workouts is sure to suffer, causing the athlete to gain fitness more slowly.

TABLE 9.1 RACING WEIGHT SCHEDULES FOR NUTRIENT TIMING

Time	Nutrient Timing	Percent Daily Caloric Intake	What to Eat
Morning Exerciser			
6:00 A.M.	Pre-workout snack		Small amount of easily absorbed high-carb drink or food (e.g., banana, sports drink)
6:15 A.M.	Workout		Sports drink according to thirst
7:30 A.M.	**Breakfast**/post-workout recovery nutrition	20–25	High-carb, moderate-protein, low-fat
10:00 A.M.	Midmorning snack	10	Any high-quality foods
12:00 P.M.	**Lunch**	20–25	Balance of high-quality foods
3:00 P.M.	Midafternoon snack	10	Any high-quality foods
6:00 P.M.	**Dinner**	20–25	Balance of high-quality foods
8:30 P.M.	Evening snack (optional)	5	Any high-quality foods
Noon Exerciser			
7:30 A.M.	**Breakfast**	20–25	Balance of high-quality foods
10:00 A.M.	Midmorning/pre-workout snack	10	High-carb, moderate-protein, low-fat
12:00 P.M.	Workout		Sports drink according to thirst
1:30 P.M.	**Lunch**/post-workout nutrition	20–25	High-carb, moderate-protein, low-fat
6:00 P.M.	**Dinner**	20–25	Balance of high-quality foods
8:30 P.M.	Evening snack	5	Any high-quality foods
Late Afternoon Exerciser			
7:30 A.M.	**Breakfast**	20–25	Balance of high-quality foods
10:00 A.M.	Midmorning snack	10	Any high-quality foods
12:00 P.M.	Lunch	20–25	Balance of high-quality foods
3:00 P.M.	Midafternoon snack/ pre-workout	10	High-carb, moderate-protein, low-fat
5:15 P.M.	Workout		Sports drink according to thirst
7:00 P.M.	**Dinner**/post-workout nutrition	20–25	High-carb, moderate-protein, low-fat
Twice-a-Day Exerciser			
6:00 A.M.	Pre-workout snack		Small amount of easily absorbed high-carb drink or food (e.g., banana, sports drink)
6:15 A.M.	Workout		Sports drink according to thirst
7:30 A.M.	**Breakfast**/post-workout recovery nutrition	20–25	High-carb, moderate-protein, low-fat
10:00 A.M.	Midmorning snack	10	Any high-quality foods
12:00 P.M.	**Lunch**	20–25	Balance of high-quality foods
3:00 P.M.	Midafternoon snack/ pre-workout	10	High-carb, moderate-protein, low-fat
5:15 P.M.	Workout		Sports drink according to thirst
7:00 P.M.	**Dinner**/post-workout nutrition	20–25	High-carb, moderate-protein, low-fat

There is a need for more formal studies of the effects of intermittent fasting on competitive endurance athletes. For now we must rely on studies of the effects of actual Ramadan fasting on various types of athletes. The findings of these studies are not likely to make you seek conversion to intermittent fasting of any kind! Sure, athletes do lose weight and body fat during Ramadan. A 2008 study involving Tunisian rugby players found significant body-weight and body-fat reductions by the fourth week of Ramadan (Bouhlel et al. 2008). But this is not the kind of weight loss that will enhance sports performance. A 2005 study involving Senegalese 400-meter sprinters showed a significant performance decline in a set of 3×250 meters during Ramadan compared to before the holy month (Faye et al. 2005). The reason was clear. Blood tests showed that the athletes were suffering from severe hypoglycemia when they exercised more than 10 hours after their last meal.

In addition to impairing endurance performance by reducing muscle and liver glycogen and blood glucose levels, intermittent fasting is likely to sabotage performance further by interfering with recovery from training. It is clear from the scientific literature that fasting after exercise retards the various recovery processes, which are inseparable from the processes by which athletes gain fitness in response to training. For this reason, intermittent fasters who consume no food in the first few hours after workouts get less out of those workouts than those who eat within the "recovery window." In conclusion, intermittent fasting is as bad an idea for endurance athletes as you probably assumed it was!

The best way for you to practice nutrient timing depends partly on when you normally train. The four nutrition schedules in Table 9.1 are based on the guidelines discussed in this chapter. Determine which schedule best reflects when your workout fits into your day—in the morning, at noon, later in the afternoon, or twice each day.

TEN

MANAGING YOUR APPETITE

ppetite is important. It is your body's internal mechanism for food intake regulation. Its job is to drive you to eat enough to meet your body's energy and micronutrient needs, and no more. The appetite mechanism works very well under normal circumstances. Obviously, it would not have survived millions of years of evolutionary testing if it did not work to the benefit of our health. But our modern lifestyle does not constitute "normal circumstances" in relation to the environment in which most of our evolution took place. Consequently, our appetite cannot be entirely relied upon to ensure that we don't overeat and thus accumulate excess body fat.

At least two major problems with our environment seem to drive this present-day mismatch. First, many of the processed foods, such as cheeseburgers, that are staples of the modern diet are far more calorically dense than most natural foods, such as carrots. We can eat 500 or even 1,000 calories in just a few minutes when dining on cheeseburgers compared to scarcely 100 calories in the same amount of time when snacking on carrots. Because the appetite is not satisfied instantaneously when food is swallowed (there's a lag time of 10 to 20 minutes), it's possible to eat far more than enough calories needed to satisfy the appetite when consuming cheeseburgers and other such foods. In essence, the modern diet does an end run around our appetite control mechanism.

The second problem with our environment in relation to appetite is the sheer abundance of food, its cheapness, and the intensity of social influences promoting overeating. Most people find they become hungry when food is put in front of them, even if they were not hungry to begin with. And in our current environment, food sits in front of us practically everywhere. Consequently, our appetite is effectively much greater than it was even 40 years ago, when food was somewhat less abundant and more expensive, and when overeating was not as intensively promoted.

Exercise is a great way to counterbalance the manner in which our modern food environment sabotages our appetite control mechanism and makes us hungrier. Exercise increases demand for calories more than it increases appetite and thereby reduces caloric excess in your diet and body-fat storage. As an endurance athlete, therefore, you are in a better position to control your body weight. However, as we well know, even many endurance athletes struggle to reach or maintain a satisfactory body weight, and we struggle in part for the same reason others do: We love cheeseburgers, and there's a fast-food joint on every corner and a fast-food advertisement every eight minutes on television.

Fortunately, it is possible to use other means beyond exercise to overcome the environmental effects on appetite. Thus, the next logical step of the Racing Weight system is managing your appetite, and it involves five strategies. Before we discuss them, let us first consider the difference between managing your appetite and controlling your appetite, and why you cannot expect to get leaner by controlling it.

MANAGING VERSUS CONTROLLING YOUR APPETITE

There are many genes that play roles in governing appetite, and there are individual differences in the presence and activity of these genes. That's why some people have larger or more insistent appetites than others. Some of those who are naturally blessed with lighter or less insistent appetites wonder why other people can't seem to control theirs. They fault these people for a lack of willpower. And new research on the role of the brain in relation to body weight suggests that they may be right to do so, although wrong to assume that those people could do something about it if only they weren't so lazy. That's because the same research that has demonstrated that some people have more willpower than others in relationship to food is also complicating the notion of willpower itself. It is generally assumed that willpower is a quality that every person is equally capable of exercising, and thus those who do not exercise willpower choose not to. So when an overweight person's weight is blamed on lack of willpower, we say that person must be "choosing" to be fat.

But consider the results of a recent study by researchers at the Oregon Research Institute (Stice et al. 2008). An MRI machine was used to monitor activity in the so-called reward center of the brains of normal-weight and overweight individuals immediately before they drank a milkshake and while they drank it. These researchers found that, on average, overweight individuals exhibited greater activity in the brain's reward area *before* they tasted the treat and less activity *as* they tasted it. In other words, overweight persons seemed to anticipate the pleasure of drinking a milkshake more intensely than normal-weight persons, but got less pleasure from the actual drinking experience.

The authors of the study hypothesized that this difference in the functioning of the reward center of the brain, which is believed to be largely genetically determined, could partly explain why overweight persons eat more—in other words, why overweight persons are overweight. Simply put, some people are destined to be forever disappointed by the eating experience. The "high" associated with eating or drinking a treat never lives up to expectations, so they are less satisfied and more disposed to try, try again for that elusive high.

Women may be genetically predisposed to have less control over their appetite than men. The results of a recent brain imaging study by Brookhaven National Laboratory suggest that men are better able than women to control their urges to eat favorite foods (Wang et al. 2009). The study involved 13 female and 10 male subjects of normal weight. Their brains were scanned on three separate occasions. On one occasion the subjects viewed, smelled, touched, and tasted, but did not eat, their favorite foods. On another occasion the subjects were instructed to inhibit their desire for the same foods prior to being tempted with them. And on a third occasion their brains were imaged without food temptation. In both of the food temptation trials, there was a significant increase in both men and women in neural activity in areas of the brain associated with hunger and food cravings. However, in the trial in which subjects were asked to resist the desire to eat, the activity level in these regions was diminished in the brains of men whereas in women it was just as high as it was when they were not asked to inhibit their desire to eat. These results suggest that, in real-world circumstances, women might have a harder time controlling food urges than men do.

It appears, then, that some people really do have less willpower than others with respect to food. However, it is important to recognize that even those who are blessed with a stronger-than-average genetically determined capacity to say "no" to favorite foods are still essentially slaves to their appetite. After all, hunger is one of our most fundamental survival instincts. When we need food, the drive to eat seizes us with a power equal to the desperation of a drowning man's desperate struggle for air. Studies of starvation and semistarvation conditions have revealed that after a short time without food, or when made to sharply reduce food intake, all humans become irritable, unhappy, and obsessed with thoughts of food. They cannot be satisfied until they are able to fill their bellies again. For this reason, controlling appetite, in the sense of con- sistently eating less than our appetite demands, is not a reliable means to lose excess body fat. Instead we must *manage* our appetite, or the amount of eating that our appetite demands. In other words, instead of trying to resist our appetite, we must shrink it, or satisfy it with fewer calories.

How does one manage one's appetite? The Racing Weight method of appetite management comprises the following five strategies:

1. Practice nutrient timing.
2. Eat mindfully.
3. Eat high-satiety foods.
4. Eat low-density foods.
5. Eat less.

That last item—"Eat less"—probably seems more like a means of controlling appetite rather than of managing it. In fact, while eating less *is* usually a means of controlling appetite, even though it is gener- ally ineffective, in some circumstances it can be a means of managing appetite, as you will see in the last section of this chapter.

PRACTICE NUTRIENT TIMING

In the preceding chapter we looked at how nutrient timing can help you reach and maintain your racing weight, primarily by manipulating energy partitioning to your advantage—that is, by steering more calories to your muscles and fewer to your fat cells. But we saw that a couple of specific nutrient timing practices also work by reducing appetite. *Eating a substantial breakfast* reduces appetite for many hours afterward, such that people tend to eat fewer total calories over the course of a day when they eat a good-size breakfast than they do when they eat a small breakfast or none at all.

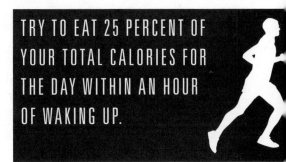

TRY TO EAT 25 PERCENT OF YOUR TOTAL CALORIES FOR THE DAY WITHIN AN HOUR OF WAKING UP.

If you refer back to the schedules in Table 9.1, you can see that all of them recommend that you try to eat at least 25 percent of your total calories for the day within an hour of waking up.

Eating frequently works in a similar way, as we discussed in Chapter 9. When people eat just two or three times per day they become very hungry between meals and therefore overeat when they do eat. But when they eat four or more times, their hunger level never becomes more than moderate, and consequently they are satisfied by modest-size meals that add up to fewer total calories over 24 hours.

Another nutrient timing practice that you can use to manage your appetite is that of *eating slowly*. Eating slowly takes advantage of the time lag between the entry of food into the stomach and the emergence of satiety in response to it. The notion that eating slowly manages appetite has been around for a long time, but only recently has it been experimentally validated. For example, in a University of Rhode Island study (Andrade et al. 2008), volunteers were encouraged to eat as much pasta as they wanted on two occasions. Once they were told to eat quickly and the other time they were told to eat slowly. When they ate quickly they consumed 646 calories in 9 minutes. When they ate slowly they consumed 579 calories in 29 minutes. This difference is not huge, and you might not want to stretch all of your meals over half an hour, but in the weight management game it's wise to do every little thing that makes even a small difference. Consistently taking perhaps 50 percent longer to finish your meals than you normally would is likely to trim a few calories here and there from your meals and, when combined with other calorie-trimming measures such as eating high-satiety foods, will eventually result in a measurable reduction of your body-fat level. And you just might enjoy your food more!

EAT MINDFULLY

Over the past 30 years, the number of calories in the average person's diet has increased significantly. This increase is widely believed to have been driven by increases in portion sizes in restaurant menu items and packaged foods that resulted from substantial decreases in the cost of producing food and competition among food businesses. The combination of this influence and that of the constant deluge of commercial advertising for food has essentially created a breach between our physical and social appetites for food.

Researchers such as consumer psychologist Brian Wansink of Cornell University, author of *Mindless Eating*, have shown that the amount of food we consume is strongly influenced by the accessibility of food, how much food is put in front of us, and social pressure to eat more, including the pressure of commercial advertising. A perfect example of the latter influence is Taco Bell's invention of a "fourth meal," a late-night meal of fast food that the television viewer is encouraged to add to his or her daily eating routine.

To reduce the effects of food overabundance on your eating, train yourself to stop eating mindlessly and instead eat "mindfully," or pay better attention to the physical signs of appetite, hunger, and fullness. The goal is to eat only when physically hungry and, when eating, to eat only until comfortably satisfied, never stuffed. As you get a better sense of how much food you really need to satisfy your physical appetite, you can also train yourself to purchase, prepare, serve, and order smaller portions that meet this standard without exceeding it.

Watch out for the different types of "hungerless eating" that might obscure your perception of your real appetite, as described in the following sections.

Emotional Eating

Often the factor that drives our eating is not physical hunger but emotions such as happiness, sadness, or even boredom. Learn to tell the difference between real, physical hunger and emotional food cravings. Physical hunger tends to come on gradually, does not involve cravings for specific foods, and goes away when you're full. Emotional eating urges come on suddenly, involve cravings for specific foods, and often don't go away even when you've eaten. And if you feel guilty after eating, chances are it was emotional eating.

Using a hunger rating scale (Figure 10.1) may help you avoid emotional eating. Rate your hunger each time you eat as a way to get in touch with your body and learn the difference between real hunger and emotional eating urges. On a 1 to 10 scale, eat only when your hunger level is 7 or above.

Another way to break away from emotional eating is to find substitutes for food that can provide the feeling of comfort you're looking for. Good substitutes might be taking a walk, calling a friend, reading a book, and doing housework.

Spontaneous Eating

Food is almost everywhere in our society, and often we eat it just because it's there, even when we're already full. This adds a lot of useless calories to one's diet. The best way to avoid spontaneous eating is to eat on a regular schedule, such as those presented in Table 9.1. In general, you should wake up each morning knowing exactly what you will eat and when and where you will eat it. When an unexpected eating opportunity arises, ask yourself, "Does this fit within my eating plan for today?" If not, take a pass.

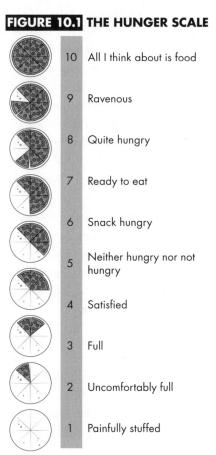

FIGURE 10.1 THE HUNGER SCALE

10	All I think about is food
9	Ravenous
8	Quite hungry
7	Ready to eat
6	Snack hungry
5	Neither hungry nor not hungry
4	Satisfied
3	Full
2	Uncomfortably full
1	Painfully stuffed

It's not necessary to take all of the spontaneity out of eating, of course. If a neighbor shows up at your front door with fresh strawberries from her garden, you would be a fool not to sample them and tell her how delicious they are before she leaves. If you have a coworker who happens to be a gourmet chef and brings leftover homemade paella to share with his officemates one Monday, you might as well eat it instead of the peanut butter and jelly sandwich you packed. But it's always best to avoid eating spontaneously when you are not really hungry. Use the hunger scale (see Figure 10.1) to decide whether to accept or decline each spontaneous eating opportunity.

Unconscious Eating

Sometimes we eat without even being fully conscious that we are doing so. For example, while watching television you might eat half a box of cookies even though you're not hungry. When you go to eat a cookie the next day, you wonder where half of them went. In Chapter 3 you were given tips on how to construct a personal food journal to keep track of calories in and calories out on a daily basis (the training and nutrition log powered by TrainingPeaks.com is one good tool). As mentioned there, it's not necessary to monitor your calorie consumption every single day once you've established a fairly regular nutritional routine. Checking in with it once in a while, though—an exercise I describe in Chapter 8 that I call "diet auditing"—is useful for keeping you on target and can help you steer clear of unconscious eating. When you perform one of these occasional "diet audits" for the purpose of matching up your calories in and calories out and balancing your energy sources, take the opportunity to spot unconscious eating occasions as well. Most people who go through this process find that they eat more than they think they do, in part because of unconscious eating. This exercise increases people's "eating awareness," making them less susceptible to eating unconsciously in the future.

Habitual Eating

Eating on a regular schedule is a good thing for two reasons. First, research has shown the body has a kind of hunger clock that operates through the release of the hunger hormone ghrelin on a circadian schedule. This schedule is adaptable, so if you consistently eat at the same times each day, your hunger clock will adjust so that you only become hungry when you're supposed to be hungry (LeSauter et al. 2009). The body's metabolism also adapts to one's eating schedule. Researchers at the University of Nottingham (Farshchi et al. 2005) showed that the resting metabolic rate was higher in volunteers when they were fed on a regular schedule than when they were fed the same amount of food on a schedule that changed from day to day. It's possible that the body slows its metabolism to conserve energy when it does not know when its next meal is coming.

Habitual eating is not always a good thing, however. The risk of becoming a slave to one's eating schedule is that it can allow you to tune out your body's signals of hunger and satiety and therefore sometimes eat when you are not really hungry and do not need calories. Just because you normally eat a snack at midafternoon does not mean you will always be hungry and in need of calories at 3:00 p.m. By all means, develop a regular eating schedule that generally provides the calories you need when you need them, but always listen to your body and be prepared to stray from your schedule when appropriate.

Clearing Your Plate

The four types of "hungerless" eating described above involve starting to eat when you're not hungry. But sometimes we start to eat when we are hungry and don't stop when we're full. Instead we keep eating until we finish the food that's in front of us or until we are uncomfortably stuffed. This type of hungerless eating is just as detrimental as the others. In fact, some nutrition experts believe that plate clearing is the single greatest contributor to the epidemic of excess weight and obesity in our society. As humans, we are inclined to eat everything that is put in front of us. Because the amount of food put in front of us has increased significantly in the past 30 years, this means we eat a lot more and gain weight.

The dangers of the plate-clearing instinct have been demonstrated in scientific research. Among the most famous studies in this area is the "self-refilling soup bowls" study designed by Brian Wansink (Wansink et al. 2005). Fifty-four subjects were invited to enjoy a bowl of soup, eating as much or as little as they liked. Half of the bowls were outfitted with a device that slowly and imperceptibly refilled them with soup as the subjects ate. On average, the subjects eating from the self-refilling bowls ate 73 percent more soup than the others, without realizing it and without feeling any fuller afterward. Less gimmicky and more real-world studies than this one (for example, studies involving bowls of different sizes) have yielded similar results.

The lesson of these studies is that you are likely to eat more food than you need if more food than you need is put in front of you. This is true even when *you* are the person putting the food in front of you. Studies have also shown that even when people are in control of the portions served, the plate is more crowded today than it was a quarter-century ago. It is not unlikely that you have been unconsciously trained to pour larger bowls of cereal than you really need to satisfy your appetite, and to pack larger lunches, and so forth. Unless you are certain that you are an exception to the norm in this regard, you may want to experiment with serving and preparing smaller portions and finding out whether they satisfy your appetite. If they do, continue to eat these smaller portions.

When you eat out and do not have control over your portion sizes, be mindful of the plate-clearing instinct and use the hunger scale to ensure that you don't fall victim to the temptation. Stop eating when you are comfortably satisfied and take the leftovers home.

EAT HIGH-SATIETY FOODS

Imagine the following two scenarios:

SCENARIO 1: You eat a large plate of pasta for lunch, only to find yourself feeling hungry again by midafternoon.

SCENARIO 2: You are overtaken by hunger during a long flight without meal service. To tide yourself over, you eat the only thing you have—a handful of almonds. When the plane lands, you realize with some surprise that you're still full.

As these two realistic (and possibly familiar) scenarios demonstrate, some foods are more filling than others. That's because some of the nutrients in foods are more filling than others. Carbohydrates such as those in pasta are not very filling. Long-chain fatty acids such as those in almonds are much more filling.

Most foods that are more filling have more calories. But not all. Some foods provide more satiety *per calorie* than others. The foods that provide the most satiety per calorie are those that contain large amounts of specific nutrients that are known to activate the body's hunger control signals more effectively than most other nutrients. These "high-satiety" nutrients include fiber, certain proteins, the aforementioned long-chain fatty acids, and possibly calcium.

By including plenty of foods that contain these nutrients in your diet, you will be able to keep your appetite satisfied throughout the day with fewer total calories. Good sources of fiber include fruits, vegetables, legumes, and whole grains. Among the most satisfying proteins are dairy proteins. Dairy products are also great sources of calcium. Among the richest sources of long-chain fatty acids are macadamia nuts, almonds, peanuts, olive oil, flaxseed oil, and other cold-pressed oils.

Natural Foods for Managing Appetite

The best way to include high-satiety foods in your diet for appetite management is in the form of small (150 or fewer calories) pre-meal appetizers consumed 10 minutes before lunch or supper. I've included ten of my favorite appetizers here. Whether you might be tempted to snack on low-quality foods while you prepare your meal, or simply eat an excessive meal once you finally sit down, you'll find these appetizers a good fix because they are packed with high-satiety ingredients. Research has shown that such appetizers reduce eating in the subsequent meal by as much as 20 percent. Each of these appetizers contains two or more foods with high-satiety nutrients proven to fill you up fast before a main meal.

Formulated Foods for Managing Appetite

In addition to natural foods, there are specially formulated weight-management products that contain high-satiety nutrients and little else. While I recommend that you generally prioritize natural foods over formulated foods in your diet, some of these formulated foods for appetite control are made from natural ingredients, and they have the advantage of providing more satiety per calorie than whole foods. These products are based on research dating back to the 1960s. At that time, scientists at Cornell and Columbia Universities discovered a hormone produced by the gut called cholecystokinin (CCK), which is released in response to eating and slows the movement of food through the stomach and sends a signal to the brain, triggering a feeling of fullness and loss of the desire to eat. Early studies on CCK showed that when it was injected into human subjects, they ate less. Subsequently, scientists discovered that certain nutrients (such as glycomacropeptide, a component of whey protein) are

NATURAL FOODS APPETIZERS

Spinach and Avocado Salad

1 cup raw spinach with ¼ cup diced tomatoes, ¼ cup diced avocado, and 1 Tbsp. olive oil–based dressing

142 calories, 15 g fat (2 g saturated fat), 5 g fiber, 2.4 g protein

---

Garden Salad

1 cup greens with tomatoes, avocado, and 1 Tbsp. olive oil-based dressing

150 calories, 10 g fat (1.5 g saturated fat), 5 g fiber, 2 g protein

---

Crackers and Cheese

4 whole wheat crackers with 1 oz. low-fat cheddar cheese

109 calories, 3 g fat (1 g saturated fat), 1 g fiber, 1 g protein

---

Lentil Soup

Example: Amy's Organic Lentil Soup, 1 cup

150 calories, 4.5 g fat (0.5 g saturated fat), 9 g fiber, 8 g protein

---

Asparagus with Almonds

4 spears steamed asparagus topped with ⅛ cup almond slivers and 1 tsp. parmesan cheese

143 calories, 11 g fat (2 g saturated fat), 6.2 g fiber, 7.5 g protein

Tomato Soup

Example: Amy's Cream of Tomato Soup, 1 cup

100 calories, 2 g fat (1.5 g saturated fat), 3 g fiber, 2 g protein

---

Baked Potato French Fries with Rosemary

Wash and skin potatoes. Cut into ½-inch slices. Drizzle with olive oil. Bake 30–40 minutes in oven at 450 degrees, turning periodically. Sprinkle with rosemary. Serving size: ½ cup.

117 calories, 6.2 g fat (0.9 g saturated fat), 0.9 g fiber, 1.2 g protein

---

Fruit-Flavored Yogurt

Example: Stonyfield Lowfat blueberry yogurt, 6 oz.

130 calories, 1.5 g fat (1 g sat fat), 2 g fiber, 6 g protein

---

Miso Soup

Boil 2¼ cups water in saucepan. Add 2 oz. tofu cut into ¼-inch cubes. Simmer 1–2 minutes. Add ½ cup chopped spinach. Simmer 1–2 more minutes. Stir in 1 tbsp. light miso paste, 2 tsp. barley miso paste. Garnish with chopped green onion. (Makes 3 servings.)

49 calories, 2.1 g fat (0 g saturated fat), 1 g fiber, 4.1 g protein

---

Toast with Peanut Butter

1 slice whole-wheat toast with 1 tsp. all-natural peanut butter

150 calories, 9 g fat (1 g saturated fat), 4 g fiber, 8 g protein

especially potent CCK stimulators, and they also discovered other satiety hormones, such as peptide YY (PYY), that have their own special nutrient stimulators (including long-chain fatty acids).

Since these discoveries, food chemists have worked to create food products that reduce hunger more with fewer calories than the regular foods that contain these nutrients. I was involved in developing a pair of these products, which are now being marketed specifically to endurance athletes: a snack bar called Forze and a snack drink bearing the same name. The drink is the more remarkable of the two. It contains only 45 to 50 calories per 8-ounce serving but is as filling as a much larger snack, thanks to its high-satiety ingredients, which include soy and whey proteins, sunflower oil, the amino acid glutamine, and fiber. Its efficacy was proven in a series of double-blind, placebo-controlled studies. In one of them, 20 subjects were given either Forze or a placebo and were then provided with a pasta lunch and instructed to consume as much food as they wished within 25 minutes. The amount of food consumed was measured and recorded. After eating their lunch, the subjects were asked to complete visual analog scale (VAS) assessments for hunger, fullness, and how much food they wanted to eat. VAS assessments were recorded immediately after lunch and every 30 minutes for the next 3 hours. The experiment was later repeated with a crossover design, meaning all of the subjects receiving Forze the first time received the placebo the second time and vice versa. On average, subjects ate 21 percent fewer calories at lunch after drinking Forze than after drinking the placebo. There was also an extension of satiety at 3 hours as measured by the VAS ratings.

While Forze is the first satiety product marketed specifically to endurance athletes, the broader category of satiety foods and beverages is growing rapidly. Other products in the category include LightFull Satiety Smoothies and FullBar snack bar.

EAT LOW-DENSITY FOODS

It is not only the nutrients within food that stimulate the release of satiety hormones such as CCK but also the stomach distension, or stretching, that occurs as food accumulates within the stomach. The more the stomach distends, the more satiety hormones are released. Therefore the volume of food has a major effect on satiety, as well as the specific nutrients in food. The number of calories in a given volume of food varies greatly among different food types. Water and fiber add volume to foods without adding calories. Therefore foods with high water and fiber contents, such as fruits and vegetables, typically provide more satiety per calorie than foods with low water and fiber contents. Foods with a low ratio of calories per unit volume are referred to as "low energy-density foods." The more such foods you include in your diet, the more easily you will satisfy your appetite without overeating.

Barbara Rolls, a well-known nutrition researcher at Pennsylvania State University, has performed a number of interesting studies on the satiety effects of foods with different levels of energy density. In one of these studies (Bell et al. 1998), women were fed either a high-density, medium-density, or low-density meal three times a day. The lunch entrée, for example, was a

> **THE VOLUME OF FOOD HAS A MAJOR EFFECT ON SATIETY, AS WELL AS THE SPECIFIC NUTRIENTS IN FOOD.**

pasta bake made from pasta shells, zucchini, broccoli, carrots, onions, tomato sauce, and parmesan, mozzarella, and ricotta cheeses. The low-density version contained more vegetables, while the medium- and high-density versions contained more shells and cheese. All participants received instructions to eat as much as they wanted. The subjects in all three groups ate the same weight of food, but the women eating the high-density meals took in 30 percent more calories than the women eating the low-density meals due to the differences in caloric density.

By improving your diet quality according to the guidelines presented in Chapter 7 you will also lower the overall energy density of your diet. Adding fruits and vegetables to your diet will serve both purposes, of course, but so will other changes such as replacing refined-grain foods with whole-grain foods. Perhaps the simplest way for many endurance athletes to reduce the energy density of their diets is to replace energy bars with fruits and vegetables as snacks. While some energy bars are very nutritious, most are also quite energy dense. No other foods even come close to fruits and vegetables in terms of minimal energy density, and few athletes eat enough fruits and vegetables, so by substituting them for your current snack choices you get two benefits.

You can enhance the appetite-satisfying effect of these changes by eating your low-density foods as appetizers or at the beginning of meals.

By triggering the initial release of satiety hormones before you begin eating the higher-density foods in your meal, you are likely to eat less of these foods, provided you listen to your body and put down the fork as soon as you feel comfortably full.

Because of their high water content, soups work especially well as meal starters. Research has shown that when people eat a light soup before a meal, they experience a feeling of fullness that causes them to eat smaller portions and fewer calories in their meal. For example, in another study by Barbara Rolls (Flood and Rolls 2007), participants who ate a bowl of soup before a lunch entrée consumed 20 percent fewer total calories (soup plus entrée) than participants who skipped the soup and went straight to the entrée.

To make this strategy most effective, eat a lighter soup containing no more than 150 calories. Lighter soup options include vegetable, tomato, chicken barley, and sweet potato.

EAT LESS

Because satiety is primarily dependent on the volume of food that is eaten, and because most people cannot sustain a diet that does not satisfy their appetite, reducing the amount of food eaten daily is not an effective weight management method for many endurance athletes. However, it can be effective for some, because in the right circumstances reducing food intake may reduce appetite, so you not only eat less but want less. The reason has to do with a hormone called *leptin*.

Leptin is an appetite-regulating hormone that is produced by fat cells. It acts on the hypothalamus, the brain's hunger center, to turn off the hunger switch. The more fat your fat cells contain, the more leptin they produce and the more your appetite shrinks.

At least that's how it works under normal circumstances. However, there appears to be a second factor that affects leptin production, and that's habitual eating patterns. If you consistently overeat, your brain cells will become leptin resistant, so your appetite remains inflated despite high circulating levels of leptin in your body.

Fortunately, this effect is reversible. If you restrain your eating for a week or so, your brain's sensitivity to the action of leptin is likely to increase. Research suggests that reducing fat intake is especially helpful in correcting leptin resistance. The degree to which you can overcome leptin resistance depends on genetic factors and possibly also on how you ate as a young child. There is evidence that some people are "hard-wired" for low leptin sensitivity and, consequently, big appetites.

Be aware that reducing food intake is likely to reduce your appetite only if you are significantly overweight and thus probably leptin resistant. Understand also that a sharp reduction in food intake will make you hungry even as it reduces your appetite. For example, if you normally eat 3,000 calories per day and you reduce your intake to 1,800 calories, your appetite might decrease to the point where it can be satisfied with 2,700 calories, but since you're only eating 1,800 calories, you're still hungry. So it's a good idea to pursue the eating-less tactic as a two-step process. First, reduce your daily caloric intake sharply—by 40 percent or thereabouts—for two weeks to reduce your appetite. Then increase it to a level that lies between this level and your former habitual level for the long term.

Try this method only if you are significantly heavier than your racing weight and have reason to believe that your appetite has been inflated by long-term overeating. And even then, try it only during the off-season, when your training load is lighter and a sharp calorie reduction is not likely to hinder your fitness development.

BEFRIEND YOUR APPETITE AGAIN

In modern society we have come to view our appetite as an enemy, not to be trusted. If not for our appetite, maintaining an optimal body weight would be easy. If the job of our appetite is to help us regulate our body weight appropriately, it appears not to be working correctly.

In fact, our appetites work just fine. What's broken is our food environment, which is full of foods that sabotage our appetite and messages that cause us to ignore it. We cannot travel back in time to a Golden Age when our appetite and our food environment existed in perfect harmony. The next best thing you can  do is practice the appetite management strategies I showed you in this chapter, which are realistic, effective, and already practiced with good results by people just like you.

TRAINING FOR RACING WEIGHT

F or many years a debate has raged between two factions of what we might loosely call the exercise community. The debate concerns the best way to exercise to get leaner. Some argue that prolonged, moderate-intensity exercise in the "fat-burning zone" is best. Supporters of this position tend to be representative of the endurance-sports faction of the exercise community. Others argue that high-intensity interval training is the best way to shed excess body fat. Supporters of this position tend to be representative of the gym-based exercise faction of the exercise community. Could it be that endurance athletes typically deem prolonged, moderate-intensity exercise to be more efficacious not because an objective analysis has led them to that conclusion but because that's the type of exercise they spend most of their time doing? And could it be that gym exercisers judge high-intensity interval training (HIIT) superior to long endurance workouts not based on fact and reason but based on their dislike for endurance workouts? The truth is, both types of exercise are effective for fat-burning, and a program that combines the two is likely to be more effective than one based on either type alone.

A big difference between endurance athletes and gym exercisers is that the primary goal of endurance athletes is to achieve maximum race performance—getting leaner is just one means to that end—whereas for most gym exercisers, getting leaner is the main point of working out. So for endurance athletes it doesn't matter which type of exercise is the better fat burner. What matters above all is finding the combination of workouts that will increase race fitness the most. But as I suggested earlier in this book, form follows function in endurance sports training (and nutrition practices). The training that makes you fittest will also make you leanest. It's no accident that the world's best endurance athletes are also the world's leanest exercisers—even more lean than the bodybuilders who care only about being lean. Training with a focus on building endurance fitness is a more reliable way to maximize fitness *and* leanness, I believe, than training with a focus on getting lean. Form follows function, after all.

Few endurance athletes train perfectly for performance. Most could benefit from making one or more specific changes to their methods. There are three changes you can make to your training to become leaner and yield better performance: increase the volume of moderate-intensity workouts, add more high-intensity training, and do more strength training.

MORE VOLUME AT MODERATE INTENSITY

The so-called fat-burning zone of exercise intensity is a concept that has spread rapidly throughout all levels of exercise culture. Nearly every person who has ever picked up a fitness magazine or experienced a single session with a personal trainer has heard of it, though few people understand exactly what it is. So let's look at the concept more closely.

Suppose you were to perform an incremental exercise test on a stationary bicycle in which you started pedaling very slowly in a low gear and then pedaled progressively faster in higher and higher gears until you were sprinting all out. At the beginning of the test your muscles would burn fat almost exclusively, and not much of it. As your intensity level increased, your rate of fat burning would steadily increase, and your muscles would also enlist more and more carbohydrate. At a still fairly moderate exercise intensity the rate of fat burning would peak and eventually begin to decrease as the rate of carbohydrate burning spiked.

By the time you reached an all-out sprint your muscles would be burning carbohydrate at an extremely high rate and no fat at all. The intensity zone surrounding the point at which the rate of fat burning peaks is your fat-burning zone. Typically it falls at roughly 59 to 64 per-

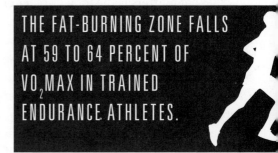

THE FAT-BURNING ZONE FALLS AT 59 TO 64 PERCENT OF VO_2MAX IN TRAINED ENDURANCE ATHLETES.

cent of VO_2max in trained endurance athletes, which corresponds to a comfortable but not dawdling pace in cycling, running, and the other endurance sports. For unfit individuals, the fat-burning zone is usually between 47 and 52 percent of VO_2max.

Exercise scientists, doctors, obesity experts, dieticians, weight-loss coaches, and personal trainers commonly advise men and women seeking to lose weight to perform aerobic exercise primarily within their individual fat-burning zone. It makes perfect sense; if your goal is to get rid of excess body fat, why not exercise at the intensity that gets rid of it faster than any other?

Exercising within the fat-burning zone is indeed an effective way to burn off excess body fat, but it is not necessarily more effective than exercising at higher intensities, where carbohydrate burning is greater and fat burning is less. The reason has to do with what happens *after* moderate-intensity and high-intensity workouts are performed. After a moderate-intensity workout, few of the food calories you eat will be used to replenish your muscle glycogen (or muscle carbohydrate) stores, because you did not have to tap deeply into those stores during the workout. Instead, calories will be used to replenish the fat stores you used. Whereas after a high-intensity workout, many of the food calories you consume will be used to replenish your depleted muscle glycogen stores and relatively few calories will be used to replenish fat stores, because you did not burn much fat during the workout. In fact, your body may even continue to mobilize fat stores after the workout to help replenish muscle glycogen. In short, if you burn mostly fat during a workout, you will store mostly fat afterward (Phelain et al. 1997). And if you burn mostly carbohydrate during a workout, you will store mostly carbohydrate afterward.

So with respect to the goal of getting leaner, it doesn't really matter which kind of calories your muscles use predominately during exercise.

What matters is the total number of calories used. The more calories your muscles use during a workout, the more likely it is that you will consume fewer total calories than your body uses over 24 hours, and if this is the case, then you are likely to experience a net loss of body fat. This will happen even if you burned mostly carbohydrate during your workout, because the body always replenishes muscle glycogen preferentially and it doesn't take a heck of a lot of calories to do it. Thus, unless your diet is carbohydrate-deficient, any exercise-induced caloric deficit will ultimately take the form of body fat loss instead of muscle glycogen loss. What matters from a fat-loss perspective is not the type but the total number of calories burned during a workout. Because high-intensity exercise burns calories faster than moderate-intensity exercise, high-intensity exercise is, in the big picture, the more efficient way to shed body fat. However, a person can do a lot more moderate-intensity exercise than high-intensity exercise, so it's moderate-intensity exercise that ultimately has the greatest potential to reduce body fat.

Some endurance coaches promote training in the fat-burning zone to increase an athlete's fat-burning capacity and ultimately increase fat-reliance in racing. Perhaps the best-known advocate of this approach is Phil Maffetone, a triathlon coach who made his name by developing a training philosophy characterized by an extreme emphasis on the importance of fat metabolism. He taught his athletes, including six-time Hawaii Ironman world champion Mark Allen, to do virtually all of their training at a very low intensity to maximize fat metabolism and stimulate physiological adaptations that increased the body's capacity for fat oxidation in subsequent workouts. (I have my doubts about whether these athletes actually held themselves back as much as their coach advised.) Over time, Maffetone believed, the athlete would be able to swim, bike, or run faster and faster at the same, low, fat-burning intensity.

Research has shown that training in the fat-burning zone does improve fat-burning capacity. However, it only improves fat-burning capacity within the fat-burning zone itself—that is, at lower exercise intensities. No matter how fit they are or in what manner they've trained, all endurance athletes rely on carbohydrate when racing at intensities that are near or above the lactate threshold. For example, a triathlete who is capable of completing an Olympic-distance triathlon in 2:20 is likely to swim, bike, and run at approximately 85 percent of VO_2max. At this intensity, the muscles get approximately 90 percent of their energy from carbohydrate and only 10 percent from fat. Thus, while the well-trained triathlete has a much greater maximal fat-burning capacity than an unfit individual, this particular training adaptation is irrelevant to performance in sprint and Olympic-distance triathlons.

The ability to swim, bike, and run faster in sprint and Olympic-distance triathlons is actually accounted for largely by increased carbohydrate-burning capacity. Indeed, it is an often-overlooked fact that training increases maximal carbohydrate-burning capacity, which occurs at 100 percent VO_2max, to a much greater degree than it increases fat-burning capacity, which remains at 60 to 65 percent of VO_2max even in the fittest athletes.

This point was illustrated by a study from the University of California–Berkeley (Bergman et al. 1999). Nine untrained subjects rode stationary bikes for 1 hour at the power output level that elicited 66 percent of their individual VO_2max. The relative contribution of fat and carbohydrate oxidation to their muscle work was estimated. The subjects then engaged in a regular cycling workout program for 9 weeks and were retested. During those 9 weeks of training, their VO_2max increased significantly, so that the power output level that elicited 66 percent of VO_2max in the first test elicited only 54 percent in the second. The rate of fat burning was higher at this absolute power output level in the second test. However, when they rode at 66 percent of their *new* VO_2max, the relative contributions of fat and carbohydrate to total energy production were unchanged from the pre-training test.

While increased fat-burning capacity resulting from training has little effect in shorter events, increased fat-burning capacity is a critical adaptation en route to improved performance in multihour events such as ultramarathons, Ironman races, and 50K cross-country ski races. Elite long-distance endurance athletes are able to oxidize more than 8 fat calories per minute during exercise, whereas the typical healthy untrained young adult is able to burn fat at only half this rate. In addition, training greatly increases the absolute power output level on the bike and the absolute speeds in swimming, running, skiing (and any other endurance sports) at which the maximal rate of fat burning occurs. Thus, while less-trained and highly trained endurance athletes alike may get the same relative proportions of their muscle energy from fat and carbohydrate, more highly trained athletes simply move a heck of a lot faster at their peak fat-burning intensity level.

The reason this is important is that in races that take more than about five and a half hours to complete, athletes cannot sustain an intensity level that exceeds their maximal rate of fat burning. That's because the body stores only enough carbohydrate, and can process only enough consumed carbohydrate, to last roughly five-and-a-half hours when working at 60–65 percent of VO_2max. Consequently, the only way to race longer and faster at this intensity level is to get more energy from fat.

ELITE LONG-DISTANCE ENDURANCE ATHLETES ARE ABLE TO OXIDIZE MORE THAN 8 FAT CALORIES PER MINUTE DURING EXERCISE.

Phil Maffetone's approach suggests that athletes seeking these adaptations need to go out of their way to get them. They don't. Normal endurance training, with its emphasis on long, moderate-intensity workouts, naturally maximizes fat-burning adaptations. There is no evidence nor is there any cause to speculate that training almost *exclusively* at moderate intensities, as Maffetone recommended, enhances fat-burning adaptations beyond the level achieved by training predominantly at moderate intensities. And there is every reason to believe that eliminating high-intensity workouts from your training would compromise your fitness in a variety of ways, including reducing your mechanical efficiency, VO_2max, and muscle power.

For example, in one study, researchers from Brigham Young University (Creer et al. 2004) separated 17 trained cyclists into two groups. One group performed only moderate-intensity training for 4 weeks. The other group included a very small amount of sprint training—just 28 minutes per week—in their training mix. Total work output increased significantly in members of the sprint group but not in the moderate-intensity group. Studies such as this one show that a little high-intensity training goes a long way to enhance performance through mechanisms that are complementary to those by which moderate-intensity training boosts performance. Increased fat-burning capacity is not the be-all and end-all of performance in endurance racing; it's just one piece of the puzzle. The endurance athlete who ignores the other pieces, most of which are associated with training at higher intensities, will pay for it.

That said, workouts that serve primarily to enhance fat-burning capacity certainly have their place in any endurance athlete's training regimen. The workouts that have the greatest effect on fat-burning capacity are those that most deplete your muscle-glycogen stores—namely, very long workouts that you finish cross-eyed and drooling. If you do not currently drive yourself this deep into the pit of fatigue in your longest workouts, you might want to consider extending them for the sake of possibly increasing your fat-burning capacity.

One of the primary mechanisms by which glycogen-depleting workouts stimulate this adaptation is the release of an immune system compound called interleukin-6 (IL-6). This chemical is released by the muscles in response to declining glycogen levels during exercise and triggers increased fat burning. This is why duration has a big effect on the fuel mix that the muscles use at moderate to moderately high intensities. In the first mile of the bike leg of an Ironman 70.3 triathlon, your muscles might get 50 percent of their fuel from fat and 50 percent from carbohydrate. In the last mile of the run leg, although your exercise intensity is unchanged, your muscles might get 75 percent of their energy from fat and only 25 percent from carbohydrate due to glycogen depletion and the compensatory effect triggered by IL-6 release.

Interestingly, IL-6 not only increases fat burning during workouts but also triggers adaptations that increase the athlete's general fat-burning capacity. The more IL-6 is released in a workout, the bigger the boost in fat-burning capacity you'll get from it. That's why it is beneficial to regularly perform endurance workouts that leave you more or less exhausted, as that's what it takes to maximize IL-6 release.

What's also interesting is that consuming carbohydrate during exercise suppresses IL-6 release and may thereby blunt IL-6-mediated increases in fat-burning capacity. Eschewing carbohydrate intake in some long workouts could force your muscles to rely more on fat fuel and make you a better fat burner. However, you should consume carbohydrate in most of your long workouts because it will enhance your performance in those workouts and thereby strengthen other fitness adaptations.

Simply doing a high overall volume of moderate-intensity training will stimulate more or less the same benefits as doing very long workouts. Like a long individual workout, a daily succession of moderately long workouts or morning and afternoon workouts will challenge your muscles to perform in a glycogen-depleted state. Even with adequate carbohydrate intake, your muscles will not be able to fully replenish their glycogen supplies between workouts, and as a result your fat-burning and glycogen storage capacities will increase (provided you periodically give your muscles a chance to fully recover).

There is ultimately more potential to increase endurance through increasing overall training volume than through increasing the duration of the longest training sessions. That's because very long training sessions are extremely taxing and create a significant recovery demand. Once your long endurance workouts exceed a certain critical duration, they begin to limit your overall training volume because they require you to take it easy for a day or two afterward. In most cases you're better off making high training volume a greater priority than single-session duration and limiting the duration of your longest endurance workouts to that which is strictly needed to ensure you can "go the distance" in races. An interesting bit of evidence in favor of this recommendation comes from a 1982 study by Ron Maughan, of Scotland's Aberdeen University (personal communication), who found that average weekly training mileage was a much better predictor of performance in a marathon than the longest distance of a single training run. Indeed, it's worth noting that elite marathon runners typically do not run any farther than the 20 to 22 miles that novice marathon runners run in their longest workouts. But whereas the novices may peak at 45 miles per week, the pros routinely exceed 120 miles.

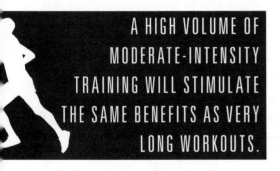

A HIGH VOLUME OF MODERATE-INTENSITY TRAINING WILL STIMULATE THE SAME BENEFITS AS VERY LONG WORKOUTS.

The same rule applies to the other endurance sports. Research suggests that overall training volume is the best predictor of performance in cycling and swimming, as well as running. More important than the length of your longest workouts or even the amount of high-intensity training you do is the total amount of time you spend training week in and week out. This does not mean that you should not do long workouts or high-intensity workouts. It simply means that in your search for improvement as an endurance athlete, you should look to increase your total training volume before you look to increase the amount of high-intensity training you do or the length of your longest workouts. You will perform best if you regularly engage in long endurance workouts and high-intensity workouts, but you must avoid putting so much effort into such workouts that your overall training volume is limited by your need for relative rest (i.e., reduced training) for recovery.

Elite athletes in each of the endurance sports train roughly the same amount—and they train a lot. Professional cyclists, for example, typically spend 30 hours a week on their bikes. Few age-group endurance athletes have the time or physical capacity to train so much. Each of us must work within our own physical and scheduling limitations. But I encourage you to maximize the volume of training you do within these limitations. High-volume training produces other benefits besides increased fat burning and glycogen storage. It also increases aerobic capacity and movement economy. In short, it will make you a faster athlete—and a leaner one, as well.

Don't rush headlong into a high-volume program, however. To avoid injury and burnout you must increase your training volume slowly, not only within a single training cycle but also from one training cycle to the next. Those marathoners who run 120 miles a week took many years to build up to that level. I myself completed my first 100-mile running week as my thirty-eighth birthday was approaching. Be patient as you work your way toward your own lifetime maximum training load.

MORE HIGH-INTENSITY TRAINING

I mentioned above that calories are burned at a higher rate during high-intensity exercise than during moderate- or low-intensity exercise. It is also the case that the body burns more calories *after* high-intensity exercise. Advocates of high-intensity exercise for weight loss make much of this fact. But as we shall see, they make too much of it. There is greater overall potential for body-fat loss through moderate-intensity exercise. And a high-volume training regimen with predominately moderate-intensity exercise will result in a higher level of endurance performance than a necessarily lower-volume program in which high-intensity training predominates. That said, many endurance athletes, especially runners, cyclists, cross-country skiers, and triathletes, do not perform enough high-intensity training to optimize their performance, probably because it can be rather unpleasant. Adding high-intensity training to your regimen will likely boost your performance and lower your body-fat percentage.

In the 1920s the legendary British exercise physiologist A. V. Hill first observed that the body's rate of oxygen consumption remains elevated for some time after exercise, and that this phenomenon is indicative of a metabolic rate that, while lower than the metabolic rate during exercise itself, remains above the normal resting metabolic rate. This phenomenon has come to be known as excess post-exercise oxygen consumption (EPOC). More recent research has determined that EPOC has two phases—a strong acute phase lasting up to 2 hours and a weaker long-term phase lasting 24 hours or more—the sum of which accounts for 6 to 15 percent of the total caloric cost of a workout, depending on its duration and intensity. Thus, if you burn 1,000 calories during a workout you can expect to burn roughly an extra 100 calories in excess of your normal resting metabolism in the hours after the workout.

Different types of workouts produce different levels of EPOC. High-intensity cardiovascular exercise (think interval sessions) results in the largest amounts of post-exercise energy consumption. Indeed, EPOC increases exponentially at exercise intensities exceeding roughly 60 percent of VO_2max. Research has also shown that the difference between high- and low-intensity workouts in terms of EPOC translates into differences between the two workout types in their effects on body composition. A recent study from the University of New South Wales, Australia (Trapp et al. 2008), found that women lost an average of 10.5 percent of their fat mass after 15 weeks on a three-times-a-week program of 20-minute workouts consisting of 8-second stationary bike sprints followed by 12-second passive recoveries. (Sounds easy, but that's 60 all-out sprints—a hellishly difficult workout.) Subjects in a control group that performed traditional endurance workouts lost considerably less fat over the same period despite spending roughly 400 percent more time pedaling.

Gym exercisers have pounced on results such as these (and other results showing that high-intensity intervals boost aerobic and anaerobic capacity in a far more time-efficient manner than conventional endurance training) to argue that high-intensity intervals are simply "better" than conventional endurance training and to imply that endurance athletes are needlessly doing too much steady-state work. However, workout duration has a big effect on EPOC, as well, and most endurance athletes routinely train longer than the 40 minutes that the controls in the study cited above rode at the peak of their training—not to mention, we seldom train as slowly as the 60 percent of VO_2max at which these subjects rode. A study conducted by researchers at the University of New Hampshire (Quinn et al. 1994) found that a 1-hour workout at 70 percent of VO_2max resulted in 55 percent more EPOC than a 40-minute workout at the same intensity (which itself produced only 14 percent more EPOC than a 20-minute workout at the same intensity).

And let's not forget that 85 to 94 percent of the total energy cost of each workout comes during the workout itself, not through EPOC. It's possible to burn a lot more calories in an exhaustive moderate-intensity workout—due to its far greater duration—than in an exhaustive maximum-intensity interval workout. In a recent review of the scientific literature on EPOC and body-weight management, researchers from the University of South Australia (LaForgia et al. 2006) concluded that "the earlier research optimism regarding an impor-

> IF YOU BURN 1,000 CALORIES DURING A WORKOUT, EXPECT TO BURN ROUGHLY 100 CALORIES IN EXCESS OF YOUR NORMAL RESTING METABOLISM IN THE HOURS AFTER THE WORKOUT.

tant role for . . . EPOC in weight loss is generally unfounded. . . . The role of exercise in the maintenance of body mass is therefore predominantly mediated via the cumulative effect of the energy expenditure during the actual exercise." In other words, for the purpose of getting lean, going long trumps going fast—although doing some of both is better still.

You would not want to perform maximum-intensity interval workouts exclusively for the sake of getting lean for the same reason that you would not want to perform them exclusively for the sake of maximizing your fitness, despite the fact that maximum-intensity interval workouts boost aerobic and anaerobic capacity in a far more time-efficient manner than conventional endurance training. I'll explain this reason through a simple thought experiment.

Suppose we took the subjects in one of these 8-week studies comparing the effects of high-intensity interval training and steady-state aerobic training and asked them to continue doing what they were doing, and not only continue doing it, but to do more and more of it as long as they kept improving. What would happen? Well, those in the HIIT group (high-intensity interval group) would be able to increase their volume of anaerobic training for a short while, but before long—indeed, probably right around the time they tried training every day—they would hit a wall, beyond which any additional increases would prove counterproductive. Meanwhile, those in the slow-and-steady group would be able to continue increasing their slow-and-steady workload, and continue getting fitter, for a long, long time. Their total training volume would be vastly greater than that of the interval group by the time they reached their plateau, and their performance level would be significantly better in longer performance tests, though probably still worse in shorter ones.

Now let's suppose that each group began to replace its respective core training type with the other group's training to stimulate further improvement, again stopping when improvement ceased. So the members of the slow-and-steady group now gradually cut back their slow-and-steady miles while adding perhaps 1 minute of high-intensity interval work for every 5 minutes of slow moderate-intensity training eliminated (this ratio of one to five is selected to avoid overtraining, as a minute of sprinting is far more stressful than a minute of cruising). At the same time, the HIIT group would gradually add moderate-intensity training while cutting just enough high-intensity interval work to see improvement and also avoid overtraining. When all was said and done, the slow-and-steady folks would find their performance plateau after having reduced their slow-and-steady training by perhaps 20 percent and having added a volume of intervals equal to no more than 20 percent of the new, reduced slow-and-steady training volume. But the interval athletes would have had to reduce their interval training by no less than 80 percent and added a volume of slow-and-steady training equal to perhaps 400 percent of their original interval volume. Both groups, of course, will now be training in precisely the same way: the way real-world competitive endurance athletes train, with a broad foundation of moderate-intensity "base" work and a thin layer of high-intensity training on top.

The lesson of this thought experiment is that you should not increase your reliance on interval training for the sake of boosting your resting metabolism or your fitness level unless you really aren't doing very much interval training. Again, though, many endurance athletes do indeed underutilize high-intensity intervals. Runners, cyclists, and cross-country skiers should do at least one workout per week that includes intervals performed at an intensity level exceeding lactate-threshold intensity, and they should also perform a second, somewhat lighter high-intensity session each week during periods of their training when they are focused on developing their speed. Swimmers and rowers should do even more, as their races are typically much shorter and more intense. Triathletes should perform supra-threshold intervals at least twice a week in swimming and once every 10 days or so in cycling and running.

If you're currently doing less interval training you will undoubtedly experience improvements in your body composition and performance by correcting this training imbalance. As with increasing your overall training volume, it is important to proceed slowly when increasing your commitment to high-intensity interval training. In fact, to avoid overtraining or injury it may be necessary to slightly reduce your overall training volume as you increase your volume of high-intensity training. When your body has adjusted to the stress of doing more high-intensity training you may then reintroduce some slower training.

STRENGTH TRAINING

During exercise, the amount of oxygen you consume depends not only on the intensity of your exercise but also on the amount of muscle mass you carry. Increased muscle metabolism is the cause of increased oxygen consumption during exercise, so the more muscle mass you have, the more oxygen you consume—hence, also, the more calories you burn at any given work rate.

Elevated muscle metabolism is also the cause of EPOC. Consequently, the more muscle mass you carry, the more EPOC you will enjoy after workouts. It's another example of the tendency for the fit to get fitter. Training increases the percentage of the body's mass that consists of muscle. This change itself increases the amount of EPOC one experiences after a workout. In other words, lean individuals get a greater post-exercise fat-burning effect than individuals carrying more fat get from the same workout.

This was shown in a recent study involving 250 Japanese male athletes between 16 and 21 years old (Tahara et al. 2008). Researchers measured the EPOC of each athlete for 40 minutes after short-duration exhaustive exercise. These values were compared against measurements of body size and composition. The researchers found that differences in fat-free body mass (which is mainly muscle) accounted for 55 percent of the individual differences in EPOC.

The lesson of this study is that, with respect to maximizing EPOC, it is best to be large and lean. Indeed, resting metabolism in general is highest in the most muscle-bound men and women. Of course, with respect to endurance performance, it is best to be *light* and lean. Therefore I do not recommend that you replace half of your endurance training with heavy weightlifting for the sake of maximizing EPOC! I do, however, recommend that all endurance athletes do a small amount of weightlifting and/or calisthenics exercises—two to three sessions per week lasting 20 minutes each will suffice.

The performance and body composition benefits of power training in cycling were demonstrated in a New Zealand study (Paton and Hopkins 2005). Researchers divided a team of cyclists into two groups. During an 8-week period within their competitive season, members of one group continued training normally while members of a second group replaced two workouts each week with high-resistance, low-cadence strength intervals. All of the cyclists performed 40-km time trials before and after the study period. Over the 8 weeks, members of the strength intervals group increased their mean time-trial power output by 7.8 percent compared to the control (or normally training) group. In addition, skinfold measurements suggested that the cyclists exposed to strength intervals lost a significant amount of body fat.

The benefits of weightlifting on running performance were demonstrated in a 2008 study by Norwegian researchers (Støren et al. 2008). Seventeen well-trained runners were divided into two groups. Members of one group continued with their normal run training while members of the other group added to their routine three weekly strength sessions consisting of four, four-repetition sets of half-squats using their four-repetition maximal load (i.e., the heaviest weight they could lift four times). After 8 weeks, members of the strength group exhibited not only the expected gains in maximal strength and rate of force development, but also significant improvements in running economy (5 percent) and in time to exhaustion at maximal aerobic running speed (21.3 percent). The control group showed no improvement in any of the measured parameters.

How could heavy half-squats enhance running economy and endurance? Previous research involving explosive strength training has shown that this type of training increases running economy by enhancing the capacity of the muscles and tendons to capture "free" impact energy and return it to the ground. Maximal strength training probably worked in a similar way.

It is worth noting that the loads used in this study were much heavier than those used by most endurance athletes in strength training. Endurance athletes are generally taught that they should use moderate loads and perform sets with large numbers of repetitions (12-rep sets are typical), because this approach imposes a strength-endurance challenge that is more relevant to endurance sports performance than the strength-power challenge imposed by lifting heavier loads. However, the point of hitting the gym if you're an endurance athlete is not to do the same type of training you do in your primary sport discipline(s). The point is to get a type of training stimulus that you are *not* getting from your endurance training. Lifting very heavy loads is exactly the sort of thing that endurance athletes should do in the gym, because it complements rather than reifies their endurance training. And this Norwegian study proves it.

This is not to say that heavy lifting is the only sort of strength training endurance athletes should do. Core training exercises such as side planks do not entail lifting heavy loads but they boost endurance performance, too, by increasing joint stability and thereby removing waste from sports movements. This was shown in a study performed by researchers at Barry University (Sato and Mokha 2009). Fourteen recreational and competitive runners participated in a 6-week core strengthening program, before and after which their running kinematics, leg stability, and 5,000-meter running performance were tested. Another 14 runners served as controls, by continuing to run during the six-week study period and not strengthening their core.

What did the researchers find in this case? Interestingly, core strength training was found not to affect the runners' ground reaction forces or leg stability (essentially balance on one leg), but it did improve their 5,000-meter race performance relative to members of the control group. The authors of the study did not speculate about why this effect was found. I wouldn't be surprised to learn that it was mediated by an improvement in running economy resulting from more efficient transfer of forces between the upper body and the legs.

To get meaningful benefits from strength training, endurance athletes should perform strength workouts lasting 20 to 40 minutes apiece two to three times per week. You can accomplish much in a small amount of time with focused and efficient workout designs. Build your workouts from a mixture of exercises that increase your maximum strength and power in sport-specific movements and exercises that increase the stability of key joints in your sport, such as the shoulders if you are a swimmer. There is no need to pad your workout with multiple exercises for the same muscle group or numerous sets of each exercise. Just get in, go hard, and get out. The appendix provides recommended strength exercises for various endurance sports.

As for maximum-intensity sport-specific strength and power development, even less is needed. I recommend that runners perform one set of 6–10 x 8–10-second sprints up a steep hill each week. Cyclists may perform either one set of 6–10 x 20-second power intervals (sprints in their highest gear) or steep hill sprints once per week. Since this type of training is difficult for cross-country skiers on actual snowfields, I recommend they use either the running or the cycling protocol just described, or both. Swimmers can and should spend more time sprinting and developing power through kicking and pulling drills, because such high-intensity work is less taxing in swimming and because pool swim races are short and require more strength and power. Triathletes should be training for strength and power in swimming, cycling, and running, of course, but they cannot do as much of each as single-sport athletes do lest they overwhelm themselves with the combination. I recommend that triathletes perform kicking and pulling drills once or twice a week in swimming and once every other week in cycling and running, on alternate weeks.

> ATHLETES IN EVERY ENDURANCE SPORT SHOULD INCORPORATE SPORT-SPECIFIC STRENGTH AND POWER TRAINING INTO THEIR REGIMEN.

With respect to strength training, then, athletes in every endurance sport should incorporate a bit of sport-specific strength and power training into their regimen—high-resistance sprints on the bike, steep uphill running sprints, and the like. These training modifications will not cause you to gain weight, but they will stimulate a slight increase in muscle mass that will in turn cause a proportional decline in fat mass by increasing your EPOC levels after workouts and by elevating your resting metabolism. Weightlifting and sport-specific strength and power training will also increase your power by conditioning your seldom-used fast-twitch muscle fibers and reduce your injury risk by improving the stability of your joints.

ANABOLIC EATING

Gains in muscle strength and power cannot be maximized through training alone. Diet also contributes to muscular adaptations to strength and power training. If muscle strength and power are major concerns for you, then you will want to practice "anabolic eating" alongside your strength and power training. Anabolic eating is eating for muscle growth. While endurance athletes are not interested in muscle growth for its own sake, gains in muscle strength and power are closely linked to increases in muscle size. Use the following anabolic eating tips to get the most out of your strength and power training. Don't worry about "bulking up." There is absolutely zero chance that you will gain a burdensome amount of muscle weight through strength and power training and anabolic eating if you are also engaging in moderate- to high-volume endurance training.

Maintain a Caloric Surplus

Research has shown that the most important dietary requirement for muscle growth is a caloric surplus. It is next to impossible to gain muscle mass if your body is burning more calories than it absorbs from food. This surplus need not be large, as muscle protein accretion is a slow process, and indeed your caloric surplus should not be large, as a large daily excess of energy intake will cause more fat storage than muscle gain. A surplus of 100 calories a day is plenty.

Eat Plenty of Protein

Before you draw any conclusions about this advice, I should warn that it's not for the reason you think. It is widely believed that very high levels of protein intake are required to maximize muscle growth, but research has shown this belief to be false. A daily protein intake of 1.2 grams of protein per kilogram of body weight is sufficient to maximize muscle growth resulting from resistance training. While this level of protein intake is greater than the recommended minimum level of 0.8 grams per kilogram per day, it does not exceed the amount that the average person actually consumes. So there is no need to increase your level of protein intake to promote muscle growth.

However, increasing your protein consumption may help you minimize the body-fat gains that often accompany muscle growth. The reason is that dietary protein is less readily converted into body fat than dietary carbohydrate and fat. Consequently, if you maintain a diet with a 100-calorie daily surplus, in which 30 percent of your calories come from protein, you are likely to gain less fat than if you maintain a diet with a 100-calorie daily surplus in which only 18 percent of your daily calories come from protein (which is average), although the amount of muscle gain is likely to be the same on both diets.

Eat Animal Foods

Animal proteins are more conducive to muscle growth than plant proteins, for a few reasons. First, they are "complete" proteins, meaning they contain all of the essential amino acids that the body cannot synthesize for itself, whereas proteins from plant foods are not complete. Second, animal proteins are more bioavailable than plant proteins, meaning they are more readily incorporated into the cells of the body. Only 78 percent of the protein contained in high-fiber legumes is actually digested, compared to 97 percent of the protein contained in animal foods. Finally, and not least important, animal foods tend to contain much larger amounts of protein than plant foods. For example, a large (1-cup) serving of brown rice contains only 4.5 grams of protein. By contrast, a small (3-ounce) serving of beef flank steak provides nearly 23 grams of protein.

For all of these reasons, you are likely to find it easier to gain muscle if you get most of your protein from animal foods such as fish and dairy products. However, it is certainly not impossible to gain muscle on a vegetarian diet. You just have to work a little harder at it. Because plant proteins are less bioavailable, you should aim for a target of 1.8 to 2.0 grams of protein per kilogram of body weight daily if you don't eat meat. Meeting this requirement will be much easier if you make regular use of vegetarian protein supplements such as soy protein shakes.

Eat Carbs and Protein After Workouts

The timing of protein consumption has a significant effect on the rate of muscle protein synthesis. Research has shown that protein consumed immediately before, during, and immediately after exercise causes more muscle protein synthesis than equal amounts of protein consumed at other times.

The optimal amount of protein consumption after exercise is 20 grams. Consuming protein with carbohydrate after workouts is proven to result in even greater amounts of muscle protein synthesis. This is because carbohydrate stimulates the release of insulin, which in turn transports the amino acids from dietary protein to the muscle cells and initiates muscle protein synthesis, as discussed in Chapter 9.

Take a Creatine Supplement

Creatine phosphate is a fuel that the muscles rely on for maximum-intensity efforts such as sprinting 100 yards. Certain precursors of creatine phosphate, such as creatine monohydrate, are taken as supplements to increase creatine phosphate stores in the muscles. Research has shown that creatine supplementation enhances gains in muscle strength, size, and power resulting from resistance training, as well as performance in repeated high-intensity intervals. While creatine is extremely popular among strength athletes and recreational weightlifters, few endurance athletes use it. Yet it is likely to be helpful to those athletes who are seeking greater muscle strength and power. Chapter 14 will discuss creatine supplementation in greater detail.

MORE IS BETTER

Because most Americans do not exercise regularly, and in fact some hate working out, general exercise recommendations, which are typically directed toward those whose primary exercise objective is to lose weight, are often focused on the value of efficiency. "Get more from less" and "Train smarter, not harder," are messages you have undoubtedly heard. But as we have seen, the most effective way to get leaner is to train for optimal performance, and it is quite clear that improved endurance performance can only come from doing more in training. That's just how it works. You cannot get better results by merely shuffling around the workouts you're already doing, and certainly not by scaling back your training, unless you are among the small minority of endurance athletes who are truly doing more training than your body can handle. Instead, something must be added. And as this chapter has shown, the list of things worth adding is short: more moderate-intensity volume, more high-intensity training, and strength training.

TWELVE

WHAT THE PROS EAT

The nutrition practices that I described and recommended to you in Chapters 7 through 10 are based on scientific research, on my own experiences as a sports nutritionist, coach, and athlete, and on what other nutritionists, coaches, and athletes have told me works for them. But do the world's best endurance athletes actually follow these practices? In truth, none follows the complete Racing Weight system as I have formulated it, because this system is new. The very reason I created it was that there was no comprehensive weight-management system for endurance athletes. I humbly expect that there will be elite athletes among those who adopt the Racing Weight system, but none has had the chance yet.

There are many endurance athletes who practice most of the individual methods that constitute the complete Racing Weight system. But there are also many who practice few of them. In fact, the nutritional habits of elite endurance athletes are a lot more varied than their training methods. To begin with, there are substantial ethnic and cultural differences. For example, elite Kenyan runners typically get more than 75 percent of their calories from carbohydrates, while elite American endurance athletes get scarcely more than half of their calories from carbs. Even within cultures, however, there are big differences in the nutritional habits practiced by individual endurance athletes. Some are extremely careful in their eating habits and other weight-management practices, others are utterly careless, and there's a whole spectrum of athletes in between.

THE NUTRITIONAL HABITS OF ELITE ENDURANCE ATHLETES ARE MORE VARIED THAN THEIR TRAINING METHODS.

Sports nutritionists generally hate to admit it, but the prevalence of championship-caliber endurance athletes who maintain low-quality diets is strong proof that at least some gifted individuals can reach the top of their sports with nutritional habits that are far sloppier than their training methods. Nobody wins championships on poor training. Swimmer Michael Phelps's famous 12,000-calories-a-day training diet includes more than a few "empty calories" from sources such as chocolate-chip pancakes and sugary energy drinks. Runner Anthony Famiglietti, a two-time Olympian and winner of multiple U.S. championships, proudly included a segment entitled "World's Worst Diet" in his self-produced DVD *Run Like Hell*. And there are many other examples. If diet is so critical to endurance performance, then how can the likes of Phelps and Famiglietti dominate on such junky diets?

The answer to this question is fourfold. First, world-class athletes have genes that are so favorable to leanness that they can generally eat more than others without gaining too much weight. Second, world-class athletes burn prodigious numbers of calories in their training—far more than most amateur athletes do—which creates further separation between the volume of low-quality foods they can eat with impunity and the volume we can eat. Third, there is a growing body of evidence that exercise can actually make up for a nutrient-poor diet in certain ways by mimicking some of the beneficial effects of vitamins, minerals, and phytonutrients. For example, in a 2009 study published in *Nutrition*, Brazilian researchers reported that exercise completely counteracted the weakening effect of a nutrient-poor diet on the antioxidant defense systems of laboratory animals (Teixeira et al. 2009). Finally, not all world-class endurance athletes can eat a lot of junk without sabotaging their performance. I have spoken with many world-class endurance athletes who say they pay a price they can feel and measure when they stray from the dietary rules that work best for them. In fact, the aforementioned Anthony Famiglietti completely transformed his lifelong pizza-and-candy diet in 2007, after it finally caught up with him in the form of chronic sinus infections, fatigue, and plummeting performance in training and races. Now he eats like Dr. Andrew Weil.

What this means for you is that you cannot use every elite endurance athlete as a dietary role model. Some of them eat in ways that would undoubtedly make you flabby and slow, even if you scaled back the calories. It's different with training. As I suggested above, most elite athletes in each endurance sport train similarly, because generally the training methods that work best for one of them work best for nearly all of them. So you can train effectively by copying what any chosen elite athlete does and scaling it back appropriately. With diet, however, you would be making a gamble.

Nevertheless, there is interest in knowing how top endurance athletes do eat, and there's no harm in imitating particular habits of individual athletes that you believe would work for you, too. With these ideas in mind I have collected one-day food diaries from fourteen of the world's best endurance athletes. I did not select them because they eat a certain way or because they model something close to the Racing Weight system. I simply made a wish list of champions and record breakers I admire and asked each of them to let the readers of this book peek inside their kitchens, as it were.

Again, these diets are not presented to you as models to follow blindly, although you certainly could do worse than to follow any one of them blindly. Instead I present them as a special source of real-world information that you are free to combine with the guidelines and recommendations in Chapters 7 through 10 of this book and your own needs and preferences to create a customized Racing Weight regimen that works best for you.

> THESE DIETS ARE NOT PRESENTED TO YOU AS MODELS TO FOLLOW BLINDLY, ALTHOUGH YOU CERTAINLY COULD DO WORSE.

JEREMIAH BISHOP

is a professional mountain bike racer with the MonaVie Cannondale team. Based in Harrisonburg, Virginia, Bishop is the winner of multiple national championships in marathon and short-track cross-country racing. Despite his high fitness level and clean diet, Bishop has high blood pressure due to genetic inheritance, which he is able to control without medication. The following one-day food journal is from an early-season training period when Bishop was intentionally eating 200 to 400 fewer calories than his body burned daily.

BREAKFAST
1 cup of oatmeal with raisins and cranberries
Optygen HP (herbal supplement)
2 cups of coffee
2 tsp. of flax oil
1 shot of MonaVie Active (açai juice supplement)

WORKOUT
2 bottles of Cytomax sports drink; 1 bottle of water;
2 Cytomax gels; 1 PowerBar
Post-workout: Cytomax recovery drink

LUNCH
Italian wedding soup
Turkey sandwich with provolone
Salad (mixed greens, carrots, cherry tomatoes)
Fresca

AFTERNOON SNACK
Fig Newman cookies
Raw Revolution bar
Black tea

DINNER
Large mixed green salad with smoked salmon, grated parmesan cheese,
    tomatoes, carrots, olives, mandarin ginger dressing
MonaVie Pulse
Red yeast rice (for treating high cholesterol)
Bio 35 Multivitamin

ANNA CUMMINS

of Bellevue, Washington, is a rower who won a gold medal in the 2008 Olympic Women's Eight and a silver medal in the same event at Athens in 2004. She is also a three-time world champion. Following is a typical day's menu during Cummins's training for Beijing, when she ate more carefully than ever in search of peak performance. "The key for me to obtain my optimal racing weight," she says, "was to eat however much I felt like eating, but to try for as many fresh fruits, veggies, and lean meats as possible." For Cummins, this meant cutting processed carbohydrates from her diet (bread, pasta, etc.) as well as foods high in sugar. She began making more frequent trips to the grocery store and preparing her meals. As a result of the changes made to her diet, Cummins found that her body became stronger and more lean for competition.

BREAKFAST
1½ cups oatmeal with a handful of walnuts, handful of berries (frozen or fresh), whole banana, dash of cinnamon, splash of milk or rice milk, sprinkle of brown sugar
1 tall glass of water to take a multivitamin and fish oil (2–3 capsules)

WORKOUT 1
1 water bottle of diluted GU$_2$O
Post-workout: Banana with peanut butter or almond butter and/or Lara bar; water bottle or a small coffee with milk and sugar

WORKOUT 2 *(strength training or light run, row, or ergometer)*
Water

MORNING SNACK
3 eggs, handful of cherry tomatoes, half of a small avocado sprinkled with salt, pepper, parmesan cheese
One piece of whole-grain toast
Small bowl of fresh fruit (5–7 strawberries)
Water

WORKOUT 3
1 bottle of water; 1 water bottle of diluted GU$_2$O
Pre-workout: Banana with almond butter or peanut butter and/or Lara bar and/or handful of trail mix

DINNER
Baby carrots dipped in hummus
Grilled chicken breast (rubbed with salt, pepper, olive oil, spices)
1 piece of corn
Spinach salad with toasted slivered almonds, cherry tomatoes, green onions, sliced mushrooms
Homemade dressing (salt, pepper, olive oil, white wine vinegar, splash of juice/ sugar)
1 sliced orange
1 piece of fresh bread from the local bakery served with butter
Water

EVENING SNACK
Whole peeled grapefruit
Handful of trail mix or nuts
1 tall glass of water to take a multivitamin and fish oil (2–3 capsules)

RYAN HALL of Mammoth Lakes, California, is the American record holder in the half-marathon (59:43) and the fastest American-born marathoner of all time (2:06:17). The food diary below was recorded a couple of weeks after Hall finished 3rd in the 2009 Boston Marathon, when he was staying at the Olympic Training Center in Chula Vista, California, "where they provide some pretty incredibly tasty and healthy eats," he said. "I usually don't eat this gourmet at home in Mammoth."

(Note: Ryan drinks 20 oz. water when he wakes up every day.)

BREAKFAST
1 cup Trader Joe's Flax Crunch cereal with Cytomax recovery shake (1 scoop) substituted for milk
1 Tbsp. of Trader Joe's sunflower seed butter

WORKOUT 1 *(run plus calisthenics)*
Lots of water

MORNING SNACK
1 piece sourdough bread with 1 Tbsp. almond butter

LUNCH
4–6 oz. steak
4–6 oz. polenta with sautéed mushrooms and onions
2–4 oz. orzo with feta and spinach
2 cups steamed veggies (broccoli, cauliflower, zucchini, yellow squash, carrots)

AFTERNOON SNACK
Sunflower-seed butter on two pieces of sourdough bread

WORKOUT 2 *(bike ride, gym workout, self-massage)*
Water

DINNER
Spinach salad with grape tomatoes, green and red peppers, mushrooms, cottage
 cheese, and Caesar dressing
4 oz. pork with ½ cup applesauce
1 cup steamed broccoli
¾ cup chipotle polenta
Piece of French bread
½ cup pasta
½ cup baked beans

EVENING SNACK
Handful of trail mix

SCOTT JUREK

of Seattle, Washington, is one of America's most accomplished ultrarunners. He has won the Western States 100 seven times, the Badwater Ultramarathon twice, and many other major ultramarathons around the world. He is also a vegan, which means he consumes no animal or animal-derived foods of any kind. Jurek explains his diet: "I eat organic foods as much as possible (probably 90 percent of my diet), and over the last year I have been trying to eat more locally grown, seasonal foods. I try to get people to think about what I eat rather than what I do not eat, as that is how I look at it." As a vegan, Jurek recognizes the importance of finding healthy alternatives when he chooses to cut something out of his diet. He focuses on eating healthy fats, whole grains, legumes, soy protein (via tempeh, tofu, miso, and fermented soy powder), nuts, seeds,

fruits, and vegetables. During peak training Jurek eats about 5,000 calories a day. Here's a one-day snapshot of his diet:

WORKOUT 1 *(run, core strength, stretching)*
CLIF shot electrolyte drink; water

BREAKFAST

2–3 servings of Green Magma probiotics supplement

Carbohydrate-protein smoothie (usually a mix of soaked almonds, dates, hemp seeds, bananas, blueberries, hemp and/or fermented soy protein powder, vanilla, maca powder, sea salt)

1–2 servings of soy yogurt mixed with 2–3 Tbsp. ground flax seeds

3–4 pieces of whole fruit

2–4 cups whole-grain cereal with dried fruit (muesli or hot cereal, mixed-grain porridge or polenta, or raw buckwheat porridge) and/or 2–4 pieces of Ezekiel sprouted-grain bread with 2–4 Tbsp. raw almond butter

MORNING SNACK

Herbal tea (raw yerba mate or green tea), or rarely one shot of espresso

Piece of fruit or energy bar

LUNCH

Large mixed green salad (dark leafy greens, sprouts, raw kale, arugula, etc., with mixed tomatoes, cucumbers, carrots, etc.)

Whole grains or whole-grain pasta, or bread, legumes (beans or lentils)

AFTERNOON SNACK

Fruit, energy bar, nuts, seeds, or dried fruit

WORKOUT 2
CLIF shot electrolyte drink; water

DINNER

Large salad (similar to lunch but with different greens and veggies like raw cabbage) or steamed or sautéed dark greens such as kale or collards, steamed vegetables, sautéed tofu or tempeh or legumes (lentils, pinto or garbanzo beans)

Potatoes, yams, squash, or whole-grain/sprouted pasta or whole grains (brown rice, quinoa, etc.)

For dessert, a homemade mixture of fresh fruit, dates, and nuts or dark chocolate

MEGAN KALMOE

(rear in photo) placed 1st with Ellen Tomek in the 2008 U.S. Olympic Trials Women's Double Sculls and was a 2005 under-23 world champion in the Women's Four. Here's how she eats during the peak summer training period.

BREAKFAST

1 cup bran flakes

½ cup organic skim milk

¼ cup blueberries

1 cup orange juice (not from concentrate)

1 whole-wheat English muffin

1 Tbsp. Smart Balance

2 Tbsp. raspberry jam

8 oz. regular drip coffee, black

WORKOUT 1

20 oz. Gatorade (from powder mix); 32 oz. water; 1 GU packet (if doing anaerobic threshold or power work)

Post-workout: 1 CLIF bar; 1 banana; 8 oz. coffee

MORNING SNACK

2 whole eggs, scrambled

2 slices whole-wheat toast

1 Tbsp. Smart Balance

8 oz. orange juice

LUNCH

1 serving leftover homemade lasagna (made with regular pasta, part-skim ricotta, part-skim mozzarella, zucchini, and ground turkey)

1½ cups raw carrots

¼ cup hummus

12 oz. brewed iced tea

AFTERNOON SNACK

1 medium apple

2 Tbsp. chunky peanut butter

2 white cheddar rice cakes

WORKOUT 2

20 oz. Gatorade (from powder); 20 oz. water

DINNER

5 slices homemade pizza (homemade white dough, homemade tomato sauce, part-skim mozzarella, fresh homegrown basil, vine tomatoes, fresh whole garlic)

Small green salad with cucumber, carrot, onion, sunflower seeds

1½ Tbsp. raspberry-walnut salad dressing

12 oz. seltzer water

1 slice angel food cake

½ cup homemade blueberry sauce (blueberries, sugar, lemon juice)

8 oz. water

HUNTER KEMPER is a three-time U.S. Olympian in triathlon, a five-time national champion, and a two-time Pan Am Games medalist. Here's what Kemper eats on a typical training day.

BREAKFAST

Full bowl of Wheaties with flaxseed sprinkled on top and skim milk

WORKOUT 1

24 oz. Amino Vital Endurance

Pre-workout: Banana

Post-workout: Protein bar with at least 20 grams of protein

WORKOUT 2

16 oz. Amino Vital Endurance

SECOND BREAKFAST *(post-workout)*

3–4-egg omelet with vegetables, ham, and American cheese

Plain bagel

2 small pancakes, lightly buttered

16 oz. fruit smoothie with a spoonful of flaxseed

16 oz. Amino Vital Pro

8 oz. orange juice

LUNCH

Turkey and cheese sandwich on a toasted whole-wheat bagel

24 oz. Amino Vital Pro

1 cup strawberry-banana yogurt

16 oz. water

Fruit medley (sliced apple, sliced banana, grapes, strawberries)

WORKOUT 3
48 oz. Amino Vital Endurance; 1 carbohydrate gel; 1 energy bar
Post-workout: Protein bar (at least 20 grams of protein); 24 oz. water and 24 oz. Amino Vital Pro for afternoon hydration

DINNER
Salad with feta cheese, pecans, and sesame dressing
Full plate of pasta with grilled chicken (1 full chicken breast)
2 pieces garlic toast
24 oz. water

EVENING SNACK
Bowl of Wheaties with skim milk and sprinkled with raisins

TERA MOODY

is a runner based in Boulder, Colorado, who finished in 5th place in the 2008 U.S. Olympic Team Trials of the Women's Marathon. She runs twice a day often, but not always. Here's her typical eating on a two-run day.

WORKOUT 1
Water
Pre-workout: Oatmeal with cinnamon; decaf coffee with soymilk; water
Post-workout: Bread with peanut butter; grapefruit; water

BREAKFAST
Scrambled eggs with bell peppers and mushrooms
Herbal tea

MORNING SNACK
Almonds
Liquid iron supplement
Emergen-C vitamin drink

LUNCH
Plain turkey sandwich
Water

WORKOUT 2
Water
Pre-workout: PowerBar Endurance drink
Post-workout: Pear

DINNER
Steak
Steamed asparagus with olive oil, garlic, salt, pepper
Baked potato
Glass of red wine

EVENING SNACK
Dark chocolate

CHIP PETERSON

won the 2005 World Open Water Swimming Championships 10K race and took silver in the 5K when he was only 18 years old. Two years later he won both events in the U.S. National Open Water Swimming Championships. Peterson set several school records as a swimmer at the University of North Carolina. Here's how he typically eats during the off-season.

WORKOUT 1
Water
Pre-workout: Cereal bar
Post-workout: Bagel with cream cheese, egg, and bacon; water

WORKOUT 2 *(strength training)*
Water
Post–workout: Gatorade recovery shake

LUNCH
Mediterranean spicy chicken wrap
Greek salad
Hummus with pita
Water

WORKOUT 3
Water
Post-workout: Apple and peanut butter; water

DINNER *(from dining hall)*
Turkey stir fry with white rice
Sesame tofu
Fruit salad cup
Cookie
Water

KIKKAN RANDALL

is an elite cross-country skier who lives in Anchorage, Alaska. She represented the United States in the 2002 and 2006 Winter Olympics. In 2008 she became the first American woman to win a World Cup cross-country ski race. Here's what Kikkan ate on September 15, 2009.

BREAKFAST
1 egg
½ cup pure egg whites
2 Tbsp. shredded cheddar cheese
2 slices Canadian bacon
2 slices whole-wheat toast
2 Tbsp. raspberry jam
4 oz. orange juice
8 oz. tea with skim milk and sugar

WORKOUT 1 *(skate rollerskiing)*
24–32 oz. PowerBar Endurance sports drink
Post-workout: 20 oz. PowerBar Recovery drink; 6 oz. fat-free yogurt; 1 medium banana

LUNCH
6-inch Subway sandwich (turkey, pepper-jack cheese, veggies, honey mustard on wheat bread)
1 small bag of Baked Lays potato chips
12 oz. lemonade
1 white-chocolate-chip macadamia nut cookie

AFTERNOON SNACK
1 cup Frosted Mini-Wheats cereal
⅔ cup skim milk
1 skim mozzarella cheese stick

WORKOUT 2 (*skate rollerskiing*)
24–32 oz. PowerBar Endurance sports drink
Post-workout: 20 oz. PowerBar Recovery drink; 2 slices
whole-wheat bread; 2 Tbsp. peanut butter; 1 Tbsp. honey

DINNER
Steak fajitas (3 oz. marinated steak, 1 cup kidney beans, 1 cup cooked onions
and bell peppers, ¼ cup shredded cheddar cheese, ½ cup fresh spinach,
½ cup fresh tomatoes, 2 large tortillas)
20 oz. water

EVENING SNACK
1 white-chocolate-chip macadamia nut cookie

SHANNON ROWBURY of San Francisco, California, is a middle-distance runner whose achievements include an NCAA national championship title in the mile, U.S. national championship titles at 1,500 and 3,000 meters, and an appearance in the finals of the 2008 Beijing Olympic 1,500 meters.

BREAKFAST
½ sprouted-grain English muffin with local honey and chunky
almond butter
½ banana
Dark-roast coffee with lots of milk
Water

WORKOUT 1
Carbohydrate-protein sports drink
Post-workout: ½ protein bar; apple; water

LUNCH
2 eggs scrambled with onion, mushroom, spinach, vine-ripened tomato, sundried
tomato, tofu, and mozzarella
Water

WORKOUT 2
Carbohydrate-protein sports drink

AFTERNOON SNACK
Carrots
Water

DINNER
Broiled salmon
Quinoa
Salad (romaine lettuce, avocado, carrots, tomatoes, olive oil, and balsamic vinegar)
Water
One piece of dark chocolate

EVENING SNACK
Protein powder with milk

PIP TAYLOR created the recipes you'll find in the next chapter. She is not only a talented chef and nutritionist but also a world-class triathlete. The Australian's career highlights include a World Cup triathlon victory, an Australia and Oceana Long-Course Triathlon Championship title, and a 3rd-place finish in the Wildflower Triathlon.

WORKOUT 1
Nothing

BREAKFAST
½ cup raw oats soaked in ½ cup plain low-fat yogurt overnight and then mixed with chopped apple
1 cup mixed berries
Small handful almonds
Water

WORKOUT 2
24 oz. Accelerade Hydro

LUNCH
Sourdough bread sandwich with lettuce, tomato, and tuna
Small tub yogurt
50 grams chocolate
Water

WORKOUT 3
24 oz. Accelerade Hydro
Post-workout: Cranberry Nut Forze bar

DINNER
Salmon fillet
Big salad with greens, roasted sweet potatoes, garlic, green beans, tomatoes, goat cheese
Apple with two slices cheese
Water

CHRISSIE WELLINGTON of England is a two-time winner of the Hawaii Ironman World Championship and has recorded more sub-9-hour Ironman finishes than any other woman. She notes that, in addition to the foods and drinks listed below, in a typical day she drinks water and Cytomax throughout the day (approximately three liters total).

WORKOUT 1
Nothing
Pre-workout: Banana; 2 Tbsp. of honey; 2 Tbsp. peanut butter; cup of coffee with milk

BREAKFAST
"Huge bowl" of porridge oats, all-bran buds, raisins, dried plums, coconut, nuts and seeds, mixed with vanilla yogurt
Cup of tea or coffee

WORKOUT 2
Cytomax sports drink; Muesli bar; carbohydrate gel
Pre-workout: Apple

LUNCH
Two bagel sandwiches with turkey and cheese
Large green salad
Handful of nuts

WORKOUT 3
Nothing
Pre-workout: Banana

DINNER
Beef steak stir fried with vegetables
Rice
Bowl of frozen fruit with yogurt

EVENING SNACK
Small bar of chocolate

SIMON WHITFIELD of Canada won the gold medal in the 2000 Olympic Triathlon in Sydney and the silver medal in the 2008 Olympic Triathlon in Beijing.

BREAKFAST
Koala Kids gluten-free cereal with almond milk and Vega oil blend
Dancing Goats dark coffee from a French press

WORKOUT 1
eLoad sports drink
Pre-workout: Half a pack of Sharkies energy chews
Post-workout: Half a pack of Sharkies energy chews

MORNING SNACK
Ezekiel sprouted-whole-grain English muffin with almond butter and
    orange honey
⅓ avocado with sea salt

WORKOUT 2
1 liter eLoad sports drink
Post-workout: ⅔ avocado with almond crackers; a bit of chocolate (75 percent cacao)

AFTERNOON SNACK
Black French-press coffee
Gluten-free wafer cookies
7 Systems vitamins
Pure blueberry juice

WORKOUT 3
500 ml water
Pre-workout: Pack of Sharkies energy chews
Post-workout: Vega protein shake (Vega oil, almond milk,
        banana, plain low-fat yogurt, 2 cups berries, Vega protein);
        small piece of chocolate

DINNER
Quinoa spinach salad with oranges, avocado, red peppers, curry mustard dressing
Pork tenderloin with maple glaze and garlic tabasco with a spice rub
Red wine (½ glass)

EVENING SNACK
Bowl of Koala Kids cereal with almond milk
Fizzy calcium-magnesium drink

PHIL ZAJICEK

is a professional cyclist who rides for the Health Net team. Not many fruits and vegetables appear in his sample one-day food diary below. That's because Phil has Crohn's disease and has difficulty digesting the fiber in these foods.

BREAKFAST
Oatmeal with brown sugar
Coffee

WORKOUT
Sports drink

LUNCH
Chipotle barbacoa burrito

AFTERNOON SNACK
Salami sandwich

DINNER
Ziti pasta with marinara sauce, parmesan cheese
Glass of red wine

EVENING SNACK
Cereal and milk

THIRTEEN

ENDURANCE FUEL

What would a diet book be without recipes? I'm joking, of course. This is not a diet book in the conventional sense. But it's not so different, either. This book is about weight management for endurance performance, and thus it's largely about food. In the preceding chapters I presented a number of guidelines for food selection and eating. So why shouldn't I present a selection of original meal recipes that are consistent with these guidelines?

Because I'm no chef, that's why! But thankfully my friend Pip Taylor, an Australian elite triathlete, nutritionist, and gourmet cook, is. I asked Pip to create a week's worth of endurance fuel—seven breakfasts, seven lunches, seven dinners, and even seven desserts—and she kindly obliged. Each recipe concludes with a listing of the nutritional facts per serving. Because some minor elements in a recipe (such as a sprinkling of nuts) may vary quite a bit in caloric content, depending upon the specific type used, the calorie counts indicated in the nutritional facts per serving will be based upon the primary ingredients. Most importantly, in addition to being healthful and oriented specifically to the nutrition needs of endurance athletes, these exclusive recipes are also easy to prepare and, most importantly, delicious!

 # BREAKFAST RECIPES

Banana Buttermilk Pancakes with Strawberries, Pecans, and Yogurt

Buttermilk is low in fat, which keeps these banana pancakes fairly low in calories and light in texture. Serve the pancakes with some fresh seasonal fruit, plain yogurt, and some chopped raw pecans.

Serves two.

INGREDIENTS

4 bananas
1 cup all-purpose flour
2 tsp. baking powder
½ tsp. mixed spice (also known as pudding spice)
2 Tbsp. brown sugar (light or dark is fine)
¾ cup well-shaken buttermilk
Fresh hulled and halved strawberries, natural yogurt, and pecans to serve

DIRECTIONS

1. Combine all ingredients except strawberries, yogurt, and pecans in a blender or food processor or alternatively mash bananas, then combine with remaining ingredients and mix well.

2. Heat a nonstick pan over medium heat and pour in batter a half-cup at a time. Cook for 2–3 minutes until bubbles appear on surface and edges start to set. Turn gently and cook a further 1–2 minutes.

3. Remove from pan and keep warm in a 200°F oven or an oven set on low while you continue with remaining batter.

Serve with fruit salad, yogurt, and some chopped pecans.

Nutritional facts per serving (daily value):			
Calories	529	Protein	12 g (24%)
Total Fat	2 g (3%)	Saturated Fat	1 g (4%)
Cholesterol	4 mg (1%)	Carbohydrate	121 g (40%)
Fiber	8 g (31%)	Sugars	47 g
Calcium	410 mg (41%)	Iron	4 mg (24%)

Bircher Muesli

This is a very simple version of soaked, bircher-style muesli. Oats are soaked overnight and the rest of the ingredients are stirred through in the morning. Alternatively, if you forget to do this the night before, add ¼ cup of water to the oats along with berries (if using frozen) and microwave on high for 30 seconds, before stirring in the yogurt and chopped apple. Substitute your favorite seasonal fresh fruits and nuts to mix things up.

Serves one.

INGREDIENTS

¾ cup rolled oats
½ cup plain yogurt
1 cup mixed berries (raspberries, blueberries, etc., frozen or fresh)
1 apple, cored and chopped (leave skin on)
1 Tbsp. raw nuts (almonds, macadamias, walnuts, etc.)

DIRECTIONS

1. The night before, combine oats, yogurt, and berries if you are using frozen ones. Leave covered in the refrigerator.

2. In the morning, stir in chopped apple and berries, if using fresh, and then top with nuts.

Nutritional facts per serving (daily value):			
Calories	452	Protein	15 g (31%)
Total Fat	8 g (13%)	Saturated Fat	3 g (17%)
Cholesterol	16 mg (5%)	Carbohydrate	84 g (28%)
Fiber	11 g (44%)	Sugars	34 g
Calcium	195 mg (19%)	Iron	3 mg (17%)

Breakfast Bread-and-Butter Pudding

This is a satisfying, sticks-to-your-ribs breakfast that is the perfect reward for a hard weekend workout or race.

Serves one to two. (Nutritional analysis for 2 servings.)

INGREDIENTS

2 thick slices sourdough bread, each cut into 8 cubes
2 large eggs, lightly beaten
2 oz. (50 g) ham, diced
½ red bell pepper, diced
¼ cup cherry tomatoes, halved
¼ cup grated cheddar cheese, plus 1 Tbsp. extra
Salt, pepper to taste
Spray oil (to grease pan)

DIRECTIONS

1. Preheat oven to 350°F. Lightly spray a large 1½-cup-capacity oven-proof ramekin dish (or use two regular-size muffin holes).

2. In a medium-size bowl gently combine eggs, ham, red pepper, tomato, and cheese. Fold in cubed bread. Season to taste.

3. Spoon this mixture into prepared ramekin, top with extra grated cheddar, then bake in preheated oven for about 20 minutes until set and golden brown.

4. Let sit for 5 minutes before eating.

Nutritional facts for two servings (daily value):	
Calories............................434	Protein..............24 g (48%)
Total Fat................13 g (20%)	Saturated Fat.......4 g (22%)
Cholesterol.........236 mg (79%)	Carbohydrate.... 55 g (18%)
Fiber......................4 g (14%)	Sugars........................ 2 g
Calcium .... 189 mg (19%)	Iron .... 4 mg (22%)

Breakfast Smoothie

An on-the-go breakfast alternative. The almond butter adds protein and essential fats to help you feel and stay full.

Serves one.

INGREDIENTS

1 banana
½ cup blueberries (frozen are best in this recipe)
½ cup natural yogurt
½ cup milk or orange juice
1 Tbsp. almond butter

DIRECTIONS

Blend all ingredients and drink.

Nutritional facts per serving (daily value):	
Calories............................389	Protein.............. 14 g (28%)
Total Fat.................. 17 g (26%)	Saturated Fat.......7 g (33%)
Cholesterol............. 28 mg (9%)	Carbohydrate.... 52 g (17%)
Fiber...................... 6 g (23%)	Sugars...................... 35 g
Calcium ....303 mg (30%)	Iron .... 1 mg (5%)

Corn Cakes

These corn cakes are great for breakfast but can also make a tasty lunch or even dinner, served with some smoked salmon and crème fraiche, or with a poached egg and baby spinach.

Makes 10–12 corn cakes—enough to serve three or four people for break-fast or two or three for lunch.

INGREDIENTS

1 cup all-purpose flour
1 tsp. baking powder
½ tsp. smoked paprika, optional. (*Note:* This is not the same
    as paprika, so if you can't find smoked paprika then omit it.)
3 green onions (scallions), finely chopped

1 Tbsp. finely chopped fresh parsley

2 large eggs, lightly beaten

1 14-oz. can creamed corn

1½ cups corn kernels (freshly cut from the cob are best but otherwise use drained, tinned corn kernels)

Fresh rocket leaves, to serve

1 avocado, pitted and sliced, to serve

2 fresh tomatoes, sliced, to serve

DIRECTIONS

1. Preheat oven to 200°F. Mix together flour, baking powder, smoked paprika, green onions, and parsley. Add egg and creamed corn and mix well. Stir in kernels, then season to taste.

2. Heat a nonstick pan on medium heat and coat lightly with olive oil. Cook heaped tablespoons of mixture, two or three at a time, for 2–3 minutes until the edges start to look cooked. Carefully turn and continue cooking a further minute or two.

3. Keep warm in a baking dish in the oven while you cook the remaining mix.

4. Serve corn cakes with rocket leaves, sliced avocado, and tomato.

Nutritional facts for four servings (daily value):	
Calories.....................377	Protein.............13 g (25%)
Total Fat.................12 g (18%)	Saturated Fat........2 g (11%)
Cholesterol.........106 mg (35%)	Carbohydrate....61 g (20%)
Fiber........................9 g (36%)	Sugars.........................7 g
Calcium ....111 mg (11%)	Iron ....4 mg (22%)

Fruit Toast with Honey, Cinnamon, Ricotta, and Fresh Figs

When figs are not in season use any other sliced fresh fruit—try blueberries, a banana, strawberries, or a peach.

Serves one.

INGREDIENTS

2 slices thick-cut sourdough fruit bread

5 oz. low-fat fresh ricotta cheese

1 Tbsp. honey

½ tsp. ground cinnamon

2 fresh figs, sliced (alternatively use fresh apple slices, apricot,
    or halved seedless grapes)

DIRECTIONS

1. Mix together ricotta, honey, and cinnamon.

2. Meanwhile toast fruit bread lightly. Spread with ricotta mix, then top
with fresh figs or alternative fruit of choice.

Nutritional facts per serving (daily value):	
Calories............................527	Protein...............21 g (41%)
Total Fat.................21 g (32%)	Saturated Fat......12 g (61%)
Cholesterol...........71 mg (24%)	Carbohydrate....69 g (23%)
Fiber........................ 6 g (23%)	Sugars...................... 37 g
Calcium .... 374 mg (37%)	Iron ....3 mg (16%)

Toasted Granola

Although this recipe requires a little cooking time, it is a great cereal to
have in the cupboard. Use the listed ingredients as a starting point—
change the fruits, seeds, and nuts to your favorites or mix it up differently
each time. If you have a very large baking dish it is worth making in sufficient quantity to fill it, as the cereal will last up to a month stored in an
airtight container. Otherwise, halve the ingredients and bake for a little
less time. Note that this recipe requires a convection oven.

Makes roughly 20 1-cup servings.

INGREDIENTS

10 cups rolled oats

2½ cups rye flakes

2½ cups barley flakes

2½ cups mixed raw, unsalted seeds and nuts (e.g., pepitas,
    pumpkin seeds, sunflower seeds, macadamias, almonds, hazelnuts)

½ cup shredded coconut

½ cup honey mixed with ½ cup warm water to dissolve

2½ cups mixed chopped dried fruits (e.g., sultanas, cranberries,
blueberries, apple, apricot, figs)

DIRECTIONS

1. Preheat convection oven to 350°F. Mix together grains (oats, barley, rye), nuts, seeds, and coconut and place in a large baking tray. Add the water and honey mix and toss well to coat the dry mix, breaking up any clumps.

2. Bake in the oven for 40–60 minutes, stirring about every 10 minutes so that the mix browns evenly. Remove from oven and toss with dried fruits.

3. When completely cool, store in an airtight container.

Serve with milk, yogurt, and fresh fruit.

Nutritional facts per serving (daily value):	
Calories 829	Protein .... 26 g (52%)
Total Fat .... 22 g (33%)	Saturated Fat .... 4 g (20%)
Cholesterol .... 0 mg (0%)	Carbohydrate .. 143 g (48%)
Fiber .... 24 g (95%)	Sugars .... 15 g
Calcium .... 93 mg (9%)	Iron .... 7 mg (38%)

LUNCH RECIPES

Asian Pork Burgers in Pita Bread

These burgers can be served in any type of bun or between toasted focaccia slices instead of the pita pockets.

Serves four.

INGREDIENTS

1¼ lbs. lean ground pork (or ground chicken)

3 green onions (scallions), chopped finely

3 cloves garlic, crushed

1 Tbsp. finely chopped fresh coriander leaves plus 2 Tbsp.
   loosely packed leaves

2 carrots cut into strips with a vegetable peeler (or grated)

1 long red chili, finely chopped

1 large egg, lightly beaten

Pinch salt

1 small head radicchio sliced into thin strips (or use purple cabbage)

1 tsp. sweet chili sauce

1 tsp. soy sauce

2 tsp. rice wine vinegar

8 leaves butter lettuce (kept whole)

4 small whole-grain pita pockets, halved crosswise

DIRECTIONS

1. In a large mixing bowl combine ground pork, green onions, garlic, chili, coriander, salt, and egg, and mix well. Shape into eight patties and leave to chill in the refrigerator for 15–20 minutes (or until needed).

2. Meanwhile, combine sweet chili sauce, soy sauce, and rice wine vinegar in a medium-size bowl. Add carrot, radicchio, and coriander leaves and toss to mix well.

3. Remove patties from refrigerator and cook on a preheated barbecue grill or frying pan over medium heat until completely cooked through (about 3 minutes per side).

4. Serve in pita pockets with carrot and radicchio salad and butter lettuce.

Nutritional facts per serving (daily value):	
Calories 482	Protein .... 33 g (66%)
Total Fat .... 25 g (39%)	Saturated Fat .... 7 g (35%)
Cholesterol .... 179 mg (60%)	Carbohydrate ..... 32 g (11%)
Fiber .... 6 g (22%)	Sugars .... 8 g
Calcium .... 141 mg (14%)	Iron .... 4 mg (23%)

Baked Potato Stuffed with Mixed Mushrooms, Sour Cream, and Chives

There are endless options for baked potato fillings. Other great options include chili con carne, creamed corn with chicken and cheddar, herbs with chopped ham and a little cheese and a can of baked beans. Also try using a sweet potato for something different. To speed things up a little you can cook the potatoes in the microwave, but if you have time and prefer a crisper shell, bake in a hot oven.

Serves two.

INGREDIENTS

1 tsp. olive oil
1 lb. mixed mushrooms such as Swiss brown, enoki, or pine, roughly chopped
½ cup chicken stock
1 Tbsp. chopped fresh chives
2 Tbsp. light sour cream
2 medium/large russet potatoes or sweet potatoes

DIRECTIONS

1. To prepare potatoes in the microwave: Pierce potatoes several times with a fork or skewer. Microwave on high for 12–15 minutes until cooked through when tested.

2. To prepare potatoes in the oven: Preheat oven to 400°F. Place potatoes (or sweet potato if you prefer) on an oven tray and bake for about 40 minutes until cooked through when tested.

3. To prepare mushroom filling: Wipe mushrooms clean with a paper towel (never wash mushrooms as they will soak up excess water).

4. Heat olive oil in a nonstick pan over medium heat. Add garlic and cook, stirring for 30 seconds. Add mushrooms and stock and continue to cook for a further 5 minutes until the mushrooms are soft and cooked through and the liquid has almost completely evaporated. Add chives and stir.

5. Remove potatoes from microwave or oven, and make a cross through the middle of each, squeezing to open out. Fill potatoes with mushroom mixture and then top each one with a spoonful of sour cream.

Nutritional facts per serving (daily value):	
Calories.............................370	Protein.............. 15 g (30%)
Total Fat.....................6 g (9%)	Saturated Fat.........2 g (9%)
Cholesterol..............8 mg (3%)	Carbohydrate.... 68 g (23%)
Fiber.......................11 g (45%)	Sugars..........................9 g
Calcium ....59 mg (6%)	Iron..................3 mg (18%)

Zucchini, Mint, and Feta Filo Pies

These are quick to make—most of the required time goes toward waiting for them to bake while they are in the oven. You could try other vegetables such as cooked spinach, chopped asparagus, green peas, corn, cherry and sun-dried tomatoes, and also vary the herbs to suit your taste.

Makes eight pies or will serve four as a light lunch.

INGREDIENTS

½ small onion, finely chopped
4 small-to-medium zucchinis, grated
4 medium eggs, lightly beaten
⅓ cup fresh mint leaves
3½ oz. feta cheese, crumbled
Salt and pepper to taste
8 sheets filo pastry (*Note:* Look for it in the supermarket freezer
    section.)
Oil spray
Premium-quality store-bought tomato chutney to serve (optional)
Salad leaves to serve (optional)

DIRECTIONS

1. Preheat oven to 350°F. Make the filling first, then set aside as you prepare the pie cases. Put grated zucchini into a strainer and push gently to remove some excess water, then put into a mixing bowl. Add onion, eggs, feta, and finely chopped mint leaves and mix, then season to taste. Set aside.

2. Try to work quickly once the filo pastry is opened so that it does not dry out. You can buy a little extra time by covering it with a dry tea towel topped with a damp cloth. Place filo in a pile so that there are eight layers on top of each other. Cut into eight pieces approximately 4 inches square.

Spray eight holes of a regular-size muffin tin lightly with oil, then take two layers of filo and place into each hole, pushing down to minimize overhang. Spray the pastry lightly, then place another two layers of filo on top, positioning them at right angles so that the whole of the muffin hole is covered. They will look a little rough and wrinkly.

3. Spoon zucchini mixture into cases until they are two-thirds full. Do not overfill as they will puff slightly as they bake and may overflow.

4. Cook in oven for 30–35 minutes until set and golden brown. Let sit for about 15 minutes before removing from muffin tin. Serve warm or at room temperature with chutney and salad.

5. Leftovers can be stored in an airtight container in the refrigerator.

Nutritional facts per serving (one serving equals one of eight pies made):			
Calories	288	Protein	14 g (29%)
Total Fat	13 g (20%)	Saturated Fat	6 g (29%)
Cholesterol	208 mg (69%)	Carbohydrate	30 g (10%)
Fiber	4 g (14%)	Sugars	5 g
Calcium	196 mg (20%)	Iron	4 mg (21%)

Fish Tacos with Avocado, Tomato, and Corn Salsa

A deceptive variety of nutrition is delivered in this delectably simple lunch recipe.

Serves two.

INGREDIENTS

2 7-oz. firm white fish fillets such as snapper or blue eye,
    cut into three strips
1 tsp. ground cumin
1 tsp. paprika
1 tsp. olive oil
1 cup fresh corn kernels (or canned corn, drained)
2 small tomatoes, chopped roughly
1 avocado, chopped

1 lime, juiced, plus extra lime wedges to serve (optional)
Sea salt and black pepper
1 small red chili, finely chopped
1 tsp. fresh coriander leaves (cilantro), finely chopped
4 small soft wheat-tortilla wraps

DIRECTIONS

1. In a shallow dish combine olive oil, paprika, and cumin and mix to a paste. Add fish strips and turn gently to coat. Set aside while you prepare the salsa.

2. Combine corn (if using fresh corn, cut the kernels from the cob and then cook in boiling water for 2 minutes) and tomato with chili, lime juice, and chopped coriander. Add chopped avocado, seasoning to taste, and mix gently.

3. Heat a frying pan to a medium-high heat. Add fish to pan and cook for 2–3 minutes (depending on thickness of fish), then turn and cook a further 1–2 minutes.

4. Meanwhile, heat tortillas by wrapping in foil and placing in oven on low temperature or by wrapping in a paper towel and microwaving for 30 seconds (or according to packet instructions).

5. Place warm tortilla on a plate, top with strips of fish and salsa. Serve two tortillas per person with lime wedges.

Nutritional facts per serving (daily value):	
Calories 635	Protein .... 46 g (92%)
Total Fat .... 25 g (38%)	Saturated Fat .... 4 g (20%)
Cholesterol .... 86 mg (29%)	Carbohydrate .... 63 g (21%)
Fiber .... 13 g (52%)	Sugars .... 7 g
Calcium .... 159 mg (16%)	Iron .... 5 mg (30%)

Goat Feta, Spinach, and Potato Frittata

Frittatas make a quick breakfast, lunch, or even dinner when served with a simple green salad and/or some crusty bread. They can be eaten hot, at room temperature, or cold, so you can prepare them in advance easily. Any variations of ingredients can be used; try using combinations of mushrooms, ham, tomato, roasted pumpkin—even cooked pasta can be added.

Serves two.

INGREDIENTS

Half of a small onion, thinly sliced
4 large eggs, lightly beaten
2½ oz. goat feta cheese (low-fat), crumbled
1 cup baby spinach leaves, washed and dried
¾ lb. potatoes, skin on
Sea salt and pepper to taste
Olive oil

DIRECTIONS

1. Preheat an oven broiler/grill to high. Meanwhile, cook potatoes until tender either in boiling water for several minutes or covered in the microwave. Slice into ½-inch thick slices and set aside.

2. Heat a nonstick oven-proof frying pan over medium heat and spray with a small amount of olive oil. Add onion and cook for 2–3 minutes, stirring until soft and starting to turn golden. Add potato slices and spinach and toss gently, adding salt and pepper to taste. Pour over eggs, stir gently from the edges of the pan inwards for 30 seconds, then crumble goat cheese over the top.

3. Allow to cook over a low/medium heat for 5–6 minutes until nearly set. Turn off the heat and place pan under the hot grill for 2–3 minutes until frittata is puffed and golden.

4. Let sit in pan for about 5 minutes, then slide out onto a board and cut into wedges.

Nutritional facts per serving (daily value):	
Calories.....................384	Protein.............. 21 g (42%)
Total Fat.................. 20 g (31%)	Saturated Fat.......9 g (43%)
Cholesterol........454 mg (151%)	Carbohydrate.... 30 g (10%)
Fiber.......................4 g (18%)	Sugars........................ 5 g
Calcium .... 261 mg (26%)	Iron ....3 mg (19%)

Salad of Roasted Pumpkin, Chickpeas, Red Onion, Chili, and Basil

This salad can be eaten hot or at room temperature or stored in the refrigerator and eaten cold the next day. It is substantial enough to be eaten on its own but also makes a good accompaniment for dinner with a grilled piece of steak, chicken, or fish.

Serves two.

INGREDIENTS

1 lb. (500 g) pumpkin, deseeded and chopped into ½-inch cubes
1 large red onion cut into 8 wedges (keeping core intact)
½ Tbsp. olive oil
15 oz. canned chickpeas, drained
½ tsp. chili flakes
2 Tbsp. shredded fresh basil leaves
Sea salt and black pepper to taste

DIRECTIONS

1. Preheat oven to 390°F. In a baking dish combine pumpkin, onion, and olive oil. Sprinkle with chili flakes and sea salt to taste.

2. Roast for 40 minutes until pumpkin is golden and starting to caramelize. Add chickpeas and basil to pumpkin and toss gently.

Nutritional facts per serving (daily value):	
Calories............................580	Protein..............27 g (55%)
Total Fat.................. 11 g (17%)	Saturated Fat.........1 g (7%)
Cholesterol...............0 mg (0%)	Carbohydrate....99 g (33%)
Fiber...................... 24 g (97%)	Sugars...................... 20 g
Calcium .... 201 mg (20%)	Iron ....10 mg (55%)

Thai Chicken and Rice-Noodle Salad

If you're going to try this recipe, note that it is worthwhile to poach a whole chicken at once. It is a healthy way to cook and will give you a very tender chicken that can be used for sandwiches and salads, tossed with pasta, and so on over several days. The liquid can also be retained and used as a stock in other recipes such as soups and risottos. Note that it takes a while to make this recipe—three hours—but you can cut down the preparation time significantly by purchasing a precooked rotisserie chicken.

Serves two.

INGREDIENTS

4-oz. packet rice vermicelli noodles
1 cup cherry tomatoes, halved
2 small cucumbers, cut into thin strips
1½ cups poached chicken meat stripped into bite-sized pieces
2 Tbsp. chopped fresh mint leaves
2 Tbsp. chopped fresh coriander leaves
1 Tbsp. sweet chili sauce
1 Tbsp. rice wine vinegar
½ tsp. sesame oil
2 tsp. fish sauce

DIRECTIONS

1. Prepare rice noodles according to packet instructions, drain, rinse under cold water, and drain again.

2. Combine sweet chili sauce, fish sauce, rice wine vinegar, and sesame oil, then set aside.

3. In a large bowl combine noodles, tomatoes, cucumber, chicken, and herbs, then toss with sauces and serve.

To poach a whole chicken:

INGREDIENTS

200 fluid oz. water
4 green onions (scallions), chopped roughly
12 cloves garlic, crushed
2-inch piece fresh ginger stem, chopped into three pieces
1½ Tbsp. sea salt
1½ Tbsp. whole peppercorns
1 stick lemon grass (white part only), crushed with the back of a knife
1 bunch coriander, stems only
2½–3¼ lbs. whole chicken, cavity cleaned

DIRECTIONS

1. Place all ingredients except chicken in a large pot and bring to a boil. Reduce heat and submerge chicken in liquid. Simmer gently for 15 minutes, then turn off heat.

2. Cover and let chicken rest in stock for 2–3 hours to cook through completely.

3. Carefully remove chicken, keeping strained stock for other recipes, and when cool enough to handle, strip meat away from bones, removing skin. Refrigerate until required unless using straight away.

Nutritional facts per serving (daily value):	
Calories.............................406	Protein.............. 36 g (72%)
Total Fat..................... 6 g (9%)	Saturated Fat.........1 g (7%)
Cholesterol...........88 mg (29%)	Carbohydrate.... 50 g (17%)
Fiber........................5 g (19%)	Sugars......................... 5 g
Calcium ....127 mg (13%)	Iron ....3 mg (19%)

White Bean Puree on Rye Toast with Tomatoes and Basil

Here's a quick lunch that provides all the essentials. Canned beans are a great staple to have in the cupboard and are an easy and tasty protein source that can be added to salads, pastas, or sandwiches, as in this recipe.

Serves one.

INGREDIENTS

1 clove garlic
15½-oz. can white cannellini or butter beans
1 fresh tomato, chopped
1 tsp. balsamic vinegar
¼ cup finely shredded basil leaves
2 slices rye bread, lightly toasted
Salt and pepper

DIRECTIONS

1. Combine garlic and beans in a food processer or blender and puree, then season to taste. Gently toss together tomato, basil, and balsamic vinegar in a small bowl.

2. Pile bean puree onto rye toast, then top with tomato and basil mixture. Add extra freshly ground black pepper.

Nutritional facts per serving (daily value):			
Calories	552	Protein	30 g (59%)
Total Fat	5 g (8%)	Saturated Fat	1 g (4%)
Cholesterol	0 mg (0%)	Carbohydrate	100 g (33%)
Fiber	24 g (97%)	Sugars	14 g
Calcium	229 mg (23%)	Iron	8 mg (42%)

 # DINNER RECIPES

Eggplant Pizzas

Serve these veggie pizzas with a simple green salad or some steamed green beans. If you have higher energy needs, pair with some crusty bread.

Serves two.

INGREDIENTS

2 medium eggplants, halved lengthwise

2 cloves garlic, crushed

14-oz. can crushed tomatoes

1 Tbsp. shredded basil leaves

1 Tbsp. roughly chopped parsley

4 slices mozzarella (or other good melting cheeses such as
    fontina or semisoft goat cheese)

Sea salt and black pepper to taste

DIRECTIONS

1. Preheat oven to 200°F. Score the cut sides of the eggplant in a criss-cross pattern, then season with sea salt. Place in a baking dish and bake for 20–30 minutes until soft all the way through when pierced with a skewer.

2. Combine garlic and tomato and halve the amount of each of the herbs and spread onto eggplant halves. Place a slice of cheese on each one, then return to oven for another 15 minutes until cheese is melted and tomato mixture is hot.

3. Remove from oven, sprinkle with remaining herbs, and season with fresh cracked black pepper.

Nutritional facts per serving (daily value):	
Calories...........................342	Protein.............20 g (40%)
Total Fat.................14 g (22%)	Saturated Fat.......8 g (39%)
Cholesterol.......... 45 mg (15%)	Carbohydrate.....41 g (14%)
Fiber......................21 g (85%)	Sugars.......................19 g
Calcium .... 365 mg (37%)	Iron ....2 mg (13%)

Fish and Chips (Salmon and Sweet Potato Chips with Cucumber Yogurt Dressing)

This fish and chips recipe is quick, healthy, and can satisfy cravings. Steaming the sweet potato first in the microwave speeds up the cooking and also means less oil is needed in the cooking process. Baking the salmon in the oven is also a quick and healthy way to cook any type of fish without additional fats.

Serves two.

INGREDIENTS

2 7-oz. salmon fillets or Atlantic char
1¼ lbs. sweet potato, skin left on, sliced into ¼-inch-thick coins
½ cup natural yogurt
2 small cucumbers, finely chopped
1 Tbsp. finely chopped parsley
Sea salt and pepper to taste
Olive oil

DIRECTIONS

1. Preheat oven to 450°F (or highest setting). Place sweet potato pieces in a microwave-safe bowl and microwave on high for 6–8 minutes until soft but still retaining their shape. Add 1 tsp. olive oil and toss.

2. Line a baking tray with parchment paper and spread out sweet potato slices in one layer. Season with sea salt and pepper, then place in preheated oven and bake for 10 minutes until potatoes are starting to brown. Using a turner or fish spatula, gently turn the sweet potato slices and push to one side of the sheet so that there is room for the fish on the same tray.

3. Season the fish lightly and place in the oven for a further 6–8 minutes until cooked to your liking.

4. Meanwhile, as the potatoes and fish are in the oven, combine the yogurt, cucumber, and parsley in a small bowl, season to taste, and mix well.

5. Serve the fish and chips with the yogurt dressing.

Nutritional facts per serving (daily value):	
Calories.............................456	Protein..............27 g (54%)
Total Fat.................. 11 g (17%)	Saturated Fat....... 3 g (13%)
Cholesterol........... 63 mg (21%)	Carbohydrate.... 63 g (21%)
Fiber.......................9 g (36%)	Sugars........................16 g
Calcium ....182 mg (18%)	Iron ....3 mg (16%)

Lemon and Rosemary Chicken Skewers with Couscous Salad

Couscous is a very athlete-friendly food: It is ready in an instant, can be eaten hot or cold, and goes well with so many different foods and flavors.

Serves two.

INGREDIENTS

¾ lb. chicken thigh fillets each cut into 6 pieces
1 tsp. chopped rosemary leaves
1 tsp. lemon zest
1 Tbsp. lemon juice
1 Tbsp. olive oil

2 cups boiling chicken stock (or water)
1 cup couscous (instant variety)
1 cup cherry tomatoes, halved
1 cup broccoli florets
1 Tbsp. almonds, roughly chopped
1 Tbsp. chopped parsley

DIRECTIONS

1. In a shallow dish, whisk lemon juice, lemon zest, olive oil, and rosemary. Add chicken pieces and turn to coat well. Put aside to marinate for 20 minutes (or leave covered in the refrigerator until needed).

2. Meanwhile soak wooden skewers in cold water for at least 30 minutes (or use metal skewers).

3. To prepare couscous salad: in a large bowl combine couscous with broccoli, then pour over boiling stock and cover with plastic wrap for 5 minutes. Fluff with a fork, add tomatoes, almonds, and parsley and mix well.

4. Thread chicken pieces onto skewers and char-grill or barbecue, turning frequently for about 4 minutes until cooked through.

Nutritional facts per serving (daily value):	
Calories............................708	Protein............51 g (101%)
Total Fat..................18 g (28%)	Saturated Fat.......4 g (18%)
Cholesterol.........137 mg (46%)	Carbohydrate....83 g (28%)
Fiber......................7 g (28%)	Sugars........................7 g
Calcium ....90 mg (9%)	Iron ....4 mg (23%)

Pearl Barley Risotto with Shrimp, Lemon, and Baby Spinach

Serves two.

INGREDIENTS

½ Tbsp. olive oil
1 small onion, finely chopped
2 cloves garlic peeled and minced
1½ cups pearl barley, rinsed under cold water and drained

½ lb. raw shrimp, peeled and deveined

2 cups chicken stock

2 cups water

1 Tbsp. lemon zest

2 cups baby spinach leaves

1 Tbsp. finely chopped fresh parsley

1 Tbsp. finely chopped fresh basil

DIRECTIONS

1. Set a large, heavy-base saucepan or pot on medium heat and cook the olive oil, onion, and garlic until soft and translucent. Add the pearl barley and stir until it is coated with the onion mixture.

2. Add the stock and cook, stirring until the liquid is absorbed (about 10–15 minutes), then add the water and continue to cook, stirring frequently until the liquid is absorbed and the barley is tender, but still al dente (firm to bite). This will be about 30–35 minutes of total cooking time.

3. Add the prawns, lemon zest, and baby spinach and stir. The prawns will only take several minutes to change color and be cooked through. Stir through the herbs and season to taste.

Note: If you don't have time to stand at the stove and stir the risotto, it can also be baked in the oven. After sautéing the onion and garlic on the stove top, add the pearl barley and the liquid (stock and water), then bake in a preheated oven at 350°F for 30–35 minutes until liquid is absorbed and barley is tender to the bite. Remove from oven, stir in shrimp, lemon zest, and spinach, and return to oven for 5–10 minutes until shrimp is pink and just cooked through.

Nutritional facts per serving (daily value):	
Calories............................800	Protein.............. 45 g (91%)
Total Fat................. 10 g (16%)	Saturated Fat....... 2 g (10%)
Cholesterol......... 177 mg (59%)	Carbohydrate.. 135 g (45%)
Fiber..................... 25 g (101%)	Sugars......................... 8 g
Calcium ....:.167 mg (17%)	Iron .... 8 mg (45%)

Potato Gnocchi with Tomato, Bacon, Thyme, and Mozzarella ✗

Potato gnocchi can be bought prepared and par-cooked. It then only takes a matter of a few minutes to heat and serve, making it another staple to keep in the cupboard for a fuss-free, last-minute meal.

Serves two.

INGREDIENTS

1 small onion, finely chopped
2 slices Canadian or back bacon, roughly chopped
2 tsp. fresh thyme leaves
14-oz. can crushed tomatoes
8 baby bocconcini balls, torn in half (or 2½-oz. fresh
    mozzarella balls, roughly chopped)
1 lb. potato gnocchi
Salt and pepper to taste

DIRECTIONS

1. Bring a large pot of salted water to boil. Meanwhile, heat a large non-stick frying pan over medium heat. Add onion and bacon and fry gently until onion is soft and translucent and bacon is cooked. Add thyme leaves and tomato and cook a further two minutes.

2. Reduce heat to very low while you add the gnocchi to the boiling water. Cook according to packet instructions; this should only take a minute or two. The gnocchi are ready when they float to the surface.

3. Drain, then add gnocchi to the pan with the tomato sauce and the mozzarella and seasoning to taste (you should not need much salt, since the bacon is salty). Turn off heat and toss well.

4. Serve immediately with extra cracked black pepper.

Nutritional facts per serving (daily value):	
Calories...........................386	Protein............. 19 g (39%)
Total Fat.................. 11 g (17%)	Saturated Fat....... 5 g (26%)
Cholesterol........... 39 mg (13%)	Carbohydrate.... 55 g (18%)
Fiber.......................3 g (13%)	Sugars........................ 8 g
Calcium .... 216 mg (22%)	Iron .... 2 mg (13%)

Stir-Fried Beef and Mushroom with Snow Peas and Hokkien Noodles

Stir-fries are really quick and easy and can be varied easily depending on what is at hand and what is in season. Try this recipe with diced chicken or prawns and vegetables such as carrot, baby bok choy, and green beans. Chop the vegetables relatively thin and roughly the same size so that they cook in the same amount of time. Experiment with different sauces by adding chili or ginger, or different types of noodles. Although this recipe calls for the use of Hokkien noodles, which are traditional rice noodles used in Southeast Asian stir fries, any type of rice noodle will do.

Serves two.

INGREDIENTS

½ Tbsp. peanut oil

¾ lb. lean beef, such as top sirloin or round steak, cut into strips

2 cloves garlic, crushed

1 small onion, sliced thin

1 cup snow peas, with strings removed

8 dried shitake mushrooms

½ lb. Hokkien noodles or any other Asian egg-based noodle

1 Tbsp. oyster sauce

1 Tbsp. soy sauce

1 Tbsp. rice wine

1 tsp. sesame oil

DIRECTIONS

1. Place Hokkien noodles in a large bowl and cover with boiling water (following packet instructions). Leave to stand, then separate noodles gently and drain. Rinse with cold water, then drain again and set aside.

2. Meanwhile, place dried mushrooms in a small bowl, cover with boiling water, and set aside for 5 minutes. Drain (reserve mushroom water to use as stock in another recipe, such as a risotto). Remove stems from mushrooms and discard, then slice caps.

3. Heat peanut oil in a wok (or large frying pan) over high heat. Stir-fry beef in two batches until browned (about 3–5 minutes), then remove. Add

onion to wok and cook until golden, then return meat to pan along with garlic, snow peas, mushrooms, oyster sauce, soy sauce, and rice wine. Cook for an additional 3 minutes, then add noodles and sesame oil.

4. Toss well until noodles are heated through, then serve immediately.

Nutritional facts per serving (daily value):	
Calories..............................823	Protein.............. 43 g (86%)
Total Fat................ 44 g (68%)	Saturated Fat....... 8 g (41%)
Cholesterol........... 83 mg (28%)	Carbohydrate.....62 g (21%)
Fiber.......................5 g (21%)	Sugars......................... 4 g
Calcium .... 96 mg (10%)	Iron .... 8 mg (42%)

Tuna Mac 'n' Cheese

Mac 'n' cheese that is good for you! Once you've mastered this recipe, vary the vegetables: Try using roasted pumpkin and peas, even add chopped cherry tomatoes, asparagus, or broccoli. You can also swap the tuna for diced ham or smoked chicken. This dish can be prepared well before you serve it, even the night before, and stored covered in the refrigerator. It will just take a little longer in the oven (about 40 minutes) to heat all the way through.

Serves four to six.

INGREDIENTS
1 lb. dried short pasta (macaroni, farfalle, penne, etc.)
1 small onion, finely chopped
2 cloves garlic, crushed
½ Tbsp. olive oil
1 15-oz. can evaporated skim milk
1 Tbsp. corn flour
½ cup water
1 6½-oz. can water-packed tuna, drained
1 large zucchini, grated
1 large carrot, grated
1 6½-oz. can corn, drained
5 oz. low-fat cheddar cheese, grated
½ cup dried breadcrumbs

DIRECTIONS

1. Preheat oven to 350°F. Bring a large pot of salted water to a boil, then add pasta. Cook according to packet instructions, drain, rinse under cold water, and drain again before setting aside.

2. Meanwhile, heat a large nonstick frying pan over medium heat. Add the olive oil, then add garlic and onion and sauté until translucent. Add zucchini, carrot, and corn and cook a further minute, then add evaporated milk. Bring to a slow simmer while stirring.

3. In a small glass bowl, combine corn flour and water and mix to dissolve, then add to pan, stirring continuously. Cook a further 2 minutes, bringing back to simmer until the mixture thickens. Turn off heat.

4. Return cooked and drained pasta to the pot and add the sauce mixture along with the tuna and 3.5 oz. of the grated cheese. Mix well, then spoon into a large baking dish. Combine the remaining cheese and breadcrumbs and sprinkle over the top.

5. Bake in preheated oven for about 30 minutes until heated through and the topping is crunchy and bubbly.

Nutritional facts per serving (daily value for 6 servings):	
Calories............................682	Protein...............38 g (77%)
Total Fat.....................6 g (9%)	Saturated Fat.........2 g (9%)
Cholesterol............22 mg (7%)	Carbohydrate...118 g (39%)
Fiber.........................7 g (29%)	Sugars........................13 g
Calcium ....232 mg (23%)	Iron ....3 mg (18%)

 # DESSERT RECIPES

Baked Apple, Cranberry, and Maple Pudding

If you prefer, substitute pears or even mixed berries for the apples in this recipe.

Serves four.

INGREDIENTS

1 tsp. butter

4 apples, peeled, cored, and quartered

¼ cup dried cranberries

1 tsp. cinnamon

2 medium eggs

½ cup all-purpose flour

⅓ cup pure maple syrup (or golden syrup)

1 cup low-fat milk

DIRECTIONS

1. Preheat oven to 350°F. Cut each apple quarter in half, then cut crosswise into four parts so you are left with small chunks.

2. In a bowl lightly whisk the eggs with the milk and maple syrup. Add the flour and cinnamon and whisk until just combined, stir in the apple and cranberries, and set aside.

3. Lightly grease a medium-size shallow baking dish. Pour apple and custard mixture into dish and bake in the oven for about 30 minutes until set, puffed, and golden.

Nutritional facts per serving (daily value):			
Calories	284	Protein	7 g (14%)
Total Fat	5 g (7%)	Saturated Fat	2 g (9%)
Cholesterol	111 mg (37%)	Carbohydrate	56 g (19%)
Fiber	3 g (11%)	Sugars	37 g
Calcium	121 mg (12%)	Iron	2 mg (10%)

Banana Cinnamon French Toast

French toast is not just for breakfast!

Serves two.

INGREDIENTS

4 slices fruit bread

1 large egg

⅓ cup low-fat milk

2 tsp. powdered sugar

2 tsp. cinnamon

2–3 medium bananas, mashed

Butter

DIRECTIONS

1. Make two sandwiches with the bread and mashed bananas. In a shallow bowl combine the egg, milk, and 1 tsp. each of cinnamon and sugar and whisk to combine. In another small bowl combine the remaining sugar and cinnamon.

2. Dip each sandwich in the egg and milk mixture and cook in a lightly greased nonstick frying pan over medium heat for about 2 minutes on each side until golden brown.

3. Serve sliced in half and sprinkled with the mixed cinnamon and sugar.

Nutritional facts per serving (daily value):	
Calories 369	Protein .... 11 g (21%)
Total Fat .... 6 g (9%)	Saturated Fat .... 2 g (9%)
Cholesterol .... 108 mg (36%)	Carbohydrate .... 74 g (25%)
Fiber .... 8 g (32%)	Sugars .... 29 g
Calcium .... 133 mg (13%)	Iron .... 3 mg (18%)

Chocolate-Cherry Custard Parfait

You can make the custard yourself, but using a low-fat, store-bought variety makes this a very quick and easy dessert treat. It is best made up the day before you serve it, or at a minimum of several hours before eating, to let the flavors develop and the custard soak through the sponge biscuits.

Serves two.

INGREDIENTS

1 cup pitted Morello canned cherries, drained,
    with ½ cup syrup reserved

1 cup low-fat chocolate custard

6 savoiardi biscuits (or Italian sponge fingers, also known
   as ladyfingers)
1 oz. dark chocolate, grated

DIRECTIONS

1. Break biscuits in half and dip briefly in syrup. Place three halves in the bottom of two 1½-cup capacity ramekin dishes or glasses.

2. Add ¼ cup of the custard to each dish followed by ¼ cup of the cherries. Repeat the layers, finishing with the cherries. Sprinkle grated chocolate over the top and leave in the refrigerator to sit for several hours or overnight.

Nutritional facts per serving (daily value):	
Calories............................326	Protein.............. 11 g (22%)
Total Fat....................8 g (13%)	Saturated Fat.......4 g (22%)
Cholesterol......... 128 mg (43%)	Carbohydrate.... 54 g (18%)
Fiber........................3 g (13%)	Sugars........................31 g
Calcium .... 252 mg (25%)	Iron .... 2 mg (11%)

Honey-Roasted Pineapple with Mint and Pistachios

Who says you can't get some of your daily fruit servings in a delicious dessert?

Serves two.

INGREDIENTS

4 ½-inch-thick pineapple slices
¼ cup honey
1 cinnamon stick
1½ oz. pistachios, shelled and chopped roughly
1 Tbsp. shredded fresh mint leaves
½ cup thick natural yogurt

DIRECTIONS

1. Preheat oven to 350°F. Cut pineapple slices in half and place in a shallow roasting pan with the cinnamon stick. Warm the honey until runny

(microwave for 1 minute or over a low-medium heat) then pour over pineapple.

2. Roast in oven for about 15 minutes, then turn pineapple pieces and continue to roast for another 10 minutes.

3. Allow to cool for 10 minutes, then top with mint and pistachios and serve with yogurt.

Nutritional facts per serving (daily value):	
Calories.............................342	Protein................7 g (15%)
Total Fat.................12 g (18%)	Saturated Fat.......2 g (12%)
Cholesterol..............8 mg (3%)	Carbohydrate....59 g (20%)
Fiber.......................5 g (19%)	Sugars......................50 g
Calcium.............140 mg (14%)	Iron.................3 mg (14%)

Orange Ricotta Cream with Poached Pears

Here's another fruit-based dessert that's as satisfying as cake.

Serves two.

INGREDIENTS

2 pears, peeled, cored, and quartered
⅓ cup sugar
1½ cups water
1 orange, juiced
½ cup low-fat vanilla yogurt
1 cup skim ricotta cheese
1 tsp. orange zest
2 tsp. powdered sugar

DIRECTIONS

1. In a medium saucepan combine water, sugar, and orange juice. Stir over medium heat until sugar is dissolved. Bring to a boil and then add the pears. Poach for about 5 minutes until pears are tender and then remove from liquid.

2. In a small bowl, whisk the ricotta, yogurt, powdered sugar, and orange zest.

3. Serve the pears with a dollop of the ricotta mixture and a little of the poaching liquid if desired.

Nutritional facts per serving (daily value):	
Calories............................331	Protein...................5 g (9%)
Total Fat.....................1 g (2%)	Saturated Fat.........1 g (3%)
Cholesterol..............4 mg (1%)	Carbohydrate....81 g (27%)
Fiber........................8 g (32%)	Sugars.......................67 g
Calcium.............161 mg (16%)	Iron...................0 mg (3%)

Pear, Raspberry, and Almond Crumble

This dessert makes a nice treat for a cold winter's night. Different fruits can be used, such as stone fruits or apples, and there is no need to add any additional sugars to the fruits. The almond meal in the topping also adds some essential fats to the nutritional profile.

Serves 8–10

INGREDIENTS

3 pears, sliced thinly (leave skin on)
10 oz. raspberries (either fresh or frozen)
1 cup all-purpose flour
1 cup almond meal (ground almonds)
¾ cup sugar
½ cup (1 stick) butter, melted

DIRECTIONS

1. Preheat oven to 350°F. Combine pears and raspberries in a large baking dish and set aside.

2. In a medium-size mixing bowl combine flour, almond meal, and sugar. Melt butter by microwaving on medium power or over low-medium heat, then add to dry ingredients. Mix well—the mixture should resemble breadcrumbs.

3. Top fruit with the crumble mix, pressing down gently, then bake in oven for about 30 minutes until the fruit begins to bubble through the crumble topping.

Nutritional facts per serving (daily value):	
Calories 501	Protein .... 7 g (15%)
Total Fat .... 25 g (39%)	Saturated Fat..... 10 g (52%)
Cholesterol ....41 mg (14%)	Carbohydrate.... 67 g (22%)
Fiber .... 9 g (35%)	Sugars .... 38 g
Calcium ....69 mg (7%)	Iron ....2 mg (12%)

Roasted Stone Fruits with Ginger

The ginger adds an appealing kick to this refreshing after-dinner treat.

Serves two.

INGREDIENTS

4 peaches or other stone fruits (apricot, plum, etc.)
½ Tbsp. crystallized ginger, finely chopped
1 Tbsp. brown sugar (light or dark is fine)
1 cup frozen yogurt or low-fat ice cream to serve (optional)

DIRECTIONS

1. Preheat oven broiler to high. Line a baking tray with parchment paper and place halved fruits cut-side up on tray. Sprinkle fruit with brown sugar and ginger and place under broiler for 5–10 minutes until caramelized on top and soft throughout.

2. Serve with frozen yogurt or low-fat ice cream if desired.

Nutritional facts per serving (daily value):	
Calories 193	Protein .... 6 g (12%)
Total Fat .... 4 g (7%)	Saturated Fat....... 3 g (13%)
Cholesterol .... 16 mg (5%)	Carbohydrate.... 35 g (12%)
Fiber ....3 g (12%)	Sugars .... 33 g
Calcium .... 167 mg (17%)	Iron .... 1 mg (4%)

FOURTEEN

THE ROLE OF SUPPLEMENTS

have two friends and colleagues whom I hold in the highest esteem, yet they could not be farther apart in their attitudes toward nutritional supplements. Donavon Guyot, the brilliant young CEO of TrainingPeaks, has never used a nutritional supplement in his entire life. That did not stop him from becoming a national-class triathlete. Brad Culp, editor of the magazine *Triathlete*, practically lives on supplements. In fact, for one week, as a sort of gonzo journalistic experiment for the magazine, he did live entirely on supplements. Frankly, I was surprised by how bad he looked, and reportedly felt, at the end of that week, given how little real food he eats normally. Nevertheless, eating like George Jetson (from the cartoon sitcom of the sixties, in which the Jetsons are a futuristic family of the year 2062) has not prevented Brad from achieving a very high level of performance as a triathlete. Indeed, at the time of this writing he owns the swim course record at Ironman Florida®.

While these two athletes serve as extreme examples, they demonstrate that using supplements for endurance performance is a personal choice, not a question with a universally right or wrong answer. Supplementation is seldom necessary, but athletes who choose to supplement will attest that it can be effective in promoting health, athletic performance, and,

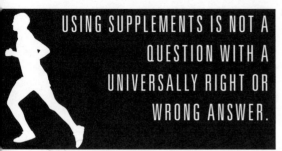

USING SUPPLEMENTS IS NOT A QUESTION WITH A UNIVERSALLY RIGHT OR WRONG ANSWER.

yes, a leaner body composition. If you don't like the very idea of supplementation, then rely on the five-step plan I have given you to realize your racing weight and don't burden yourself with fears that this choice will hold you back. If you are open to supplementation, then you are not likely to regret making an informed decision to try one or two of the few nutritional supplements that promote leanness, either directly or indirectly.

I chose to make this chapter on supplementation the last chapter of the book to emphasize the point that supplementation should not be used as a primary means to pursue your racing weight. Improving your diet quality, balancing your energy sources, practicing nutrient timing, managing your appetite, and training properly should come first. And if you do all of these things consistently, you will likely find that there is nothing left for supplements to do for you—no flab left to fry. But again, selective supplementation may get you there faster.

In this chapter I will discuss six supplements that, based on scientific research and in some cases also on my own experience, I believe worth consideration: beta-alanine, calcium, conjugated linoleic acid (CLA), creatine, fiber, fish oil, green tea extract, and whey protein. In case you're curious, I myself use creatine, fish oil, and whey protein (as well as an herbal supplement called ARX that increases aerobic performance but has nothing to do with weight management).

BETA-ALANINE

As with many other sports nutrition supplements, the jury is still out on beta-alanine. What the jury is specifically trying to decide is whether it increases endurance performance directly, by increasing resistance to fatigue at high intensities, and perhaps indirectly, by boosting the results that endurance athletes derive from speed training. There is also some evidence that beta-alanine supplementation might make endurance athletes leaner by increasing lean muscle mass.

Beta-alanine is a non-essential amino acid that is obtained in the diet primarily from meats containing carnosine, a naturally occurring peptide made up of beta-alanine and l-histidine. Beta-alanine serves a variety of functions in the body, but perhaps its most important role is to help formulate carnosine, which is not absorbed intact from food sources.

BETA-ALANINE is a non-essential amino acid that formulates the antioxidant (carnosine) believed to help muscles fight fatigue, improve results from speed training, and increase lean muscle mass.

Unproven, but some endurance athletes may find it worth a try.

Carnosine has long been celebrated as an "antiaging" compound because it is an antioxidant, it prevents glycation (a process whereby excess sugar in the bloodstream damages body proteins, contributing to Alzheimer's disease and other problems), and it extends the life span of individual cells. But more recently, scientists have discovered that carnosine has a significant role in exercise performance. Specifically, it helps the muscles maintain normal acidity levels during intense exercise, when there is a tendency for the muscles to become too acidic, hastening fatigue.

Early studies on beta-alanine supplementation found that it increased anaerobic endurance, or fatigue resistance, in prolonged or repeated efforts at very high intensities. But then came a spate of studies with contradictory results. For example, researchers at the University of Ghent, Belgium, and the University of Chichester, England, investigated whether beta-alanine supplementation would raise the carnosine concentration in the calf muscles of trained sprinters and whether it would enhance performance in a pair of strength-endurance tests and a single-sprint race simulation (Derave et al. 2007). Fifteen male sprinters with 400-meter times under 52 seconds took either a beta-alanine supplement or a placebo daily for four weeks. The athletes completed three performance tests both before and after the supplementation period: a 400-meter sprint, five sets of 30 maximal-effort leg extensions, and a maximal-duration isometric contraction of the quadriceps. Supplementation increased the carnosine concentration of the gastrocnemius muscle in the calf by 37 percent, compared to a 16 percent increase in the placebo group. In the multiple-set strength test, the beta-alanine group increased its maximal torque significantly more than the placebo group in the first two sets but not the last three. Supplementation had no effect on isometric endurance or 400-meter sprint time.

Researchers at the University of Oklahoma (Smith, Moon et al. 2009) found no significant effect of beta-alanine supplementation in their study. Forty-six men were separated into three groups. Members of two groups completed a 6-week program of high-intensity interval training while those in the third group did not exercise. One of the two exercise groups received supplemental beta-alanine while the other received a placebo. Before and after the 6-week study period members of all groups performed a maximum-effort exercise test consisting of four 2-minute bouts on a cycling ergometer. The researchers used electromyography (EMG) sensors to measure the muscles' work efficiency and their threshold of fatigue. Members of both exercise groups exhibited significant improvements in both of these measures, while members of the non-exercise group showed no improvement. There was no difference in the degree of improvement seen in the beta-alanine and placebo groups.

I don't know what it was about this study and its roundly negative results that inspired the same researchers to continue investigating the effects of beta-alanine supplementation on body composition and endurance performance when combined with high-intensity interval training—but they did, and surprisingly, they found a clear benefit this time (Smith, Walter et al. 2009). Forty-six men were divided into two groups, one of which received supplemental beta-alanine daily and the other of which received a placebo while engaged in a 6-week program of high-intensity interval training. All subjects were tested for VO_2peak, ventilatory threshold, total work performed at 100 percent of VO_2peak, and time to fatigue at three points: before training, after 3 weeks, and after all 6 weeks of training were completed. At 6 weeks, members of the beta-alanine group exhibited greater improvements in VO_2peak, total work done, time to fatigue, and lean body mass. The authors of the study, which was published in the *Journal of the International Society of Sports Nutrition*, concluded, "The use of [high-intensity interval training] to induce significant aerobic improvements is effective and efficient. Chronic [beta-alanine] supplementation may further enhance [high-intensity interval training], improving endurance performance and lean body mass."

Now a study from the Catholic University of Leuven, Belgium, has shown that beta-alanine supplementation may enhance performance in endurance cycling—albeit only sprint performance within endurance cycling (Van Thienen et al. 2009). The study was well designed. Moderately to well-trained cyclists received either beta-alanine supplementation or a placebo daily for 8 weeks. Before and again after the intervention all of the subjects performed a 10-minute time trial and a 30-second sprint at the end of a simulated 110-minute cycling race. Beta-alanine supplementation did not improve performance in the time trial compared to the placebo, but in the closing sprint, it improved mean power output by 5 percent and peak power output by 11.4 percent.

So, is beta-alanine performance enhancing or not? And more specifically, is it beneficial to endurance performance or not? Based on how divided the literature on these questions remains, it could be a while before we know definitively. But since it does no harm and might do some good, some endurance athletes may reasonably conclude it's worth a try.

I actually tried it for a while a couple of years ago. I honestly couldn't say whether it helped me, as my training was not going well at the time for other reasons. I should note that there is one strange but harmless side effect of beta-alanine supplementation, which affects roughly half of those who take it and affected me. "Parathesia" is a fancy name for a transient and benign tingling sensation in the upper extremities resulting from beta-alanine's actions as a neurotransmitter. Some people find it very uncomfortable, but I liked it. It made me want to train like a madman. That's something—however, I no longer use this supplement.

CALCIUM

A number of years ago, obesity researcher Michael Zemel caused a stir when he published a study in which he found that adding yogurt to the diets of obese men caused them to lose substantial amounts of body fat (Zemel et al. 2005). In follow-up studies, he singled out calcium as the cause of the effect (although he also found that calcium only had the effect when consumed in dairy foods). The apparent reason is that calcium reduces production of a hormone called calcitriol that promotes fat storage.

CALCIUM reduces the production of the hormone (calcitriol) that promotes fat storage.

If calcium intake is low, increasing daily intake to 1,300 milligrams could improve body composition.

Zemel's follow-up research revealed that adding dairy foods to the diet causes weight loss only in those who consume substantially less than the recommended 1,300 mg of calcium per day. Nevertheless, he actually patented the claim that dairy foods promote weight loss and sold it to the dairy industry, which then began using the claim on product labels. If you remember those labels, then you may also be aware that they have disappeared. That's because studies by other researchers failed to support Zemel's findings, and, as a result, the dairy industry faced mounting pressure to abandon the claim.

Recently, however, the *British Journal of Nutrition* published a study that did support Zemel's original finding—except that it involved calcium pills, not dairy foods. The study, conducted at Laval University in Canada, involved obese women who consumed just 600 mg of calcium per day, on average (Major et al. 2009). All of the women were placed on a 15-week, reduced-calorie diet. Half the women received supplemental calcium. After 15 weeks, the calcium-supplemented women had lost an average of 13.2 pounds, whereas the nonsupplemented women had lost only 2.2 pounds.

The study's authors did not share Zemel's explanation for the calcium effect. They suggested that the brain can detect calcium deficiency in the body, which it attempts to correct by driving increased food intake. However it works, there is increasing agreement among obesity researchers that calcium supplementation and increased intake of calcium-rich foods can promote fat loss in those whose calcium intake is currently low.

CALCIUM REDUCES PRODUCTION OF A HORMONE THAT PROMOTES FAT STORAGE.

Since the average American adult consumes only 500 to 700 mg daily, increased calcium intake through dairy foods or supplements may be a realistic way for many people to achieve a leaner body composition. It is probably less likely to make a significant difference for the typical endurance athlete than it does for those who are severely overweight, but there's no harm in experimenting, and there are other benefits associated with adequate calcium intake, including healthier bones, of course. Aim for a total daily calcium intake of approximately 1,300 mg and see what happens.

CONJUGATED LINOLEIC ACID (CLA)

Conjugated linoleic acid (CLA) is a fatty acid found primarily in meat and cheese. It was only discovered within the past 20 years. Research on the effects of CLA in animals has shown that it prevents tumor growth, increases insulin sensitivity, and reduces body-fat accumulation. However, few human studies have duplicated these benefits.

CLA is a fatty acid found primarily in meat and cheese, believed to prevent weight gain.

Athletes prone to seasonal weight gain should consider using this supplement in the off-season.

A recent review from the University of Reading, England, concluded that "the consensus from seventeen published studies in human subjects is that CLA does not affect body weight or body composition" and that "[u]ntil more is known, CLA supplementation in man should be considered with caution" (Tricon and Yaqoob 2006).

However, the results of a new study suggest that CLA supplementation may help prevent weight gain during times when people are most susceptible to storing extra fat—such as the holidays. The study was performed at the University of Wisconsin and involved 40 overweight men and women. For six months, half the subjects received a daily dose of

CLA IS WORTH CONSIDERING FOR OFF-SEASON (WINTER) USE.

CLA (3.2 mg) and the other received a placebo, all in double-blind fashion. Those receiving the CLA supplement lost 2.2 pounds during the study period, while members of the placebo group gained 1.5 pounds on average. Their weight gain was concentrated during the holiday period (Thanksgiving to New Year's).

These results may not sound too impressive, but keep in mind that holiday weight gain may account for half of the overall weight gain that normally occurs during adulthood. In light of this fact, CLA is worth considering, perhaps as a supplement for off-season (winter) use.

CREATINE

CREATINE (more specifi-
cally, the compound cre-
atine phosphate) occurs
naturally in the body and
is one of the most impor-
tant sources of energy for
high-intensity (anaerobic)
muscle contraction.

Some athletes may find
better performance and
more rewarding speed
and strength workouts
with this supplement, but
weight gain is a concern for
runners and most cyclists.

Creatine has a stronger beneficial impact on athletic performance than any other safe and legal dietary supplement. The only problem is that, while it does wonderful things for strength, sprint, and power athletes, it has little proven beneficial effect on endurance performance. Nevertheless, it may still be worth taking.

There are numerous supplemental forms of creatine, the most common of which is creatine monohydrate. All of these compounds are precursors to a slightly different compound called creatine phosphate, which occurs naturally in the body and is one of the most important sources of energy for high-intensity (anaerobic) muscle contraction. Creatine phosphate provides energy so rapidly that it is the muscles' primary energy source for maximum-intensity efforts such as heavy weightlifting and sprinting.

According to a comprehensive review of creatine studies by researchers at Baylor University, short-term creatine supplementation has been reported to improve maximal power and strength by 5 to 15 percent (Kreider 2003). It increases the amount of work performed during multiple sets of maximal-effort weightlifting by the same amount. It increases performance in a single sprint by 1 to 5 percent, and in multiple sprints by 5 to 15 percent. Moreover, when daily creatine supplementation is combined with appropriate training over a period of weeks, fitness gains are significantly enhanced. In other words, the same workouts result in faster muscle growth, strength gains, and improvements in high-intensity performance when daily creatine supplementation is added.

When combined with proper training, creatine supplementation improves body composition, primarily by increasing muscle mass. But even a small increase in muscle mass can itself reduce body-fat stores by increasing metabolism. Many endurance athletes avoid creatine because they fear that it will cause them to gain weight, but substantial weight gain is unlikely when creatine is taken by athletes who are burning hundreds of calories every day through aerobic exercise and doing very little of the types of exercise that stimulate muscle growth.

The reason endurance athletes might want to consider using creatine is that, although creatine does not affect performance in any type of exercise lasting longer than 90 seconds, it can help endurance athletes perform better and get more out of their speed and strength workouts. Since creatine clearly enhances performance in these types of training, it could indirectly enhance your race performances by boosting the fitness gains you derive from doing short intervals and lifting weights. This was shown in a 1998 German study involving triathletes (Engelhardt et al. 1998). Researchers had a group of triathletes perform an endurance test that included short maximum-intensity sprints on two occasions: before and after five days of creatine supplementation. They found that while their endurance performance was unchanged in the second test, they put out 18 percent more power in the sprints after creatine supplementation.

My experience with creatine has been that this supplement does indeed enhance the strength and power gains I get from lifting weights and doing plyometrics (jumping drills). It also makes a noticeable difference in my body composition, increasing my muscle mass and decreasing my body-fat stores with minimal effect on my body weight. When I am focused on running, even the two pounds I gain on creatine are more than I want, so I now use creatine only when focused on triathlon training, when the power I gain with creatine is worth the cost of a little added body weight.

The actual race performance gains I derive from creatine supplementation are negligible—perhaps 1 percent at most. And they don't come cheaply. A 200-serving canister of unflavored creatine monohydrate powder (the most economical type of creatine supplement) costs about $40.

It's generally recommended that one begin supplementation with a 4- to 7-day loading period during which one takes 20 g per day (four doses of 5 g each), but in fact this loading phase is unnecessary. You can simply start at a dosage of 2.5 to 5 g per day and stay there. Because insulin is needed to drive creatine into the muscle cells, you should mix the powder into fruit juice (or take the pills with fruit juice). Otherwise you can buy the supplement as a flavored drink mix that includes carbohydrate to stimulate insulin release.

FIBER

FIBER helps to regulate toxins, minerals, and nutrients for optimal health.

Aim for a daily total of roughly 14 grams of fiber per 1,000 calories.

Dietary fiber encompasses two kinds of highly complex carbohydrates that are almost completely indigestible. Insoluble fiber (mainly cellulose) serves as an important structural material in plants. It does not provide nutrition to humans but benefits us instead by absorbing and neutralizing toxins and by contributing to well-hydrated, bulky solid waste that is easily passed. Water-soluble fiber helps the body absorb minerals and helps remove nutrient excesses, including cholesterol, from the body. Examples of fiber-rich foods are whole grains, green leafy vegetables, and beans.

Adequate fiber intake is essential for optimal health; conversely, inadequate fiber intake is associated with a variety of diseases and health conditions. Specifically, a high-fiber diet reduces the risk of obesity, type 2 diabetes, cardiovascular disease, and constipation. One of the reasons these diseases and conditions are so prevalent in our society is that we do not consume enough dietary fiber. The U.S. government recommends that people consume 14 grams of fiber per 1,000 calories daily. The average American is lucky to consume 14 total grams of fiber daily (while consuming well in excess of 2,000 calories).

Excess body fat is the primary cause of cardiovascular disease and type 2 diabetes. A high-fiber diet may reduce the risk of cardiovascular disease and type 2 diabetes by reducing body-fat storage. Fiber slows digestion so we feel fuller longer and consequently eat less. Therefore getting enough fiber in your diet is quite beneficial with respect to promoting leanness. A recent review on the health benefits of fiber by researchers at the University of Kentucky concluded that fiber supplementation in obese individuals significantly enhances weight loss (Anderson et al. 2009). It is likely to have a small effect in those who are already fairly lean, but then, if you are already fairly lean, you don't need a big weight-loss effect from any supplement.

Natural foods such as fruits and vegetables are the best sources of dietary fiber, but fiber supplements can be a good backup source. If you are currently getting less than 14 grams of fiber per 1,000 calories daily and you're finding it difficult to add more whole grains, fruits, or vegetables to your diet, use a fiber supplement such as ground flaxseeds, Metamucil, or Fiber One. Use it according to label directions and aim for a total of roughly 14 grams of fiber per 1,000 calories daily from food and supplement sources combined.

FISH OIL

We looked at some of the health benefits of omega-3 fatty acids in Chapter 7. There we also saw that it is difficult to get enough omega-3 fats to support optimal health unless you eat certain types of fish consistently, at least twice a week. While I often eat fish this frequently, I don't always, so I take a fish oil supplement (fish oil is the richest source of omega-3) daily to ensure that I am never deficient, and I encourage you to do the same.

> FISH OIL reduces inflammation, enhances brain function, improves vascular health, and is also believed to help endurance athletes get leaner.
>
> Take a daily dosage of 2 to 3 grams of EPA and DHA (combined).

In addition to reducing systemic inflammation, enhancing brain function, and improving vascular health, omega-3 fats may also help endurance athletes get leaner, in both direct and indirect ways. The direct way is an apparent modification of fat metabolism through altered gene expression. Studies in the 1990s found that fat deposition in animals was reduced by omega-3 fat supplementation. Subsequent human studies have produced mixed results. Among the studies with favorable results was one performed by researchers at the University of South Australia and published in 2007 (Hill et al. 2007). Overweight volunteers were divided into three groups: For 12 weeks, some took a fish oil supplement, others exercised, and a third group did both. Interestingly, fish oil and exercise independently yielded significant reductions in fat mass, but there was no additive effect. These results suggest that fish oil supplementation may not reduce body-fat levels in those who already exercise.

However, scientists recently have begun to investigate the effects of fish oil supplementation on exercise physiology, and some of the findings in this area suggest that fish oil (or other omega-3 fat) supplementation could increase training capacity and thus improve body composition to the degree that this extra capacity is exploited. For example, researchers from the University of Wollongong, Australia (Peoples et al. 2008), investigated whether supplementation with omega-3-rich fish oil would reduce oxygen demand during exercise in humans, as it had been shown to do previously in laboratory animals. Sixteen cyclists received either fish oil or a placebo daily for 8 weeks. All subjects completed maximal-oxygen-consumption and submaximal-ride-to-exhaustion tests both before and after the intervention. Fish oil supplementation did not increase peak oxygen consumption or peak power in the maximum oxygen consumption test and did not increase time to exhaustion in the ride-to-exhaustion test. However, it did reduce oxygen consumption at each level of power output in both tests. The authors of the study speculated that fish oil achieved this effect by creating more pliable arteries with greater dilating capacity that allow more blood flow.

The two most important omega-3 fats are DHA and EPA. A daily dosage of 2 to 3 grams of EPA and DHA (combined) is recommended.

GREEN TEA EXTRACT

GREEN TEA EXTRACT increases fat burning both at rest and during exercise, which could lead to greater endurance.

Try a total of 690 milligrams of green tea catechins daily.

Green tea contains a high concentration of catechins, a type of antioxidant. It appears that green tea catechins increase fat oxidation by reducing the activity of free radicals that inhibit fat metabolism. There is evidence that green tea extract increases fat burning both at rest and during exercise. Increased fat burning at rest translates into body-fat loss. Increased fat burning during exercise could translate into greater endurance, which could be exploited for additional body-fat loss.

Don't expect a massive amount of fat loss from green tea extract supplementation, but do expect some. In a 2009 review of research on green tea extracts and weight loss, researchers from Maastricht University in the Netherlands reported that catechins, the primary antioxidant in green tea, have a "small positive effect" on weight loss and weight loss maintenance, yielding an average weight loss of about 3 pounds in short-term studies (Hursel et al. 2009).

Regarding green tea extract and exercise, a couple of Japanese studies have shown that green tea extract supplementation increases endurance in mice, but as yet, there have been no studies showing an ergogenic (performance enhancing) effect of green tea extract supplementation in humans. In a recent human study from the University of Birmingham,

> GREEN TEA EXTRACT MAY DELAY FATIGUE DURING PROLONGED MODERATE-INTENSITY EFFORTS.

England, however, acute supplementation with green tea extract increased fat burning during moderate-intensity exercise by 17 percent (Venables et al. 2008). These results suggest a strong possibility that green tea extract could delay fatigue during prolonged moderate-intensity efforts. The supplement used in this study provided 336 mg of catechins.

WHEY PROTEIN

Whey protein is used primarily as a muscle growth supplement by weightlifters and strength athletes. Research demonstrates that they have good reason to do so. A number of studies have shown that strength and muscle mass gains are significantly enhanced by whey protein supplementation.

> WHEY PROTEIN enhances strength and muscle mass gains.
>
> Try a dosage of 20 grams of whey protein for a significant satiating effect.

In recent years, whey protein has gained increasing popularity as a weight-loss supplement. Science validates this usage as well. In Chapter 4, I described a study in which whey protein supplementation doubled the amount of fat loss that was achieved through a 10-week resistance-training program. It appeared that whey achieved this result by reducing appetite, as the subjects ate approximately 14 percent less when they included whey protein shakes in their diet than when they did not.

Researchers at the University of Toronto recently reviewed all of the existing literature on whey protein, appetite, and eating (Luhovyy et al. 2007). Their conclusion, published in the *Journal of the American College of Nutrition*, asserts that "[w]hey protein has potential as a functional food component to contribute to the regulation of body weight by providing satiety signals that affect both short-term and long-term food intake regulation."

Whey protein appears to reduce appetite through several different mechanisms. For example, some of the peptides, or protein fractions, in whey protein stimulate the release of gut hormones that create a feeling of satiety, or fullness. Whey protein also reduces appetite by increasing blood amino-acid levels. It also helps regulate insulin levels.

Whey protein supplementation is very easy. Most supplements are flavored drink mixes. Just add a scoop of powder in your preferred flavor to water, stir it, and drink. You can also add the powder to smoothies, oatmeal, yogurt, and other foods. A dosage of 20 grams of whey protein is adequate for a significant satiating effect.

In addition to protein powders, there are so-called satiety foods that contain whey protein, often in combination with other satiety-stimulating nutrients. For example, Forze GPS nutrition bars and shakes contain whey protein in combination with soy protein, calcium, fiber, and long-chain fatty acids.

RECOMMENDED STRENGTH EXERCISES FOR ENDURANCE ATHLETES

T he following are 30 strength exercises for endurance athletes: five each for all endurance athletes, cross-country skiers, cyclists, rowers, runners, swimmers, and triathletes. Note that the five strength exercises for triathletes include two from the list for swimmers, two from the list for runners, and one from the list for cyclists.

It is wise to start with an adaptation phase if these exercises are new or you are not currently strength training. Spend 2 to 3 weeks practicing the movements with very light loads (in the case of non-body-weight eaxercises) to get the coordination down. Then you can move on to heavier loads.

EXERCISES FOR ALL ENDURANCE ATHLETES

1. Side Plank

Strengthens the lateral core stabilizers to improve the stability of the spine, pelvis, and hips during athletic activities

Lie on your side with your ankles together and your torso propped up by your upper arm. Lift your hips upward until your body forms a diagonal plank from ankles to neck. Hold this position for 20 to 30 seconds, making sure you don't allow your hips to sag toward the floor. (Watch yourself in a mirror to make sure you're not sagging.) Switch to the other side and repeat the exercise.

2. Supine Plank

Strengthens the gluteals and hamstrings

Lie face up on the floor with your knees bent 90 degrees and your feet flat on the floor. Contract your gluteals and lift your hips until your body forms a straight line from neck to knees. Hold this position for 5 seconds, keeping your buttocks squeezed together, then return to the start position. Complete 10 repetitions.

3. Prone Plank

Builds the endurance of the spinal stabilizers

Lie on the floor on your stomach, with your upper body supported on your forearms and your toes pressing into the ground. Maintain a 90-degree bend in your elbows and make sure they are placed directly underneath the shoulders. Tighten your entire core area and lift your hips up and in line with your legs and torso. Hold this position for up to 30 seconds without allowing your hips to sag. If you can hold the prone plank position longer than 30 seconds, make it more challenging by doing it with your left foot elevated a few inches above the floor for 15 seconds, then your right foot elevated for 15 seconds.

4. Cable Trunk Rotation

Strengthens the trunk rotational stabilizers to improve the stability of the spine, pelvis, and hips during athletic activities

Stand with your left side facing a cable pulley station. Attach a D-handle at shoulder height and begin with your trunk rotated toward the weight stack and your arms fully extended with the handle grasped in both hands. Keeping your arms extended and your hands in line with the center of your chest, rotate your trunk to the right. Keep your abdominal muscles tightened and avoid hunching your shoulders as you do so. Stop when your hands are at about the "ten or eleven o'clock" position (with the "twelve o'clock" position being hands directly out in front of you), then return to the starting position. Repeat 10 to 12 times, then reverse your position and perform a set twisting in the opposite direction.

5. Swiss Ball Hyperextension

Strengthens the lower back muscles to improve the stability of the spine, pelvis, and hips during athletic activities

Lie face down on a Swiss ball with your upper thighs, pelvic area, and stomach supported by the ball and only your toes touching the floor and your arms extended directly forward, Superman-style. Contract your lower back muscles and lift your torso upward, keeping your arms in line with your spine. Extend your spine as much as possible, then return to the starting position. Repeat 12 to 15 times.

STRENGTH EXERCISES FOR CROSS-COUNTRY SKIERS

1. Romanian Dead Lift

Strengthens the hamstrings, gluteals, and lower back for a more powerful leg action

Stand with your feet close together, knees bent very slightly, with a dumbbell next to each foot. Set your core, and then bend forward at the waist and grab the dumbbells. With arms at your side and knees locked in the slightly bent position, return to a standing position. Pause briefly and then bend forward to do another repetition.

2. Step-up

Strengthens the gluteals, hamstrings, and quadriceps, and corrects muscular imbalance in the thigh muscles

Stand facing an exercise bench or a step (12 to 18 inches high) while holding a dumbbell in each hand at your sides. Step up onto the bench with your left foot, and then push off your left heel as you raise your right leg so that you're standing on the bench. Step back down with your right leg. Continue stepping up and down, pushing with your left leg and carrying your right leg along for the ride, until you complete a full set, then switch legs and repeat with your right leg doing the work.

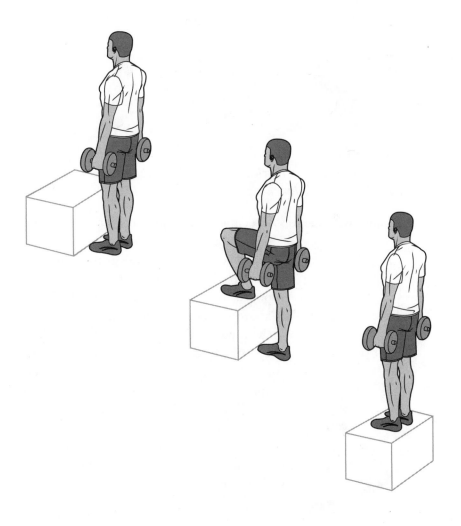

3. Stability Ball Roll-out

Strengthens the rotator cuff, scapular stabilizers, and abdominals, and corrects imbalances in the shoulder girdle and trunk

Kneel on the floor facing the ball, lean forward slightly, and place your forearms on top of the ball. Pull your belly button toward your spine. Slowly roll the ball forward by extending your forearms out in front of you and allowing your body to tilt toward the floor. Concentrate on maintaining perfect alignment of your spine. Stop just before you're forced to arch your back. Hold this position for 3 seconds and then return to the start position, exhaling as you do so. Do up to 12 repetitions.

4. Cable Face Pull

Strengthens upper-back muscles as well as the elbow flexors and grip. The external rotation helps to prevent shoulder problems

Set up a pulley with the rope attachment just above forehead level. Stand facing the pulley in a split stance and hold the rope with a neutral grip (palms and face in). Your arms are extended straight out in front of you with the hands slightly above shoulder height. Pull the center of the rope attachment toward your forehead by retracting the shoulder blades and forcing the elbows out (not down). As the rope approaches your face, your shoulder blades should be pulled back and down, with the chest high and your hands coming even with your ears. You should feel the resistance in your midback and in the back of your shoulders.

5. Side Step-up

Strengthens the quadriceps and hips for a more stable and efficient leg action

Stand with your right side facing an exercise bench or step while holding a dumbbell in your left hand with your left arm relaxed at your side. Set your core. Place your right foot on the step and then straighten your right leg completely so you're now standing on the step with your left leg unsupported. Be sure not to push off the floor with your left ankle—make your right leg do all the work of lifting your body to the height of the bench. Now step back down. After completing a full set, reverse your position and repeat with your left leg doing the work.

STRENGTH EXERCISES FOR CYCLISTS

1. Elevated Reverse Lunge

Strengthens the quadriceps for a more powerful pedal stroke

Stand on a 4-to-6-inch step with your arms resting at your sides and a dumbbell in each hand. Take a big step backward with one leg and bend both knees until the back foot hits the ground and the back knee almost grazes the floor. Then thrust powerfully upward and forward off the back foot to return to the starting position. Be sure to maintain an upright torso posture throughout the movement. Complete 10 repetitions with one leg, rest, then work the opposite leg.

2. Barbell Squat

Strengthens the gluteals, hamstrings, and quads for a more powerful pedal stroke

Stand with your feet slightly more than shoulder-width apart. Begin with a weighted barbell resting against your upper back and your hands grasping the bar on either side halfway between your neck and the weight plates. Draw your navel toward your spine, then lower your buttocks toward the floor as though sitting in a chair. Stop when your thighs are almost parallel to the floor, then return to the starting position. Complete 10 repetitions.

3. Good Morning

Strengthens the lower back to reduce the risk of low-back pain resulting from cycling

Stand tall with your feet placed slightly farther than shoulder-width apart and your arms extended straight upward, palms facing forward, with a light dumb-bell (optional) in each hand. Tighten your core. Bend forward at the waist (avoid rounding your back) and reach the dumbbells toward your toes, going as far as you can without bending at the knees. Try to keep your arms more or less in line with your torso all the way down. Now return slowly to the upright position, standing tall with arms over-head. Again, maintain a neutral spine. *Do not perform this exercise if you have a history of low-back injury, or if you have any reason to believe you might be prone to low-back pain.*

4. Bent-over Cable Shoulder Lateral Extension

Strengthens the upper back and rear shoulders to correct the forward rounding of the shoulders that frequently develops in cyclists

Stand in a wide stance with your knees slightly bent and your left side facing a cable pulley station with a D-handle connected to the low attachment point. Grasp the handle in your right hand using an underhand grip. Bend forward 45 degrees from the hips. Begin with your right arm extended toward the floor and the handle positioned directly underneath your breastbone. Tighten your core. Now pull the handle outward and upward until your right arm is fully extended away from your body and parallel to the floor. Pause briefly and return to the starting position. Complete 10 to 12 repetitions, then reverse your position and work the left shoulder.

5. Gluteal-Hamstring Raise

Strengthens the gluteals and hamstrings to generate more power during the pull phase of the pedal stroke

Lie face down on the floor and have a partner press your lower legs down into the floor just so your body can only move from the knees up. With your arms in standard push-up position, give a slight push off the floor while you contract your hamstrings and lift your body (from knees to head) upward until you are in a fully upright kneeling position. Try to keep your torso erect throughout the movement and use the hamstrings

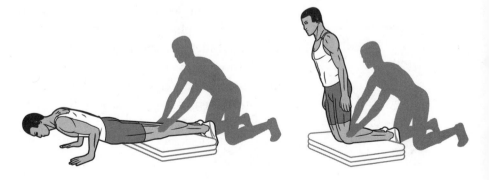

to pull your body up and the gluteals to finish the movement by tilting the pelvis back (just think of popping the hips forward to get your body upright). Lower yourself back to the floor.

STRENGTH EXERCISES FOR ROWERS

1. Cable Pull-Through

Targets the posterior chain (hamstrings, gluteals, and lower back) for efficient transfer of force from the legs to the upper body in rowing

Stand facing away from a cable column with the rope attachment set in the bottom position. Set your feet slightly farther than shoulder-width apart, so you have room to reach between your legs with both arms fully extended, and grasp the rope. Bend your knees slightly and bend forward slightly at the hips to counterbalance the pull of the rope, keeping your weight on your heels. To initiate the movement, let the weight pull your hips back as if someone had a rope around your waist and was pulling you backward. Now begin tilting your torso forward from the hips (not the waist) and allow the weight to pull your extended arms between your legs. Avoid rounding your back. The lowering phase ends when the torso is just short of parallel with the floor, at which point you'll push through the heels and use your posterior chain to pull the rope forward between your legs and straighten your body back to the starting position. Push your hips forward and squeeze your gluteals to lock out. Stand upright; don't lean back!

2. Overhead Squat

Strengthens the gluteals, hamstrings, quadriceps, core, and upper back for a more powerful leg action

Stand with your feet slightly wider than shoulder-width apart, toes turned out slightly. Grab a rolled-up towel with an overhand grip, hands shoulder-width apart, and raise it overhead so your shoulders are roughly in line with your heels. Squat down as far as possible without letting your knees jut out past your toes. Return to standing to complete one full rep. Do 10 to 15 repetitions.

3. Cable Front Shoulder Raise

Strengthen the front shoulder muscles to prevent shoulder-muscle strength imbalances

Stand facing away from a door gym or cable pulley station. Connect a handle to the low attachment point and grasp it in your right hand with your right arm relaxed at your side, palm facing the door or cable pulley station. Set your core. Contract the muscles on the front of your shoulder and lift the handle forward and upward, going just past the point where your arm is parallel to the floor. Pause briefly and return to the starting position. After completing a full set, work the left shoulder.

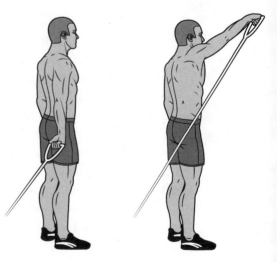

4. Straight-Arm Lat Pull-down
Strengthens the lower trapezius and keeps the shoulders healthy

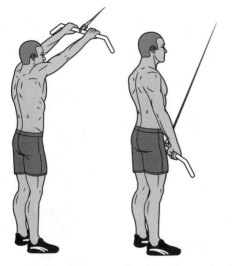

Stand facing a cable column or pulldown machine with a straight-bar attachment. Grasp the bar with a pronated (palms-down) grip and your arms extended straight in front of you with the bar at shoulder height. Keeping your torso upright and initiating the movement with your shoulder blades and upper arms, pull the bar down until it touches your upper thighs while keeping the wrists and elbows straight. When this exercise is performed correctly, you'll feel it in your midback, right at the base of your shoulder blades.

5. L-over
Strengthens the deep abdominal and oblique muscles

Lie face up with your arms resting at your sides and your palms flat on the floor. Extend your legs directly toward the ceiling, touch your feet together, and point your toes. Set your core. Keeping your big toes side-by-side, tip your legs 12 to 18 inches to the right by twisting at the hip, so that your right gluteal comes off the floor. Fight the pull of gravity by maintaining stability with your abdominals and obliques. Pause for a moment, then return slowly to the starting position, again using your core muscles to control the movement. Repeat on the left side, and continue alternating from right to left until you have completed a full set.

STRENGTH EXERCISES FOR RUNNERS

1. One-Leg Squat

Trains the hip abductors and external rotators to maintain hip stability during a single-leg movement similar to running

Stand on your right foot and bend the left leg slightly to elevate the left foot a few inches above the floor. Lower your buttocks slowly toward the floor, keeping most of your weight on the heel of your support foot. Reach the left leg either behind your body (easier) or in front of your body (harder) to keep it out of the way and to help maintain balance. Squat as low as you can go without your buttocks swinging outward (a sign that the targeted muscles have become overwhelmed and that other muscles have been activated to take up the slack). Return to the starting position. Do 8 to 10 squats on each foot.

2. Split Squat Jump

Increases stride power by simulating the stride action with exaggerated upward thrust

Start in a split stance with your right foot flat on the ground and your left leg slightly bent with only the left forefoot touching the ground a half step behind the right. Lower yourself down into a deep squat, then leap upward as high as possible. In midair, reverse the position of your legs. When you land, sink down immediately into another squat, then leap again. Use your arms for balance and to generate extra upward thrust with each leap. Complete 10 to 20 jumps in each stance.

3. X-Band Walk

Strengthens the hip abductors to increase the stability of the hips and pelvis during running

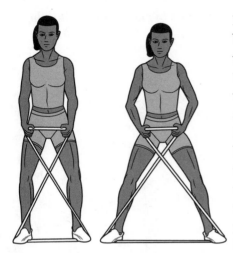

Loop a half-inch or one-inch exercise band under both feet and stand on top of it. Your feet should be roughly 12 inches apart at the start. Cross the ends of the band to form an X and grasp one end in each hand. Pull your chest up and shoulders back and keep tension on the band throughout. Start walking sideways with small lateral steps. The leg that's on the side of the direction you're moving will have to overcome the band's tension to take each step. Make sure that you keep the hips and shoulders level, and don't deviate forward or backward as you step to the side. When this exercise is performed correctly, you'll feel the movement in your gluteals. Complete 10 steps in one direction, then 10 more moving in the opposite direction.

4. VMO Dip

Strengthens the vastus medialis (the quadriceps muscle terminating in a small bulge just above the medial side of the kneecap) to improve the stability of the knee during running

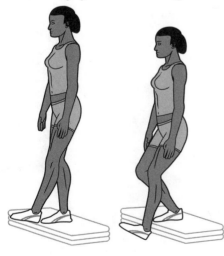

Stand on an exercise step that's 8 to 12 inches high. Pick up your left foot and slowly reach it toward the floor in front of the step by bending your right knee. Allow your left heel to touch the floor but don't put any weight on it. Return to the starting position. Complete 8 to 12 repetitions, then switch legs.

5. Suitcase Dead Lift

Enhances the ability to resist medial tilting of the body (a major cause of joint instability and overuse injuries) during the stance phase of running

Stand with your arms hanging at your sides and a dumbbell in one hand. Push your hips back, bend the knees, and reach the dumbbell down as close to the floor as you can without rounding your lower back. Now stand up again. Don't allow your torso to tilt to either side while performing this movement. Complete 10 repetitions, rest for 30 seconds, then repeat the exercise while holding the dumbbell in the opposite hand.

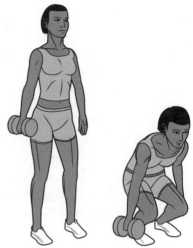

STRENGTH EXERCISES FOR SWIMMERS

1. Cable High-Low Pull

Creates a more powerful freestyle arm pull by simulating the arm pull action under load, strengthening the upper and midback muscles

Stand with your left side facing a cable pulley station with a D-handle attached at shoulder-to-head height. Bend your knees and place your feet slightly more than shoulder-width apart. Use both hands to grab the handle. Your arms should be almost fully extended with your trunk twisted to the left. Now pull the handle from this position across your body and toward the floor, stopping when your hands are outside your right ankle. This is a compound movement that involves twisting your torso to the right, shifting your weight from your left foot to

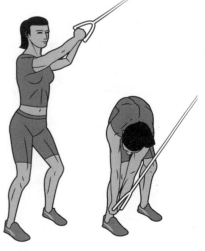

your right foot, bending toward the floor, and using your shoulders to pull the handle across your body. Concentrate on initiating the movement with your trunk muscles. At the bottom of the movement, pause briefly, then smoothly return to the starting position. Complete 10 repetitions. Reverse your position and repeat the exercise.

2. Cable Low-High Pull
Strengthens the muscles responsible for body rotation during freestyle swimming for a more efficient stroke

Connect a D-handle to a cable pulley station at ankle height. Stand in a wide stance with your left side facing the cable pulley station and most of your weight on the left foot. Grasp the handle in both hands, beginning with the handle just outside your lower left shin. Using both arms, pull the cable upward and across your body, keeping your arms straight and finishing with your hands above your right shoulder. Avoid rounding your back. Return smoothly to the starting position. Complete 10 repetitions. Reverse your position and repeat the exercise.

3. Push-up and Reach

Strengthens the chest, triceps, and shoulder stabilizers for greater shoulder stability and reduced risk of "swimmer's shoulder"

Begin by doing a standard push-up. At the top of the movement, when your arms are completely straight, twist your body to the right and reach straight toward the ceiling with your right arm. Follow the movement of your hand with your eyes. Pause for one second, then put that hand back down and twist left, reaching up with your left hand. One push-up with reaches to both sides counts as one repetition. Do 10 to 15 repetitions. If you can't do at least 10 regular push-ups, do half push-ups (where you lower your chest only halfway to the floor).

4. Cable Shoulder External Rotation

Strengthens the rotator cuff muscles to reduce the risk of injury

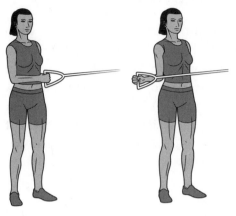

Stand with your left side facing a cable pulley station. Grasp the D-handle in your right hand and begin with your right arm bent 90 degrees so that your forearm is pointing toward the cable pulley station across your belly. Now rotate your shoulder externally and pull the handle across your body, keeping your elbow and upper arm pressed against your right side. Return to the starting position. Complete 10 repetitions, then repeat the exercise with your left arm.

5. One-Arm Dumbbell Snatch

Attenuates muscle imbalances created by swimming by essentially reversing the freestyle arm-pull action

Assume a wide stance with a single dumbbell placed on the floor between your feet. Bend your knees, tilt forward from the hips, and grasp the dumbbell with your right hand using an overhand grip (knuckles facing

forward). Begin with your right arm fully extended. The objective of this exercise is to lift the dumbbell in a straight line from the floor to a point directly overhead. To do this, begin by contracting your gluteals, hamstrings, and lower back so that the dumbbell rises to thigh height as you assume an upright standing position. From this point, keep the dumbbell moving in a straight line close to your body by bending your elbow and pulling from the shoulder. As the dumbbell approaches head level rotate and extend your arm until it is pointing toward the ceiling. Pause briefly, then reverse the movement, allowing the dumbbell to come to rest again on the floor briefly before initiating the next lift. Complete 10 to 12 repetitions, then switch to the right arm.

STRENGTH EXERCISES FOR TRIATHLETES

1. Elevated Reverse Lunge
Strengthens the quadriceps for a more powerful pedal stroke

Stand on a 4-to-6-inch step with your arms resting at your sides and a dumbbell in each hand. Take a big step backward with one leg and bend both knees until the back foot hits the ground and the back knee almost grazes the floor. Then thrust power- fully upward and forward off the back foot to return to the starting position. Be sure to maintain an upright torso pos- ture throughout the movement. Complete 10 repetitions with one leg, rest, then work the opposite leg.

2. One-Leg Squat
Trains the hip abductors and external rotators to maintain hip stability during a single-leg movement similar to running

Stand on your right foot and bend the left leg slightly to elevate the left foot a few inches above the floor. Lower your buttocks slowly toward the floor, keeping most of your weight on the heel of your support foot. Reach the left leg either behind your body (easier) or in front of your body (harder) to keep it out of the way and to help maintain balance. Squat as low as you can go without your buttocks swinging outward (a sign that the targeted muscles have become overwhelmed and that other muscles have been activated to take up the slack). Return to the starting position. Do 8 to 10 squats on each foot.

3. Suitcase Dead Lift

Enhances the ability to resist medial tilting of the body (a major cause of joint instability and overuse injuries) during the stance phase of running

Stand with your arms hanging at your sides and a dumbbell in one hand. Push your hips back, bend the knees, and reach the dumbbell down as close to the floor as you can without rounding your lower back. Now stand up again. Don't allow your torso to tilt to either side while performing this movement. Complete 10 repetitions, rest for 30 seconds, then repeat the exercise while holding the dumbbell in the opposite hand.

4. Push-up and Reach

Strengthens the chest, triceps, and shoulder stabilizers for greater shoulder stability and reduced risk of "swimmer's shoulder"

Begin by doing a standard push-up. At the top of the movement, when your arms are completely straight, twist your body to the right and reach straight toward the ceiling with your right arm. Follow the movement of your hand with your eyes. Pause for one second, then put that hand back down and twist left, reaching up with your left hand. One push-up with reaches to both sides counts as one repetition.

Do 10 to 15 repetitions. If you can't do at least 10 regular push-ups, do half push-ups (where you lower your chest only halfway to the floor).

5. One-Arm Dumbbell Snatch

Attenuates muscle imbalances created by swimming by essentially reversing the freestyle arm-pull action

Assume a wide stance with a single dumbbell placed on the floor between your feet. Bend your knees, tilt forward from the hips, and grasp the dumbbell with your right hand using an overhand grip (knuckles facing forward). Begin with your right arm fully extended. The objective of this exercise is to lift the dumbbell in a straight line from the floor to a point directly overhead. To do this, begin by contracting your gluteals, hamstrings, and lower back so that the dumbbell rises to thigh height as you assume an upright standing position. From this point, keep the dumbbell moving in a straight line close to your body by bending your elbow and pulling from the shoulder. As the dumbbell approaches head level rotate and extend your arm until it is pointing toward the ceiling. Pause briefly, then reverse the movement, allowing the dumbbell to come to rest again on the floor briefly before initiating the next lift. Complete 10 to 12 repetitions, then switch to the right arm.

REFERENCES

Achten, J., S. L. Halson, L. Moseley, M. P. Rayson, A. Casey, and A. E. Jeukendrup. 2004. Higher Dietary Carbohydrate Content During Intensified Running Training Results in Better Maintenance of Performance and Mood State. *Journal of Applied Physiology* 96: 1331–40.

Amorim, A. R., S. Rössner, M. Neovius, P. M. Lourenço, and Y. Linné. 2007. Does Excess Pregnancy Weight Gain Constitute a Major Risk for Increasing Long-Term BMI? *Obesity* 15(5): 1278–86.

Anderson, J. W., P. Baird, R. H. Davis Jr., S. Ferreri, M. Knudtson, A. Koraym, V. Waters, and C. L. Williams. 2009. Health Benefits of Dietary Fiber. *Nutrition Review* 67(4): 188–205.

Andrade, A. M., G. W. Greene, and K. J. Melanson. 2008. Eating Slowly Led to Decreases in Energy Intake Within Meals in Healthy Women. *Journal of the American Dietetic Association* 108(7): 1186–91.

Avlonitou, E., E. Georgiou, G. Douskas, and A. Louizi. 1997. Estimation of Body Composition in Competitive Swimmers by Means of Three Different Techniques. *International Journal of Sports Medicine* 18: 363–68.

Baer, J. T., and J. A. Frentsos. 1997. Increased Energy and Nutrient Intake During Training and Competition Improves Elite Triathletes' Endurance Performance. *International Journal of Sport Nutrition* 7(1): 61–71.

Bakshi, R., Y. Bhambhani, and H. Madill. 1991. The Effects of Task Preference on Performance During Purposeful and Non-purposeful Activities. *American Journal of Occupational Therapy* 45(10): 912–16.

271

Barrack, M. T., M. J. Rauh, H. S. Barkai, and J. F. Nichols. 2008. Dietary Restraint and Low Bone Mass in Female Adolescent Endurance Runners. *American Journal of Clinical Nutrition* 87(1): 36–43.

Beelen, M., R. Koopman, A. P. Gijsen, H. Vandereyt, A. K. Kies, H. Kuipers, W. H. Saris, and L. J. van Loon. 2008. Protein Coingestion Stimulates Muscle Protein Synthesis During Resistance-Type Exercise. *American Journal of Physiology, Endocrinology, and Metabolism* 295(1): E70–77.

Bell, E. A., V. H. Castellanos, C. L. Pelkman, M. L. Thorwart, and B. J. Rolls. 1998. Energy Density of Foods Affects Energy Intake in Normal-Weight Women. *American Journal of Clinical Nutrition* 67(3): 412–20.

Berardi, J. M., T. B. Price, E. E. Noreen, and P. W. Lemon. 2006. Postexercise Muscle Glycogen Recovery Enhanced with a Carbohydrate-Protein Supplement. *Medicine and Science in Sports and Exercise* 38(6): 1106–13.

Bergman, B. C., G. E. Butterfield, E. E. Wolfel, G. A. Casazza, G. D. Lopaschuk, and G. A. Brooks. 1999. Evaluation of Exercise and Training on Muscle Lipid Metabolism. *American Journal of Physiology* 276: E106–17.

Bes-Rastrollo, M., N. M. Wedick, M. A. Martinez-Gonzalez, T. Y. Li, L. Sampson, and F. B. Hu. 2009. Prospective Study of Nut Consumption, Long-Term Weight Change, and Obesity Risk in Women. *American Journal of Clinical Nutrition* 89(6): 1913–19.

Bouhlel, E., M. Denguezli, M. Zaouali, Z. Tabka, and R. J. Shephard. 2008. Ramadan Fasting Effects on Plasma Leptin, Adiponectin Concentrations, and Body Composition in Trained Young Men. *International Journal of Sport Nutrition and Exercise Metabolism* 18(6): 617–27.

Ciccolo, J. T., J. B. Bartholomew, M. Stults-Kolehmainen, J. Seifert, and R. Portman. 2009. Relationship Between Body Weight and Health-Related Quality of Life Amongst a Large Group of Highly Active Individuals. Paper presented at the Society for Behavioral Medicine, Montreal, Canada.

Creer, A. R., M. D. Ricard, R. K. Conlee, G. L. Hoyt, and A. C. Parcell. 2004. Neural, Metabolic, and Performance Adaptations to Four Weeks of High Intensity Sprint-Interval Training in Trained Cyclists. *International Journal of Sports Medicine* 25(2): 92–98.

Cureton, K. J., and P. B. Sparling. 1980. Distance Running, Performance, and Metabolic Responses to Running in Men and Women with Excess Weight Experimentally Equated. *Medicine and Science in Sports and Exercise* 12(4): 288–94.

Davis, J. M., S. Sadri, R. G. Sargent, and D. Ward. 1989. Weight Control and Calorie Expenditure: Thermogenic Effect of Pre-prandial and Post-prandial Exercise. *Addictive Behaviors* 14(3): 347–51.

De Castro, J. M. 2007. The Time of Day and the Proportions of Macronutrients Eaten Are Related to Total Daily Food Intake. *British Journal of Nutrition* 98(5): 1077–83.

Derave, W., M. S. Ozdemir, R. C. Harris, A. Pottier, H. Reyngoudt, K. Koppo, J. A. Wise, and E. Achten. 2007. Beta-Alanine Supplementation Augments Muscle Carnosine Content and Attenuates Fatigue During Repeated Isokinetic Contraction Bouts in Trained Sprinters. *Journal of Applied Physiology* 103(5): 1736–43.

Deutz, R. C., D. Benardot, D. E. Martin, and M. M. Cody. 2000. Relationship Between Energy Deficits and Body Composition in Elite Female Gymnasts and Runners. *Medicine and Science in Sports and Exercise* 32(3): 659–68.

Engelhardt, M., G. Neumann, A. Berbalk, and I. Reuter. 1998. Creatine Supplementation in Endurance Sports. *Medicine and Science in Sports and Exercise* 30(7): 1123–29.

Erlenbusch, M., M. Haub, K. Munoz, S. MacConnie, and B. Stillwell. 2005. Effect of High-Fat or High-Carbohydrate Diets on Endurance Exercise: A Meta-analysis. *International Journal of Sport Nutrition and Exercise Metabolism* 15(1): 1–14.

Farshchi, H. R., M. A. Taylor, and I. A. Macdonald. 2005. Beneficial Metabolic Effects of Regular Meal Frequency on Dietary Thermogenesis, Insulin Sensitivity, and Fasting Lipid Profiles in Healthy Obese Women. *American Journal of Clinical Nutrition* 81(1): 16–24.

Faye, J., A. Fall, L. Badji, F. Cisse, H. Stephan, and P. Tine. 2005. Effects of Ramadan Fast on Weight, Performance, and Glycemia During Training for Resistance. *Dakar Med* 50(3): 146–51.

Fleming, J., M. J. Sharman, N. G. Avery, D. M. Love, A. L. Gómez, T. P. Scheet, W. J. Kraemer, and J. S. Volek. 2003. Endurance Capacity and High-Intensity Exercise Performance Responses to a High-Fat Diet. *International Journal of Sport Nutrition and Exercise Metabolism* 13(4): 466–78.

Flood, J. E., and B. J. Rolls. 2007. Soup Preloads in a Variety of Forms Reduce Meal Energy Intake. *Appetite* 49(3): 626–34.

Fudge, B. W., C. Easton, D. Kingsmore, F. K. Kiplamai, V. O. Onywera, K. R. Westerterp, B. Kayser, T. D. Noakes, and Y. P. Pitsiladis. 2008. Elite Kenyan Endurance Runners Are Hydrated Day-to-Day with ad Libitum Fluid Intake. *Medicine and Science in Sports and Exercise* 40(6): 1171–79.

Fudge, B. W., K. R. Westerterp, F. K. Kiplamai, V. O. Onywera, M. K. Boit, B. Kayser, and Y. P. Pitsiladis. 2006. Evidence of Negative Energy Balance Using Doubly Labeled Water in Elite Kenyan Endurance Runners Prior to Competition. *British Journal of Nutrition* 95(1): 59–66.

Gaine, P. C., M. A. Pikosky, D. R. Bolster, W. F. Martin, C. M. Maresh, and N. R. Rodriguez. 2007. Postexercise Whole-Body Protein Turnover Response to Three Levels of Protein Intake. *Medicine and Science in Sports and Exercise* 39(3): 480–86.

Giovannini, M., E. Verduci, S. Scaglioni, E. Salvatici, M. Bonza, E. Riva, and C. Agostoni. 2008. Breakfast: A Good Habit, Not a Repetitive Custom. *Journal of International Medical Research* 36(4): 613–24.

Good, C. K., N. Holschuh, A. M. Albertson, and A. L. Eldridge. 2008. Whole Grain Consumption and Body Mass Index in Adult Women: An Analysis of NHANES 1999–2000 and the USDA Pyramid Servings Database. *Journal of the American College of Nutrition* 27(1): 80–87.

Goodman-Larson, A., K. Johnson, and K. Shevlin. 2003. The Effect of Meal Frequency on Preprandial Resting Metabolic Rate. *University of Wisconsin–La Crosse Journal of Undergraduate Research* 6: 1–4.

Gordon, C. M., K. C. DePeter, H. A. Feldman, E. Grace, and S. J. Emans. 2004. Prevalence of Vitamin D Deficiency Among Healthy Adolescents. *Archives of Pediatric & Adolescent Medicine* 158(6): 531–37.

Gordon-Larsen, P., N. Hou, S. Sidney, B. Sternfeld, C. E. Lewis, D. R. Jacobs Jr., and B. M. Popkin. 2009. Fifteen-Year Longitudinal Trends in Walking Patterns and Their Impact on Weight Change. *American Journal of Clinical Nutrition* 89(1): 19–26.

Gorin, A. A., S. Phelan, R. R. Wing, and J. O. Hill. 2004. Promoting Long-Term Weight Control: Does Dieting Consistency Matter? *International Journal of Obesity and Related Metabolic Disorders* 28(2): 278–81.

Havenar, J. M., and M. Lochbaum. 2007. Differences in Participation Motives of First-Time Marathon Finishers and Pre-race Dropouts. *Journal of Sport Behavior* 30(3): 270–79.

Hecht, S., D. Vigil, J. Luftman, A. Vasco, I. Gardner, L. Huston, and R. Contreras. 2007. Body Composition Analysis and Performance in Triathletes. Paper presented at the Annual Meeting of the American Medical Society for Sports Medicine, Albuquerque, New Mexico.

Hill, A. M., J. D. Buckley, K. J. Murphy, and P. R. Howe. 2007. Combining Fish-Oil Supplements with Regular Aerobic Exercise Improves Body Composition and Cardiovascular Disease Risk Factors. *American Journal of Clinical Nutrition* 85(5): 1267–74.

Hollis, J. F., C. M. Gullion, V. J. Stevens, P. J. Brantley, L. J. Appel, J. D. Ard, C. M. Champagne, A. Dalcin, T. P. Erlinger, K. Funk, D. Laferriere, P. H. Lin, C. M. Loria, C. Samuel-Hodge, W. M. Vollmer, and L. P. Svetkey. 2008. Weight Loss During the Intensive Intervention Phase of the Weight-Loss Maintenance Trial. *American Journal of Preventive Medicine* 35(2): 118–26.

Horvath, P. J., C. K. Eagen, N. M. Fisher, J. J. Leddy, and D. R. Pendergast. 2000. The Effects of Varying Levels of Dietary Fat on Performance and Metabolism in Trained Male and Female Runners. *Journal of the American College of Nutrition* 19(1): 52–60.

Hsu, F. C., L. Lenchik, B. J. Nicklas, K. Lohman, T. C. Register, J. Mychaleckyj, C. D. Langefeld, B. I. Freedman, D. W. Bowden, and J. J. Carr. 2005. Heritability of Body Composition Measured by DXA in the Diabetes Heart Study. *Obesity Research* 13(2): 312–19.

Hursel, R., W. Viechtbauer, and M. S. Westerterp-Plantenga. 2009. The Effects of Green Tea on Weight Loss and Weight Maintenance: A Meta-analysis. *International Journal of Obesity (London)* 33: 956–61.

Kerksick, C., T. Harvey, J. Stout, B. Campbell, C. Wilborn, R. Kreider, D. Kalman, T. Ziegenfuss, H. Lopez, J. Landis, J. L. Ivy, and J. Antonio. 2008. International Society of Sports Nutrition Position Stand: Nutrient Timing. *Journal of the International Society of Sports Nutrition* 5: 17.

Koutedakis, Y., P. J. Pacy, R. M. Quevedo, D. J. Millward, R. Hesp, C. Boreham, and N. C. Sharp. 1994. The Effects of Two Different Periods of Weight-Reduction on Selected Performance Parameters in Elite Lightweight Oarswomen. *International Journal of Sports Medicine* 15(8): 472–77.

Kreider, R. B. 2003. Effects of Creatine Supplementation on Performance and Training Adaptations. *Molecular and Cellular Biochemistry* 244(1–2): 89–94.

Kreider, R. B., B. C. Leutholotz, F. I. Katch, and V. L. Katch. 2009. *Exercise and Sport Nutrition: Principles, Promises, Science, and Recommendations.* Santa Barbara, Calif.: Fitness Technologies Press.

LaForgia, J., R. T. Withers, and C. J. Gore. 2006. Effects of Exercise Intensity and Duration on the Excess Post-exercise Oxygen Consumption. *Journal of Sports Science* (12): 1247–64.

Lambert, E. V., J. H. Goedecke, C. Zyle, K. Murphy, J. A. Hawley, S. C. Dennis, and T. D. Noakes. 2001. High-Fat Diet Versus Habitual Diet Prior to Carbohydrate Loading: Effects on Exercise Metabolism and Cycling Performance. *International Journal of Sport Nutrition and Exercise Metabolism* 11(2): 209–25.

LeSauter, J., N. Hoque, M. Weintraub, D. W. Pfaff, and R. Silver. 2009. Stomach Ghrelin-Secreting Cells as Food-Entrainable Circadian Clocks. *Proceedings of the National Academy of Sciences* 106(32): 13582–87.

Lewis, B. A., B. H. Marcus, R. R. Pate, and A. L. Dunn. 2002. Psychosocial Mediators of Physical Activity Behavior Among Adults and Children. *American Journal of Preventive Medicine* 23 (2 Supplement): 26–35.

REFERENCES

Lockwood, C. M., J. R. Moon, S. E. Tobkin, A. A. Walter, A. E. Smith, V. J. Dalbo, J. T. Cramer, and J. R. Stout. 2008. Minimal Nutritional Intervention with High-Protein/ Low-Carbohydrate and Low-Fat, Nutrient-Dense Food Supplement Improves Body Composition and Exercise Benefits in Overweight Adults. *Nutrition & Metabolism* 5: 11.

Luhovyy, B. L., T. Akhavan, and G. H. Anderson. 2007. Whey Proteins in the Regulation of Food Intake and Satiety. *Journal of the American College of Nutrition* 26(6): 704S–12S.

Macdermid, P. W., and S. R. Stannard. 2006. A Whey-Supplemented, High-Protein Diet Versus a High-Carbohydrate Diet: Effects on Endurance Cycling Performance. *International Journal of Sport Nutrition and Exercise Metabolism* 16(1): 65–77.

MacLean, P. S., J. A. Higgins, H. R. Wyatt, E. L. Melanson, G. C. Johnson, M. R. Jackman, E. D. Giles, I. E. Brown, and J. O. Hill. 2009. Regular Exercise Attenuates the Metabolic Drive to Regain Weight After Long-Term Weight Loss. *American Journal of Physiology—Regulatory, Integrative, and Comparative Physiology* 297(3): R793–802.

Major, G. C., F. P. Alarie, J. Doré, and A. Tremblay. 2009. Calcium Plus Vitamin D Supplementation and Fat Mass Loss in Female Very Low-Calcium Consumers: Potential Link with a Calcium-Specific Appetite Control. *British Journal of Nutrition* 101(5): 659–63.

Mann, T., A. J. Tomiyama, E. Westling, A. M. Lew, B. Samuels, and J. Chatman. 2007. Medicare's Search for Effective Obesity Treatments: Diets Are Not the Answer. *American Psychologist* 62(3): 220–33.

Marcora, S. M., A. Bosio, and H. M. de Morree. 2008. Locomotor Muscle Fatigue Increases Cardiorespiratory Responses and Reduces Performance During Intense Cycling Exercise Independently from Metabolic Stress. *American Journal of Physiology— Regulatory, Integrative, and Comparative Physiology* 294(3): R874–83.

Martinez-Lagunas, V., Z. Ding, J. R. Bernard, B. Wang, and J. L. Ivy. 2009. The Effect of a Low-Carbohydrate Protein Beverage on Endurance Performance. Unpublished manuscript. University of Texas–Austin.

Mattson, M. P., and R. Wan. 2005. Beneficial Effects of Intermittent Fasting and Caloric Restriction on the Cardiovascular and Cerebrovascular Systems. *Journal of Nutritional Biochemistry* 16(3): 29–37.

McArdle, W. D., F. I. Katch, and V. L. Katch. 2005. *Sports and Exercise Nutrition*. Philadelphia, Pa.: Lippincott, Williams & Wilkins.

Michels, K. B., and A. A. Wolk. 2002. A Prospective Study of Variety of Healthy Foods and Mortality in Women. *International Journal of Epidemiology* 31: 847–54.

Mustelin, L., K. H. Pietiläinen, A. Rissanen, A. R. Sovijärvi, P. Piirilä, J. Naukkarinen, L. Peltonen, J. Kaprio, and H. Yki-Järvinen. 2008. Acquired Obesity and Poor Physical Fitness Impair Expression of Genes of Mitochondrial Oxidative Phosphorylation in Monozygotic Twins Discordant for Obesity. *American Journal of Physiology, Endocrinology, and Metabolism* 295(1): E148–54.

Olson, C. M., M. S. Strawderman, and B. A. Dennison. 2008. Maternal Weight Gain During Pregnancy and Child Weight at Age 3 Years. *Maternal and Child Health Journal*, Sept. 26.

Onywera, V. O., F. K. Kiplamai, M. K. Boit, and Y. P. Pitsiladis. 2004. Food and Macronutrient Intake of Elite Kenyan Distance Runners. *International Journal of Sport Nutrition and Exercise Metabolism* 14(6): 709–19.

Paton, C. D., and W. G. Hopkins. 2005. Combining Explosive and High-Resistance Training Improves Performance in Competitive Cyclists. *Journal of Strength and Conditioning Research* 19(4): 826–30.

Peoples, G. E., P. L. McLennan, P. R. Howe, and H. Groeller. 2008. Fish Oil Reduces Heart Rate and Oxygen Consumption During Exercise. *Journal of Cardiovascular Pharmacology* 52(6): 540–47.

Phelain, J. F., E. Reinke, M. A. Harris, and C. L. Melby. 1997. Postexercise Energy Expenditure and Substrate Oxidation in Young Women Resulting from Exercise Bouts of Different Intensity. *Journal of the American College of Nutrition* 16(2): 140–46.

Phillips, S. M. 2004. Protein Requirements and Supplementation in Strength Sports. *Nutrition* 20(7–8): 689–95.

Quinn, T. J., N. B. Vroman, and R. Kertzer. 1994. Postexercise Oxygen Consumption in Trained Females: Effect of Exercise Duration. *Medicine and Science in Sports and Exercise* 26(7): 908–13.

Racette, S. B., E. P. Weiss, K. B. Schechtman, K. Steger-May, D. T. Villareal, K. A. Obert, and J. O. Holloszy. 2008. Influence of Weekend Lifestyle Patterns on Body Weight. *Obesity* 16(8): 1826–30.

Rasmussen, K. M., and A. L. Yaktine. 2009. Weight Gain During Pregnancy: Reexamining the Guidelines. Washington, D.C.: National Academies Press.

Rennie, M. J., and K. D. Tipton. 2000. Protein and Amino Acid Metabolism During and After Exercise and the Effects of Nutrition. *Annual Review of Nutrition* 20: 457–83.

Ritland, L. M., D. L. Alekel, O. A. Matvienko, K. B. Hanson, J. W. Stewart, L. N. Hanson, M. B. Reddy, M. D. Van Loan, and U. Genschel. 2008. Centrally Located Body Fat Is Related to Appetitive Hormones in Healthy Postmenopausal Women. *European Journal of Endocrinology* 158(6): 889–97.

Roberts, S. B., and J. Mayer. 2000. Holiday Weight Gain: Fact or Fiction? *Nutrition Reviews* 58(12): 378–79.

Rosenbaum, M., J. Hirsch, D. A. Gallagher, and R. L. Leibel. 2008. Long-Term Persistence of Adaptive Thermogenesis in Subjects Who Have Maintained a Reduced Body Weight. *American Journal of Clinical Nutrition* 88(4): 906–12.

Rowlands, D. S., and W. G. Hopkins. 2002. Effects of High-Fat and High-Carbohydrate Diets on Metabolism and Performance in Cycling. *Metabolism* 51(6): 678–90.

Sato, K., and M. Mokha. 2009. Does Core Strength Training Influence Running Kinetics, Lower-Extremity Stability, and 5,000-M Performance in Runners? *Journal of Strength and Conditioning Research* 23(1): 133–40.

Saunders, M. J., M. D. Kane, and M. K. Todd. 2004. Effects of Carbohydrate-Protein Beverage on Cycling Endurance and Muscle Damage. *Medicine and Science in Sports and Exercise* 36(7): 1233–38.

Sherman, W. M., and G. S. Wimer. 1991. Insufficient Dietary Carbohydrate During Training: Does It Impair Athletic Performance? *International Journal of Sport Nutrition* 1(1): 28–44.

Sherman, W. M., J. A. Doyle, D. R. Lamb, and R. H. Strauss. 1993. Dietary Carbohydrate, Muscle Glycogen, and Exercise Performance During 7 Days of Training. *American Journal of Clinical Nutrition* 57(1): 27–31.

Slater, G. J., A. J. Rice, K. Sharpe, D. Jenkins, and A. G. Hahn. 2007. Influence of Nutrient Intake After Weigh-in on Lightweight Rowing Performance. *Medicine and Science in Sports and Exercise* 39(1): 184–91.

Smeets, A. J., and M. S. Westerterp-Plantenga. 2008. Acute Effects on Metabolism and Appetite Profile of One Meal Difference in the Lower Range of Meal Frequency. *British Journal of Nutrition* 99(6): 1316–21.

Smith, A. E., A. A. Walter, J. L. Graef, K. L. Kendall, J. R. Moon, C. M. Lockwood, D. H. Fukuda, T. W. Beck, J. T. Cramer, and J. R. Stout. 2009. Effects of Beta-Alanine Supplementation and High-Intensity Interval Training on Endurance Performance and Body Composition in Men: A Double-Blind Trial. *Journal of the International Society of Sports Nutrition* 6: 5.

Smith, A. E., J. R. Moon, K. L. Kendall, J. L. Graef, C. M. Lockwood, A. A.Walter, T. W. Beck, J. T. Cramer, and J. R. Stout. 2009. The Effects of Beta-Alanine Supplementation and High-Intensity Interval Training on Neuromuscular Fatigue and Muscle Function. *European Journal of Applied Physiology* 105(3): 357–63.

Stice, E., S. Spoor, C. Bohon, M. G. Veldhuizen, and D. M. Small. 2008. Relation of Reward from Food Intake and Anticipated Food Intake to Obesity: A Functional Magnetic Resonance Imaging Study. *Journal of Abnormal Psychology* 117(4): 924–35.

Støren, O., J. Helgerud, E. M. Støa, and J. Hoff. 2008. Maximal Strength Training Improves Running Economy in Distance Runners. *Medicine and Science in Sports and Exercise* 40(6): 1087–92.

Stuebe, A. M., E. Oken, and M. W. Gillman. 2009. Associations of Diet and Physical Activity During Pregnancy with Risk of Excessive Gestational Weight Gain. *American Journal of Obstetrics and Gynecology* 201(1): 58.E1–8.

Stults-Kolehmainen, M., J. T. Ciccolo, J. B. Bartholomew, J. Seifert, and R. Portman. 2009. Age-Related Changes in Motivation to Exercise Among Highly Active Individuals. *Annals of Behavioral Medicine* Supplement 1: D168.

Tahara, Y., K. Moji, S. Honda, R. Nakao, N. Tsunawake, R. Fukuda, K. Aoyagi, and N. Mascie-Taylor. 2008. Fat-Free Mass and Excess Post-exercise Oxygen Consumption in the 40 Minutes After Short-Duration Exhaustive Exercise in Young Male Japanese Athletes. *Journal of Physiological Anthropology* 27(3): 139–43.

Teixeira, A., L. Müller, A. A. dos Santos, P. Reckziegel, T. Emanuelli, J. B. Rocha, and M. E. Bürger. 2009. Beneficial Effects of Gradual Intense Exercise in Tissues of Rats Fed with a Diet Deficient in Vitamins and Minerals: A Pilot Study. *Nutrition* 25(5): 590–96.

Thomson, R., G. D. Brinkworth, J. D. Buckley, M. Noakes, and P. M. Clifton. 2007. Good Agreement Between Bioelectrical Impedance and Dual-Energy X-ray Absorptiometry for Estimating Changes in Body Composition During Weight Loss in Overweight Young Women. *Clinical Nutrition* 26(6): 771–77.

Tomten, S. E., and A. T. Høstmark. 2009. Serum Vitamin E Concentration and Osmotic Fragility in Female Long-Distance Runners. *Journal of Sports Sciences* 27(1): 69–76.

Trapp, E. G., D. J. Chisholm, J. Freund, and S. H. Boutcher. 2008. The Effects of High-Intensity Intermittent Exercise Training on Fat Loss and Fasting Insulin Levels of Young Women. *International Journal of Obesity (London)* 32(4): 684–91.

Tricon, S., and P. Yaqoob. 2006. Conjugated Linoleic Acid and Human Health: A Critical Evaluation of the Evidence. *Current Opinion in Clinical Nutrition and Metabolic Care* 9(2): 105–10.

Van Pelt, R. E., K. P. Davy, E. T. Stevenson, T. M. Wilson, P. P. Jones, C. A. Desouza, and D. R. Seals. 1998. Smaller Differences in Total and Regional Adiposity with Age in Women who Regularly Perform Endurance Exercise. *American Journal of Physiology* 275 (4 Pt. 1): E626–34.

Van Thienen, R., K. Van Proeyen, B. Vanden Eynde, J. Puype, T. Lefere, and P. Hespel. 2009. Beta-Alanine Improves Sprint Performance in Endurance Cycling. *Medicine and Science in Sports and Exercise* 41(4): 898–903.

Vander Wal, J. S., J. M. Marth, P. Khosla, K. L. Jen, and N. V. Dhurandhar. 2005. Short-Term Effect of Eggs on Satiety in Overweight and Obese Subjects. *Journal of the American College of Nutrition* 24(6): 510–15.

VanWormer, J. J., A. M. Martinez, B. C. Martinson, A. L. Crain, G. A. Benson, D. L. Cosentino, and N. P. Pronk. 2009. Self-Weighing Promotes Weight Loss for Obese Adults. *American Journal of Preventive Medicine* 36(1): 70–73.

Venables, M. C., C. J. Hulston, H. R. Cox, and A. E. Jeukendrup. 2008. Green Tea Extract Ingestion, Fat Oxidation, and Glucose Tolerance in Healthy Humans. *American Journal of Clinical Nutrition* 87(3): 778–84.

Walker, L. O. 2007. Managing Excessive Weight Gain During Pregnancy and the Postpartum Period. *Journal of Obstetric, Gynecologic, & Neonatal Nursing* 36(5): 490–500.

Wang, G. J., N. D. Volkow, F. Telang, M. Jayne, Y. Ma, K. Pradhan, W. Zhu, C. T. Wong, P. K. Thanos, A. Geliebter, A. Biegon, and J. S. Fowler. 2009. Evidence of Gender Differences in the Ability to Inhibit Brain Activation Elicited by Food Stimulation. *Proceedings of the National Academy of Sciences USA* 106(4): 1249–54.

Wansink, B., J. E. Painter, and J. North. 2005. Bottomless Bowls: Why Visual Cues of Portion Size May Influence Intake. *Obesity Research* 13(1): 93–100.

Watras, A. C., A. C. Buchholz, R. N. Close, Z. Zhang, and D. A. Schoeller. 2007. The Role of Conjugated Linoleic Acid in Reducing Body Fat and Preventing Holiday Weight Gain. *International Journal of Obesity (London)* 31(3): 481–87.

Weigle, D. S., P. A. Breen, C. C. Matthys, H. S. Callahan, K. E. Meeuws, V. R. Burden, and J. Q. Purnell. 2005. A High-Protein Diet Induces Reductions in Appetite, ad Libitum Caloric Intake, and Body Weight Despite Compensatory Changes in Diurnal Plasma Leptin and Ghrelin Concentrations. *American Journal of Clinical Nutrition* 82(1): 41–48.

White, L. J., R. H. Dressendorfer, E. Holland, S. C. McCoy, and M. A. Ferguson. 2005. Increased Caloric Intake Soon After Exercise in Cold Water. *International Journal of Sport Nutrition and Exercise Metabolism* 15(1): 38–47.

Williams, M. B., P. B. Raven, D. L. Fogt, and J. L. Ivy. 2003. Effects of Recovery Beverages on Glycogen Restoration and Endurance Exercise Performance. *Journal of Strength and Conditioning Research* 17(1): 12–19.

Williams, P. T. 2007. Maintaining Vigorous Activity Attenuates 7-Year Weight Gain in 8,340 Runners. *Medicine and Science in Sports and Exercise* 39(5): 801–9.

Yanovski, J. A., S. Z. Yanovski, K. N. Sovik, T. T. Nguyen, P. M. O'Niel, and N. G. Sebring. 2000. A Prospective Study of Holiday Weight Gain. *New England Journal of Medicine* 342(12): 861–67.

Zemel, M. B., J. Richards, A. Milstead, and P. Campbell. 2005. Effects of Calcium and Dairy on Body Composition and Weight Loss in African-American Adults. *Obesity Research* 13(7): 1218–25.

INDEX

Aerobic capacity, 15, 25, 105, 171, 173, 175, 236
Alcohol, 58
Allen, Mark, 124
Alzheimer's disease, 237
Amino acids, 67, 139, 140, 160, 182, 237
Anabolic eating, 77, 78, 80, 181–183
Anaerobic capacity, 175
Anthropometric variables, 11–12, 18, 19
Antioxidants, 101, 102, 186
Appetite, 147; cravings and, 81; formulated foods for, 157, 160; managing, 7, 27, 58, 60, 135–136, 148–150, 156, 157, 160, 163
Armstrong, Lance, 9–11, 12, 18
Atkins, Robert, 112

Backstedt, Magnus, 13
Badmann, Natascha, 84
Barbell squat, 256
Basal metabolic rate (BMR), 44, 49, 50, 51, 52

Bastianelli, Marta, 2
Bent-over cable shoulder lateral extension, 257
Berardi, John, 136, 142
Beta-alanine, 236–239
Bishop, Jeremiah: diet of, 188
Blood glucose, 93, 95, 135–136, 146
Blood lactate, 94
Body composition, 12, 15–16, 23, 25, 31, 36, 40, 137, 144; beta-alanine and, 238; lean, 102, 103, 105, 113, 236; macronutrients and, 113; managing, 5, 41, 69, 74, 76; optimal, 22, 29, 132; performance and, 27, 28, 76, 177, 178; tracking, 27–29, 29 (table), 41
Body fat, 11, 13, 34, 45, 63, 132, 138; accumulation of, 60, 106, 147, 182, 241; excess, 25, 244; fasting and, 146; levels, 18, 28, 42, 77; losing, 19, 36, 69, 71, 125, 152, 165, 168, 178, 242, 245; loss, 35, 146, 168,

173, 246; measuring, 32, 33, 42,
44; performance and, 19, 28, 29;
storage, 142, 148
Body-fat percentage, 11, 14, 15, 16, 17,
18, 22, 31, 32, 32–33 (table), 60,
133, 173; inherited/lifestyle, 26;
lowering, 34, 72; measuring, 28,
29, 34–35, 36, 37, 41–52; optimal,
34–35; performance and, 19
Body mass, 22, 54, 175, 177;
distribution, 11; lean, 34, 77, 238;
performance and, 77
Body mass index (BMI), 3, 24, 25
Body weight, 3, 4, 23, 40, 66, 112,
144; attaining, 25; brain and, 149;
carbohydrates/fat/protein and,
118–119; factors affecting, 41;
fluctuation in, 56; ideal, 24, 25,
132; loss of, 146; macronutrients
and, 113; managing, 2, 5, 69, 74, 76,
118–119, 163, 175; minimizing, 71;
performance and, 16, 22, 27, 28, 29,
76; reduced-calorie diet and, 73;
tables, 24; tracking, 29 (table), 37,
41–52, 72
Bone mineral density (BMD), 42, 75
Brain, 144; body weight and, 149;
function/enhancing, 245; hunger/
food cravings and, 150; reward
center of, 149
Breakfast, 133, 134, 151

Cable face pull, 254
Cable front shoulder raise, 259
Cable high-low pull, 263–264
Cable low-high pull, 264
Cable pull-through, 258
Cable shoulder external rotation, 266
Cable trunk rotation, 251
Calcitrol, 104, 239, 240
Calcium, 103, 236, 239–240, 241
Caloric density, 103, 113, 161
Caloric intake, 119, 120, 127, 163
Caloric surplus, 80, 106, 181, 182

Calories, 66, 96, 111, 132; carbohydrates
and, 80, 186; consuming, 40, 135,
138, 154, 168; counting, 45, 46–47,
46–47 (table), 48–49, 51, 52, 64–65,
74; cutting, 7, 58, 152; information
on, 47, 48; sources of, 112, 126;
tracking, 127, 154
Calories in, 40, 80, 132, 133; counting,
41, 45–49, 64, 81
Calories out, 40; counting, 37, 41,
49–52, 64, 81; nonworkout, 50–51;
workout, 50, 51–52, 64, 168, 173
Carbohydrates, 19, 103, 111, 112, 134,
156; burning, 117, 132, 143, 167–168,
169; calories and, 80, 119, 186;
consuming, 122, 123, 126, 127, 139,
143, 171; counting, 115–120; energy
from, 65, 169; fat and, 117, 123, 166;
fatigue and, 120; high-/low-GI,
94; inadequate, 128 (table), 129;
insulin and, 243; muscle-glycogen
stores and, 116; performance and,
116, 118, 120, 137; protein and, 132;
recommended daily intake of, 118
(table); reducing, 65–67, 116, 168;
training load and, 114, 115, 118, 127;
weight gain and, 112; after workouts,
182–183
Carmichael, Chris, 10
Carnosine, 237
Catechins, 247
Cholecystokinin (CCK), 157, 160
Conjugated linoleic acid (CLA), 236, 241
Cortisol, 59
Cravings, 81, 150, 153
Creatine, 183, 236, 242–243
Cross-country skiing, 12–13, 169, 180;
performance test for, 29–30;
seasonal training for, 70 (table);
strength exercises for, 252–255;
weight management challenges of,
70
Culp, Brad, 77, 235
Cummins, Anna, 15; diet of, 189–190

Cycling, 13–14, 180; performance test for, 30; strength exercises for, 255–258; weight management challenges for, 71–72

Dairy foods, 101, 119; low-fat, 104, 107; weight loss and, 240; whole-milk, 106–107
De la Vega, Rafael, 39–40
Dehydration, 44, 73, 139
DEXA, 42, 43, 44, 45
DHA, 245, 246
Diabetes, 94, 244
Dibaba, Tirunesh, 15
Diet audits, 65, 127, 128, 154
Diet quality, 93, 95–98, 99, 100; improving, 6, 107–108, 134, 161
Diet Quality Index, 95, 96
Diet Quality Score (DQS), 98–99, 101, 102, 105; by food type, 99 (table); increasing, 99, 100, 107, 108, 108 (table), 109
Diets, 5, 7–8, 20, 35; analysis of, 39, 129;
endurance athletes and, 113–114, 123, 125; healthy, 60, 98; high-carbohydrate, 112, 113, 114, 115, 116, 117; high-fat, 112, 113, 120, 121, 122; high-fiber, 244; high-protein, 67, 112, 113, 124, 125; high-quality, 93, 113, 134; low-carbohydrate, 112, 113, 114, 115, 116, 117; low-fat, 76, 111–112, 113, 121; low-protein, 124, 125; low-quality, 186; moderation in, 95, 98, 116, 121; modern, 65, 106, 126, 147, 148; modifying, 36, 39, 54, 128; performance and, 80, 126, 137; proportionality in, 95, 98; training load and, 117; variety in, 95, 98; vegetarian, 182
DQS. See Diet Quality Score

Eating: anabolic, 77, 181–183; cutting back on, 150, 162; early, 133–135;
exercise and, 137–143; emotional, 153; frequent, 151; habits, 46, 78, 154–155; hungerless, 152, 155; mindful, 150, 152–156; plan for, 153; recording, 39, 65; schedules, 133, 155; slow, 151; spontaneous, 153–154; timing, 135–137
Elevated reverse lunge, 255, 267
Endurance, 1, 71, 247; increasing, 121, 172; isometric, 237, 238; strength, 179, 237
Endurance athletes, 4, 166, 169; carbohydrates and, 118, 120; diets and, 113–114, 123, 125; exercises for, 250–252; fat and, 120, 121; protein and, 124, 125
Endurance performance, 8, 83, 139, 173, 177, 179, 186, 242; anthropometric variables and, 19; beta-alanine and, 236, 238, 239; body composition and, 76; body weight and, 76; carbohydrates and, 118; diets and, 126; fasting and, 144, 146; health and, 6; high-fat diets and, 120; managing, 37, 93; protein and, 124; supplements and, 235; weight management and, 203
Endurance tests, 115, 120, 121, 243
Endurance training, 19, 63, 81, 172, 174, 179, 181; as acquired taste, 86–87
Energy, 7, 65, 81, 147, 169; balance, 127; deficits, 133; free, 14; increased, 138; meals and, 137; sources, 6, 19, 111, 127
Energy gels, 138, 140
Energy partitioning, 6, 132, 138
EPA, 245, 246
EPOC. See Post-exercise oxygen consumption
Ergogenic products, 140, 142
Evans, Cadel, 14
Exercise, 60, 61, 63, 64, 171, 250–252; eating and, 137–143;

enjoying, 87–91; introduction to, 86; leanness and, 165; strength, 249–269; tests, 166

Famiglietti, Anthony: diet of, 186, 187
Fasting, 134, 144, 146
Fat, 31, 66, 95, 111, 113, 114, 118, 120–123, 132, 134; carbohydrates and, 117, 123; consuming, 126, 127; energy from, 169; essential, 104–105; excess, 119, 126; gaining, 63, 64, 65, 112; healthy, 108; inadequate, 128 (table), 129; loss, 74, 168, 174, 180, 245; muscle and, 143; off-season, 55, 56; percentage of, 72, 112; saturated, 95, 100, 103; unsaturated, 103; weight/composition and, 28
Fat burning, 121, 137, 138, 169, 173; capacity for, 170, 171; carbohydrates and, 166; increased, 122, 168, 170–171, 246, 247; workouts and, 170–171; zones, 165–166, 167, 168
Fat intake, 123; endurance and, 121; leptin and, 162
Fat oxidation, 121, 122
Fat storage, 27, 132, 181; calcitrol and, 239; calcium and, 240
Fatigue, 80, 94, 120, 187, 238, 247; resisting, 115, 236
Fiber, 102, 160, 161, 236, 243, 244–245
Fish oil, 236, 245–246
Fitness, 86, 87, 88, 89, 144, 163; changes in, 80, 171; gains in, 1, 143, 166, 176, 243; level of, 26; managing, 37; off-season, 56; peak, 22, 54; race, 27, 31, 36, 166; tests, 44, 116
Fogt, Darwin, 1, 3
Food intake, 54, 163; regulation of, 147, 248
Food journals, 8, 37, 40, 48
Foods: accessibility of, 152; animal, 182; calorie-dense, 106; categories of, 100–101; comfort, 59; dairy, 101, 104, 106–107, 119, 240; fiber-rich, 244; formulated, 157, 160; high-calorie, 4; high-carbohydrate, 119, 119 (table); high-density, 162; high-glycemic, 137; high-quality, 94–95, 99, 100, 101–105, 107, 108, 113, 119, 119 (table), 134, 137; high-satiety, 150, 152, 156–157, 160; junk, 98, 100, 101, 134, 187; low-calorie, 4; low-density, 150, 160–162; low-glycemic, 137; low-quality, 94, 100, 101, 105–107, 109, 113, 134; natural, 94–95, 147, 157, 244; processed, 94, 113, 147–148; substituting, 108, 108 (table); wholesome, 21, 99, 100, 161
Forze, 160, 248
Freeman, Kris, 13
Fruit, 101–102, 244

Gebrselassie, Haile, 15
Genetics, 26, 61, 84, 136, 148
Ghrelin, 154
Glutamine, 160
Glutathione, 101
Gluteal-hamstring raise, 257–258
Glycemic index (GI), 93, 94, 95
Glycogen, 116, 137, 143, 173; depletion of, 117, 122, 171; liver, 142, 146. *See also* Muscle glycogen
Good morning, 256
Grains, whole, 103–104, 105, 161, 244
Green tea extract, 236, 246–247
Guyot, Donovan, 235
Gym exercisers, 165, 166, 174

Half-squats, 178
Hall, Ryan, 53; diet of, 190–191
Hausler, Tony, 84
Health, 6, 24, 37; weight and, 53
Healthy Eating Index, 95
Height-weight ratio, 24, 50

Heisenberg uncertainty principle, 36–37
High-carbohydrate diets, 112, 113, 114, 116; performance and, 115, 117
High-fat diets, 112, 113, 121; endurance performance and, 120; fat oxidation and, 122; lactate threshold and, 122
High-intensity interval training (HIIT), 165, 174, 175, 176, 177
High-intensity training, 166, 167, 170, 172, 173–177, 180, 183; calories for, 168; performance and, 173
Hill, A. V., 173–174
Holidays, weight gain during, 58–59, 241
Hormones, 59, 160, 162, 248
Howarth, Wesley, 85
Hunger, 160; blood glucose and, 136; brain and, 150; controlling, 156; foods and, 102; primary cause of, 136; real, 153; signals of, 155
Hunger clock, 154
Hunger scale, 153, 153 (fig.), 156
Hydration, 43, 44
Hydrostatic weighing, 42
Hypoglycemia, 146

Injuries, 21, 54, 173; overuse, 39; risk of, 2, 74, 75, 180
Insulin, 183, 243, 248; sensitivity, 25, 26, 241
Interleukin-6 (IL-6), 171
Interval training, 243; high-intensity, 165, 174, 175, 176, 177, 183, 238
Ironman, 2, 17, 80, 81, 84, 91, 124, 168, 169, 171, 235

Joint stability, 180
Juices, 102
Jurek, Scott: diet of, 191–192

Kalmoe, Megan: diet of, 193–194
Karnazes, Dean, 124

Katch, Frank, 15
Katz, David, 96
Kemper, Hunter: diet of, 194–195
Kicking drills, 180
Kouros, Yiannis, 81, 117

L-over, 260
Lactate threshold, 122, 176
Leanness, 7, 27, 53, 54, 74, 75, 133, 168, 186; exercise and, 165; importance of, 11, 18–19, 62, 123, 142; maximizing, 166
Lee, Bryan, 86–87, 89, 90
LeMond, Greg, 9
Leptin resistance, 162
Lifestyle, 5, 7, 20, 26, 62, 88, 90, 147
Lightness, 27, 74, 75
Lindquist, Barb, 17
Long-chain fatty acids, 156, 157, 160

Macronutrients, 6, 111; body composition/body weight and, 113; breakdown of, 114, 126–127; inadequate, 128, 128 (table), 129; intake ranges for, 125–129, 126 (fig.)
Maffetone, Phil, 168, 170
Maughan, Ron, 172
McArdle, William, 15
Meals, 46, 136, 137, 151, 161
Medications, weight gain and, 57
Menopause, 60–61
Menstruation, 60–61, 76
Metabolism, 26, 27, 51, 61, 80, 132; aerobic, 15; energy conservation and, 155; fat, 168, 246; fuel, 122; increase in, 135, 143; resting, 40, 135, 174, 176, 177, 180
Micronutrients, 7, 147
Minerals, 102, 103
Moderate-intensity training, 71, 165, 167, 170, 171, 175, 176, 183; body-fat loss and, 173; calories for, 168; volume at, 166

Moody, Tera: diet of, 195–196

Morken, David, 91

Motivation, 20, 70, 85–86

Mountain biking, 14; performance test for, 30; weight management challenges of, 27

Muscle, 132; damage, 139; fast-twitch, 180; gaining, 63, 78, 182; repair, 21, 142

Muscle glycogen, 115, 171; reducing, 139, 146, 168; replenishing, 142, 143, 167, 168; storing, 22, 62, 122, 136

Muscle growth, 15, 76, 78; caloric surplus and, 181; proteins and, 182; stimulating, 181, 243

Muscle mass, 15, 132; increase in, 77, 177, 180, 181, 242; lean, 11, 237; losing, 74, 124–125; maintaining, 69; whey protein and, 247

Muscle protein, synthesis, 78, 140, 142, 181, 183

Netzer, Corinne, 47

Neurotransmitters, 59, 239

Newby-Fraser, Paula, 84

Nitrogen balance, negative, 124, 125

Nutrients, 95, 98, 103, 160; effects of, 131–132; racing weight and, 145 (table); satiety and, 157, 161, 248; timing, 6–7, 132, 137, 138, 143–144, 145 (table), 146, 150, 151–152, 156

Nutrition, 5, 12, 39, 79, 113, 119, 185, 203–204, 243; balanced, 101; fine-tuning, 23; periodization, 54; protocols for, 142–143; sloppy, 186; training and, 55

Nutrient logs, 48, 154

NuVal scoring, 96, 96 (table), 97, 97 (fig.), 98

Obesity, 26, 155, 240, 244

O'Brien, Andy, 11

Off-season: diet for, 64, 73; discipline during, 55, 163; fitness during, 56; holiday season and, 58–59; weight gain during, 54, 55, 62–67

Omega-3 fatty acids, 104, 105, 245, 246

Omega-6 fatty acids, 104

One-arm dumbbell snatch, 266–267, 269

One-leg squat, 261, 267–268

Optimal body weight, 22, 24–25, 28, 29, 93, 163; determining, 25, 34, 35; maintaining, 52

Optimal performance weight, 4, 5, 7, 21, 25, 28, 32, 55, 70, 114; determining, 22–23, 26, 27, 31, 34; lifestyle and, 26; maintaining, 52; reaching, 22, 23, 27, 42, 53

Ornish, Dean, 111

Overeating, 136, 147, 148, 156, 161, 163

Overhead squat, 259

Overtraining, 21, 54, 79, 176

Overweight, 3, 27, 57, 60, 65, 112, 149, 156, 163, 240

Oxygen consumption, 177, 246

Pantani, Marco, 12, 13

Peptides, 160, 247

Performance, 3, 11, 21, 121, 176; aerobic, 105, 236; beta-alanine and, 238–239; body composition and, 27, 28, 76, 177, 178; body fat and, 19, 28, 29; body weight and, 16, 22, 27, 28, 29, 76, 77; carbohydrates and, 116, 118, 120, 137; creatine and, 243; decrease in, 79, 125, 146, 187; diets and, 80, 126, 137; high-carbohydrate diets and, 115, 117; high-intensity, 22, 173, 242; hydration and, 44, 140; improving, 1, 5, 7, 36, 79, 122, 129, 134, 141, 143, 170, 177; level of, 12, 19, 22; macronutrients and, 113; maximum, 5, 7, 27, 32, 53–54, 69, 114, 125; protein and, 124, 125; tests, 27, 29–31, 176; tracking, 27–29, 29 (table), 72; training,

113, 119, 166; weight and, 4, 28, 62, 71, 72, 81, 83, 146. *See also* Endurance performance; Optimal performance weight

Personal trainers, 166, 167

Peterson, Chip: diet of, 196–197

Phelps, Michael, 78, 186

Phillips, Stuart, 66

Phytonutrients, 101, 102

Plate-clearing instinct, 155–156

Plyometrics, 243

Portions, 46, 47, 48, 101, 152, 156

Post-exercise oxygen consumption (EPOC), 174–175, 177, 178, 180

Potts, Andy, 78, 79, 80

Power, 77, 170, 178, 180; gains in, 71, 76, 78, 181, 183, 243; maintaining, 69; peak, 246; weight and, 72

Power-to-weight ratio, 13, 71

Pregnancy, weight gain during, 59–60

Premenstrual syndrome (PMS), 60

Prone plank, 251

Protein, 111, 112, 114, 118, 134; animal, 182; appetite regulatory, 60; calories from, 65; carbohydrates and, 132; consuming, 65, 66–67, 123–125, 126, 127, 131, 132, 139, 140, 143, 181–182, 182–183; dairy, 157; fractions, 248; inadequate, 128 (table), 129; lean, 102–103; muscle growth and, 182; performance and, 124, 125; plant, 182; powders, 248; shift to, 65–67; whey, 236, 247–248

Pulling drills, 180

Push-up and reach, 265, 268–269

Racing weight, 19, 22, 55, 72, 79, 93, 114, 123, 163; appetite management and, 150; diets and, 125; estimating, 20, 23, 24–27; maintaining, 7, 40, 69, 151; nutrients and, 145 (table); optimal, 2, 49; reaching, 7, 8, 40, 41, 69, 151; supplements and, 236; training weight and, 53

Racing Weight program, 5, 6, 7–8, 28, 70, 143, 148, 185, 187

Radcliffe, Paula, 16

Ramadan, fasting during, 144, 146

Randall, Kikkan: diet of, 197–198

Recipes, 8, 203; breakfast, 204–210; dessert, 228–234; dinner, 220–228; lunch, 210–220

Recovery, 115, 140, 143, 146, 172, 174

Redgrave, Steve, 15

Reid, Peter, 2

Rennie, Mike, 66

Ritzenhein, Dathan, 2

Rolls, Barbara, 161, 162

Romanian dead lift, 252

Rowbury, Shannon: diet of, 198–199

Rowers, 72, 73–74; strength exercises for, 258–260

Rowing, 14–15; performance test for, 30; weight management challenges of, 72

Runners, strength exercises for, 261–263

Running, 15–16, 180; economy, 16, 74, 178; performance test for, 30; volume/maintaining, 74; weight management challenges for, 74–76

Rupp, Galen, 2

Satiety, 106, 150, 151, 152, 160, 247; food volume and, 162; per calorie, 156, 157, 161; signals of, 155, 248

Saunders, Michael, 141

Scales, 23, 32, 44–45, 49, 52

Sears, Barry, 112

Sherman, William, 116

Side plank, 250

Side step-up, 255

Sleep quality, 25, 59

Snacking, 46, 81, 160

Split squat jump, 261

Sports drinks, 139, 140, 141, 142

Stability ball roll-out, 254

Step-up, 253

Straight-arm lat pull-down, 260

Strength, 63, 180, 237; building, 77, 78, 179, 181, 183, 243; muscle, 76, 183; whey protein and, 247

Strength exercises, 249–252; for cross-country skiers, 252–255; for cyclists, 255–258; for rowers, 258–260; for runners, 261–263; for swimmers, 263–267; for triathletes, 267–269

Strength training, 63, 78, 166, 177–180, 183, 249

Suitcase dead lift, 263, 268

Supine plank, 250

Supplements, 8, 65, 235–247; carbohydrate-protein, 140, 142; endurance performance and, 235; racing weight and, 236; whey protein, 65

Swimming, 16–17; performance test for, 30; strength exercises for, 263–267; weight management challenges for, 76–78

Swiss ball hyperextension, 252

Systemic inflammation, 95, 245

Taylor, Pip, 8, 203; diet of, 199–200

Torres, Dara, 11, 12, 78

Tour de France, 9, 10–11, 12, 13, 14, 56

Training, 5, 7, 35, 113, 119; anaerobic, 175; base-level, 54; changes in, 23, 31, 65, 169, 180; consistent/progressive, 21; controlling, 11; core, 179; cross, 64, 144; cycles, 62; early/eating for, 134; fat-burning and, 170–171; glycogen-depleting, 171; high-intensity, 166, 167, 168, 170, 172, 173–177, 180, 183; high-intensity interval, 165, 174, 175, 176, 177; nutrition and, 55, 134, 182–183; peak, 53, 54, 55, 56, 63, 65; resistance, 78, 181, 183, 247;

scheduling, 91, 173; strength, 63, 78, 166, 177–180, 183, 249; speed, 237; sprint, 170; weight, 77. *See also* Endurance training; Moderate-intensity training

Training load, 116, 119, 126–127, 173; carbohydrates and, 114, 115, 118, 127; diet and, 117; peak, 79

Training logs, 48, 154

TrainingPeaks, 39, 45, 49, 154, 235

Training volume, 114, 176, 177; increasing, 172, 173; maintaining, 74

Triathletes, strength exercises for, 267–269

Triathlon, 17–18, 31, 86, 243; weight management challenges for, 78–81

Ullrich, Jan, 12, 55–56

Vegetables, 102, 244

Vegetarians, 125

Visser, Ysbrand, 144

Vitamins, 76, 102, 103, 104

VMO dip, 262

VO2 max, 71, 120, 121, 141, 167, 168, 169, 170, 174

Wansink, Brian, 152, 155

Water, 102, 140, 142, 161; endurance exercise and, 138–139

Weight, 31, 42, 126; conserving, 80; health and, 53; height and, 24; off-season, 55; performance and, 4, 62, 71, 72, 81, 146; power and, 72; regaining, 58, 62; tracking, 27–29. *See also* Body weight; Optimal body weight; Optimal performance weight; Racing weight

Weight gain, 4, 35, 108, 155, 180; carbohydrates and, 112; fat and, 112; holidays and, 58–59, 241; medications and, 57; off-season, 54, 55, 62–67; pregnancy and, 59–60; preventing, 59, 62; in spurts, 56–62; stress-related, 59; on weekends, 57–58

Weight loss, 2, 22, 41, 57, 83, 84, 85, 86, 87, 93, 135; dairy foods and, 240; fasting and, 146; limiting, 74; maintaining, 40, 61–62, 247; program, 40, 73; strategy, 5; supplements for, 247

Weight management, 5, 6, 94, 141, 151, 186, 236; challenges of, 69–70; comprehensive system for, 185; effective, 162; performance and, 28, 83, 203

Weightlifting, 35, 131, 178, 180, 243, 246; creatine and, 183, 242

Weil, Andrew, 187

Welch, Greg, 17

Wellington, Chrissie: diet of, 200–201

Whey protein, 236, 247–248

Whitfield, Simon: diet of, 201–202

Whole grains, 103–104, 105, 161, 244

Wolf, Robb, 144

X-band walk, 262

Zabriskie, David, 13

Zajicek, Phil: diet of, 202

Zemel, Michael, 239, 240

Zohlman, Lee, 39

Zone Diet, 112, 124

ABOUT THE AUTHOR

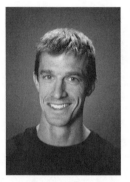

MATT FITZGERALD took up writing when he was nine years old. He became a runner two years later after running the last mile of the 1983 Boston Marathon with his father (who, of course, ran the whole thing). More than a quarter century later, Matt is still running, writing, and competing in triathlons. He has authored or coauthored more than 17 books and written for numerous national publications and websites, including *Outside* and *Runner's World*. Currently he serves as a senior editor for *Triathlete* magazine and senior producer for the Competitor Running Web site (running.competitor.com). His special expertise is endurance sports nutrition. He wrote *Performance Nutrition for Runners*, has been a consultant to several sports nutrition companies, and is a certified sports nutritionist. Matt lives in San Diego with his wife, Nataki.

PIP TAYLOR is a professional triathlete from Australia and author of the recipes in Chapter 13. She inherited her athletic talent and love of sport from her parents, who are both competitive rowers. Pip started swimming before she could walk and also competed in track and field throughout her youth. She took up triathlon after graduating from high school and met with immediate success. Her first major win came in 2003 at a World Cup Triathlon in Manchester, England. She has since won several other international events, including Memphis in May, the Oceana and Australia Long Course Championship, and Vineman Ironman 70.3. Pip has a passion for food that she expresses through cooking and as a sports nutritionist. She earned an undergraduate degree in human life science and a postgraduate qualification in sports nutrition through the International Olympic Committee. She writes a monthly nutrition column for *Triathlete* magazine.